The Gothic Romance Wave

The Gothic Romance Wave

A Critical History of the Mass Market Novels, 1960–1993

LORI A. PAIGE

McFarland & Company, Inc., Publishers
Jefferson, North Carolina

ISBN (print) 978-1-4766-7565-7
ISBN (ebook) 978-1-4766-3417-3

LIBRARY OF CONGRESS CATALOGUING DATA ARE AVAILABLE

BRITISH LIBRARY CATALOGUING DATA ARE AVAILABLE

© 2018 Lori A. Paige. All rights reserved

No part of this book may be reproduced or transmitted in any form or by any means, electronic or mechanical, including photocopying or recording, or by any information storage and retrieval system, without permission in writing from the publisher.

Front cover image © 2018 miss_j/Grape_vein/iStock

Printed in the United States of America

*McFarland & Company, Inc., Publishers
Box 611, Jefferson, North Carolina 28640
www.mcfarlandpub.com*

Table of Contents

Acknowledgments	vi
Preface	1
1. The Gathering Mist	9
2. Shadowed Beginnings: The Mass Market Gothic, 1764–1840	23
3. A Dark Blossom: Gothic Novels, 1840–1960	38
4. Gothic Flower Power: The Gothic Explosion, 1960–1970	54
5. Gilded Peak and Gloomy Valley: 1970s Gothic	72
6. Destined for Darkness: The Gothic Heroine	89
7. Melancholy Males and Demon Lovers: The Gothic Hero	105
8. Numinous Melodrama: The Appeal of the Gothic	120
9. Critics on the Gothic: The Flame and the Pitchfork	135
10. Fading Shadows: Where Did the Gothic Go?	150
Chapter Notes	165
Bibliography	179
Index	183

Acknowledgments

I would like to extend sincere thanks and appreciation to Dean Susanne Swanker and American International College for granting me a sabbatical in the fall of 2015 to pursue my gothic dreams unfettered. This work could not exist without the assistance of my friends and colleagues in the English Department and on the third floor of Lee Hall. I would also like to thank Julie Bodnar in the AIC Writing Center for her assistance and Rachael Salyer, who shared my passion for dog-eared gothics and offered many useful suggestions during the course of this project.

Preface

Swirling fog surrounds the young woman as she makes her way along the threadlike path that leads to the tall iron gates that rise toward the inky sky, their angry spikes silhouetted against an eerie full moon.

Despite her shocked protests and desperate entreaties, her hired driver has refused to take her any farther, so she must struggle over the treacherous path while dragging her cases and trying not to slip on the loose gravel. On either side of her, forlorn marshland and fetid bog stretch off into the distance, threatening injury or even death to those who blunder into their menacing clutches.

Despite several close calls in the obfuscating mist and a mishap that nearly results in a sprained ankle, she arrives at her goal: the imposing door of the ancestral manor house. Above her, eerily glowing windows peer down on her like rows of malevolent eyes. From somewhere in the distance, a macabre laugh reaches her ears. She shivers and reassures herself that it is only a nightbird.

Hesitantly she knocks. Why did no one come to meet her at the station? The various letters she received confirmed that they were expecting her. Then again, she has never met any of the writers of those letters. Could there have been some mistake? If so, how will she ever get back to town? How will she survive a night in this bleak, remote wilderness?

At last, the heavy door swings open with a groan. At the threshold stands a beady-eyed older woman who introduces herself as the housekeeper and is plainly not pleased to see her. Nonetheless, she motions the visitor inside and conducts her to a gloomy, high-ceilinged sitting room that fills her with nervous dread. If only she could live the last few days over again, she thinks, she would never have come to this frightening place.

As she is wondering whether she should grab her cases and flee, the door opens again and a tall, elegantly dressed man enters. This is the master of the house, the person she has come to see. Dark, imposing, and almost impossibly handsome, he surveys her trembling form with vaguely disapproving eyes and sarcastically welcomes her to the house. He apologizes for not sending a servant

Preface

to meet her, but things at the manor have been running less than smoothly since the accidents began—but the less said about that, and the unfortunate death that resulted, the better. He is nevertheless pleased that she has arrived safely. His words are edged with sardonic laughter as he hopes she will prove strong enough not to flee, like so many others have done before her.

Conflicting emotions riot through her during his unnerving speech. Oddly, she both fears and finds herself attracted to this odd man. She knows the next few weeks in this house will call upon every ounce of courage she possesses. At the same time, she senses that something life-changing awaits ... if only she can survive in this strange place, with these even stranger people, long enough to seize her destiny.

The passage above represents a gentle pastiche, perhaps shading into affectionate parody, of the typical mass market gothic romance of the 1960s and early 1970s. Fans of the genre will instantly recognize all the standard elements: naïve but hopeful ingénue, foreboding atmosphere complete with gloomy, crumbling manor house or castle, charismatic but intimidating aristocrat hero. The story might be set in the Victorian period, the swinging '60s, or the newly permissive '70s. Faithful readers, of which there were many, eagerly revisited the familiar story of the disenfranchised heroine escaping all manner of domestic perils while she staked her claim to both the house and its master.

Today, when the mass market gothic romance is remembered at all, it is usually as a source of nostalgia, much like a purple lava lamp or a favorite pair of faded bell bottoms. These quaint yellowed paperbacks, without exception featuring a willowy young woman fleeing from a sinister house while a single light glows in an upper window, prompt reactions ranging from wry amusement to outright condescension. Yet, in its heyday, the genre blazed a path of amazing commercial success. Modern readers may snicker at the apparent sameness of the themes, titles, and artwork, but these very elements likely contributed to the genre's high sales. Because "Gothic romance covers were easy to pick out," as Jennifer McKnight-Trontz notes in her study of romance novel covers from the 1940s through the 1980s, consumers in search of a particular type of story had no difficulty locating and identifying their preferred reading material. Soon gothics became widely available in the grocery and department stores where their target audience—overwhelmingly female—tended to shop. As a result, women purchased these inexpensive books steadily and in large quantities. "[B]y the later 1960s works of top

Preface

Gothic authors outsold the works of equivalent writers in all other categories of paperback fiction, including mysteries, science fiction, and Westerns," writes McKnight-Trontz.[1]

Curiously, while the mass market gothic romance has attracted little critical attention, the last half-century has brought newfound respect for and renewed interest in the original gothic novel, now acknowledged as the predecessor of all modern romance, mystery, and horror novels. The 18th-century Gothic novel, also immensely popular in its day, is routinely invoked in a variety of genre and canon studies, since it is impossible to discuss the rise of modern fiction (not to mention modern literary feminism) without referring to it in some capacity. In general, such studies focus on a few of the better-known examples of the traditional late 18th- and early 19th-century Gothic, such as Horace Walpole's seminal *Castle of Otranto*, Matthew Lewis' shocker *The Monk*, and Ann Radcliffe's masterpiece, *The Mysteries of Udolpho* (best known as the inspiration for the young Jane Austen's Gothic parody *Northanger Abbey*). The greatest critical respect has been reserved for Victorian examples such as *Jane Eyre*, *Wuthering Heights*, *The Picture of Dorian Gray*, and *Dracula*, works that still enjoy popularity among the general public and continue to generate a steady stream of scholarly studies, monographs, and articles.

From that point, however, critical interest dwindles. From the 1940s to the early 1970s, popular Gothic fiction dominated the commercial publishing market. Women were buying books and reading as never before, and many of those women chose Gothics. Sales of various Gothic titles from just one mass market author, Dan "Marilyn" Ross, have been estimated at over 17 million copies. Yet one rarely sees any in-depth discussion of modern gothic writing, even that which has stood the test of time, such as Daphne du Maurier's *Rebecca* (1938). It is even rarer to encounter more than brief mentions of the best-selling novels of Victoria Holt, Mary Stewart, and Phyllis Whitney. Clearly, scholars' tendency to stop soon after 1897 with the publication of *Dracula* has eliminated a huge body of work (whether or not it can justifiably be called literature in its highest cultural sense) and left an untapped reservoir of works ripe for study. Like its 18th-century precursor, the mass market gothic romance has spawned many heirs as well as a few red-headed stepchildren. By the time its popularity waned in the late 1970s and finally faded in the early 1990s, it had given birth to contemporary fiction categories like modern horror, urban fantasy, paranormal romance, and vampire erotica. Even the recent publishing mega-sensation *Fifty Shades of Grey* can trace its ancestry directly to the gothic novels of the 1960s (whether this is a point in either the book or the genre's favor remains an open question).

The rise of the mass market gothic in the 1960s and '70s also (and not coincidentally) overlaps what is now known as "second-wave" feminism and what was once known as the "women's lib" movement. Because the novels seem so quaint and chaste in contrast to today's fare (*Fifty Shades* perhaps the most extreme case), it is easy to overlook or misinterpret their positive and occasionally even progressive attitude toward the heroine and gender relations. Though classic Gothics were traditionally set in that most patriarchal of structures, the feudal castle or manor house, the mass market gothics added a new twist—the woman is now an agent of change, liberation, and transformation, not only for the architectural structure itself but for the man who inhabits it. In *Jane Eyre*, the work on which most mass market gothic romances were based, the hero and heroine (at least upon first glance) represent the two extremes of Victorian psychology, sentimentality and brutish cynicism, which heightens the conflict (as well as the attraction) between them. This dynamic is present in almost every modern gothic romance as well, perhaps for good reason. The world inhabited by the gothic hero and heroine both is and is not like our own. There, the feisty heroine can assert her wit and her rights (and rights to the hero's love) without needing to summon the rhetoric of feminism, the politics of women's rights, or other controversial and perhaps distressing issues.[2] Since many mass market gothic romances were set in the 19th century, the characters can (and often do) speak of women's rights as a new but relatively non-threatening idea. Sojourning in the world of carriage rides, formal dinners, and petticoats may have provided many female readers with a welcome escape from the social upheavals of 1960s, but the imbedded social commentary may well have made an impression on them.

Female readers, it should be remembered, supported the steady production of gothics with the money they earned in their own modern careers, and they demanded stories centered on the heroine's perspective (often in the first person narrative style). Though today it is common for romance novels to present the male point of view in alternating chapters or scenes, in the mass market gothic, the lead male character's main function is to serve as the heroine's love object, and we see him through her eyes and interpret his behavior through her words. Likewise, readers preferred tales written by (at least ostensibly) an author who shared their own feminine identity. Though many of the novels were actually the work of men (among them popular

Preface

modern authors like Dean Koontz), they usually took women's names for marketing purposes. This upends the Victorian tradition by which women novelists, such as the Brontë sisters and George Eliot, took male names in hopes of being taken more seriously by readers and critics. In the mass market gothic romance, the traditional male viewpoint is distinctly secondary to that of the heroine and the (presumed) female novelist. From beginning to end, it is a woman's story to tell.

The argument has sometimes been made that the covers symbolize a panicked flight from enforced domesticity, with a woman running from a patriarchal castle or manor house, often in skimpy clothing and bare feet, her eyes and mouth wide open in fear, the very picture of vulnerability. However, this scenario rarely occurs within the text itself. In the stories, the woman may be in reduced circumstances, but she almost always enters the house with an agenda of her own devising and forges her way through its labyrinthine corridors without flinching (or fleeing). In some stories, she arrives at the house seeking gainful employment or planning to right some wrong from the past. In others, she must adjust to a new marriage or attempt to negotiate a relationship with a man she suspects might be thinking about murdering her. While she pursues these short-term goals, she generally manages to solve a mystery or two, defeat a curse that is plaguing the house, and rescue the hero or some other vulnerable member of his family. Far from reflecting a misogynistic attitude, mass market gothic romances depict a world in which women actually hold all the power, even if few of the characters realize it at first. Though critics like Joanna Russ have claimed that mass market gothic romances have no real connection to the original 18th-century prototypes,[3] these novels may bridge the gap between the traditional, naïve heroines of Ann Radcliffe and postmodern, liberated, and sexually aware female protagonists like Anita Blake.

Given these possible interpretations, it seems even more surprising that the mass market gothic romance has been called sexist, sub-literate, formulaic tripe for the masses, perhaps deliberately engineered by some nefarious patriarchal cabal and fed to women for the purpose of forcing them into dependent subservience, a kind of literary Soylent Green. It might as well be noted at once that much of the prejudice leveled against Gothics and other types of mass market romance novels is the result of a long-established and culturally ingrained sexism. One need only mention "romance novels" in a room full of people to discover that, miraculously, almost everyone present is an expert on the entire genre's history, form, and relevance.[4] Curiously, the obvious follow-up question "How many romances have you actually read?" yields little more than blank stares and embarrassed murmurs. When it comes to gothic romances, the usual assumption is that the books all involve a haunted house, a passive (even wimpy) heroine who screams all the time, and a hero who might be a vampire or werewolf.[5] Another common remark is that the novels' relative chastity is a sign of repression, either in the characters or author (perhaps a result of the Victorian architecture and clothing often featured on the covers). The truth is, however, that while many gothics do share staple elements, there is considerable variation among the many titles as well as clear distinctions between subgenres. The tendency to characterize and even critique romance novels (of which the mass market gothic romance is an important subset) on the basis of an extremely limited (or even nonexistent) sampling has been exposed by Pamela Regis,[6] whose spirited defense of the genre built on similar works by Jayne Ann Krentz and others.[7]

On the other hand, a mention of the mass market gothic romance, without reference to its place in the larger context of women's romantic fiction, can yield more satisfying results. Depending on the age of one's interlocutor, the response might be either "Oh, gosh, I remember those! I read tons of them when I was a teenager!" or "You mean stuff like Victoria Holt and Mary Stewart? My mother [or grandmother or aunt] had shelves and shelves of those. She loved them!" Evidence gathered during the research phase of this project suggests that a loyal fan base of indeterminate size still exists for the classic Nixon-era gothic novel. Up until the early 1990s, when gothic paperbacks became almost impossible to find in bookstores, the homegrown newsletter *Gothic Journal* regularly printed letters from aficionados desperate for a fix. Today, eBay auctions sell large lots of old gothic paperbacks for healthy and even startling dollar amounts. Current books on the shelves at Barnes and Noble feature covers that echo the famous "woman running from a house" (though sometimes she is now facing the structure in question). Young adult novels, in particular, feature overt gothic elements that must seem new to their teenaged readers. The advent of digital publishing has brought back many of the original books, most long out of print and neglected, in eBook form. Many authors and fans of the genre feel that the mass market gothic is poised for a comeback. Whether that prediction will come true remains to be seen.

Perhaps some of the misunderstandings concerning the merits of romance novels in general, and gothic novels in particular, arise from attempts to consider them as texts with specifically literary agendas. Instead, romance

Preface

novels, like the folk ballads that came before them, are actually expected to retell an established formulaic tale, the outcome of which would be already known by its audience. The audience, in turn, is expected to respond to the story emotionally, taking it as a paradigm for certain aspects of modern living.

Walpole, Radcliffe, and Clara Reeve, among others, ushered in the first wave of popular gothic novels, which captivated 18th-century audiences and quite possibly created the romance novel as we know it today. The second gothic wave swept the publishing world in the late 1960s and early 1970s, leaving echoes that are still felt in popular fiction (and popular culture as a whole) today. The present study seeks to write the missing chapters of the gothic story by placing it back into this framework, restoring it to its proper context, and enumerating the sound critical and aesthetic reasons for doing so. In particular, the late 20th century gothic will be examined in its cultural context, which encompasses feminism, Vietnam, youth culture, the sexual revolution, and the growth of the modern media and mass market publishing industry.

Since the 20th century mass market gothic was aimed at middle-class female readers ranging in age from the teens to late middle age, a surprisingly broad category, the books even allow us to analyze how this market-conscious publishing enterprise (with print ads for cigarettes, recipe clubs, and other products sometimes bound into the middle of the books) reflected and in some cases challenged or rejected traditional female roles.

My research began with several large lots of vintage gothics purchased from an online auction site. Spread out for sorting and cataloguing, the books covered half a dozen tables and shelves, filling an entire academic office. Covers in all color schemes, featuring manor houses, castles, and running women in everything from nightgowns to 1970s leisure suits adorned every flat surface. The occasional smile or outright laughter produced by flipping through the books expressed genuine, though not unexpected, delight. As a passionate and lifelong *Dark Shadows* fan, I had dabbled in gothic literature for almost as long as I could read. In the 1980s, I even met one of the most prolific mass market gothic romance authors of all time, Dan "Marilyn" Ross, over dinner with some other fans. After decades of more conventional academic work (in particular the study of Victorian literature), returning to those brittle paperbacks was like coming home to my own little lichen-covered castle.

Reading the books also brought renewed pleasure. Though few aspired to literary gravity, many or even most of the stories turned out to be surprisingly fast-paced, intricately plotted, with appealing characters that are seldom as broadly drawn as critics imply (though admittedly a few of the novels fell flat). Though there is always romance, the mystery usually takes precedence and the suspense runs high. Unlike "serious" novels, gothics move quickly from one plot point to another, rather in the manner of 1950s pulp fiction, with heroines involved in literally breakneck action sequences (a good many on horseback or in cars mysteriously without brakes). Far from dreary sameness, the books exhibited great creativity and heightened emotion that provided a thoroughly entertaining experience. Though many had predictable outcomes, now and then a truly unique twist would give a novel added interest. The addictive quality often attributed to genre novels of this sort was also evident. Finishing one book led right into starting the next. On some occasions I devoured two full-length gothics in a single sitting. There was not a hint of drudgery in the research, which began to worry me—surely scholarship should not be so entertaining. Was I doing it wrong?

Further reflection suggested that I was on the right track. Modern academic departments have given popular culture of all types new respectability. Courses and textbooks have appeared on everything from *Star Trek* to detective novels to classic rock 'n' roll. In the wake of *Twilight*'s popularity, courses and scholarly studies on vampire fiction and film have popped up like mushrooms. Against this backdrop, the romance novel is still struggling to come into its own, with gothic novels clinging to its sturdy, though partially ripped, bodice. It is hoped that this study will be a positive step in that direction.

1

The Gathering Mist

> Glancing back, she saw the old house watching her, looking after her like some giant beetle certain of its victim's return. Why did she feel that way about the derelict old house, she questioned herself. Why didn't she just see it as a thing of splintered boards and sagging roof line? Why did it have its own malevolent presence for her? She couldn't blame that on Amantha's dire words. She had felt the house's malignant presence the first moment she had stood before it.
> —*House at Hawk's End* by Claudette Nicole
> [Jon Messmann], 1971

Every modern study of the gothic must begin by providing some definition of the term as the researcher plans to use it. This is not as easy a task as it might appear. Having gone through several permutations in both academic and popular usage, the word has come to mean so many things to so many people that Mary McCarthy once denied the possibility of a definition at all. "[T]he range of items called gothic are too great," she declared in 1973.[1] More recently, Victoria Nelson decided to add a "k" in her book *Gothicka* in order to distinguish popular perceptions of the genre from genuine medieval gothic.[2]

Just a few of the common definitions bandied about in various contexts have included the following:

1. The original reference to Goths and Vandals, barbarian tribes thought to have destroyed Classical society and art. By extension, the word came to be associated with an eccentric and somewhat tongue-in-cheek passion for antiquarian kitsch.

2. Popular novels of the 18th and early 19th century featuring elements of horror and romance, sometimes involving the supernatural but sometimes explaining curious events as machinations of the villain. Examples include *The Castle of Otranto*, Orientalist works like *Vathek*, and Ann Radcliffe's nov-

The Gothic Romance Wave

els (along with her many contemporary imitators). Early Victorian examples might include Polidori's *The Vampyr* and the successful penny dreadful *Varney the Vampire*.

3. Later 19th- and early 20th-century literary works, most often starting with *Jane Eyre* and *Wuthering Heights* and usually ending with *Rebecca* (1938). *Frankenstein* and *Dracula* are often mentioned, though they are often split off into a separate "horror" or "gothic horror" category. Other examples might include *The Picture of Dorian Gray* and *The Turn of the Screw*, and on the other side of the Atlantic, the works of Edgar Allen Poe.

4. Modern horror, like Stephen King or Anne Rice. A subcategory might be Southern Gothics like the short stories of Flannery O'Connor and Truman Capote's *Other Voices, Other Rooms*.

5. Contemporary "Goth" subculture, encompassing many different mediums that share an affinity for grotesque themes. This sense of the word has been personified by young adults who favor heavy black makeup and clothing, tattoos, and multiple facial piercings.

6. A subgenre of popular women's romance fiction with standardized covers and titles, with plots generally based on variations of *Jane Eyre* and *Rebecca*. The genre achieved incredible popularity in the mid–1960s and retained a devoted following until 1993, when the Zebra line, the last to bear the "gothic" label on the spine, sputtered out.

It is probably obvious that the final entry in the above list will provide the focus for the present discussion. However, it should be equally obvious that all of the entries are connected at some level (even the heavily made-up teenagers may have an interest in the works of, say, Poe or Anne Rice). In order to distinguish the paperback romance novels from both their predecessors and their successors, earlier works will be designated with a capital G, while the paperbacks of the 1960s and 1970s will be referred to as gothics (with a lowercase g) or as mass market gothic romances. These designations imply no judgment about the quality or importance of the novels mentioned; they are meant merely to separate the books published and marketed in the modern commercial sense from earlier works, even those that were mass-produced by the standards of the time.

Literary merit, in fact, is almost superfluous when it comes to gothic sensibilities; it is not too far a stretch to claim, as Clive Bloom did, that the hastily written and sometimes shoddily packaged penny dreadfuls of the early Victorian era had a greater effect on modern media than any number of care-

1. The Gathering Mist

fully composed masterworks: "It is a curious fact," he notes, "that more sense of the gothic comes through in the unconscious popular memory of such anonymous writers and their numerous 'forgotten' stories than from the classic authors."[3] Certainly the penny dreadfuls helped create the mass market gothic romance. Fast-paced, over the top, with creatures and lurid settings aplenty, these stories prefigured both the pulp novels and the classic horror films that would come one hundred years later. Today, *Varney the Vampire* is the best known of these titles,[4] but the character of Sweeney Todd and at least one werewolf also made their pop-fiction debuts here.

The penny dreadfuls resembled the mass market gothic romances in more than their subject matter. They, too, remained immune to criticism from the highbrow set and enjoyed immense popularity and steady sales despite the grumblings of the self-appointed social guardians who wished to save the public from its own poor taste. Another thing the books had in common was a recognizable format and appearance, which consumers could use to locate the type of story they were looking for. When mass market gothic romances were derided for their supposed similarity, it is actually the covers and not necessarily the stories inside them that their detractors noticed. Virtually every mass market gothic romance features a standardized cover, a title suggesting hijinks in a gloomy house, and the label "gothic" on both the spine and upper right corner, where it could easily be seen no matter which way the book was shelved in the marketplace. This practice perfected one the penny dreadfuls and, later, the pulp novels of the 1940s and 1950s began—an early example of what we would today call "branding," a visual signal used to attract fans of the genre who are faced with a large and varied book display. In many cases, the gothic covers bear little or no relation to the story inside (sometimes hilariously so). In certain cases, as *Gothic Journal* would later document, even the titles were publisher-created to enhance genre conformity.

The cover art of mass market Gothics, affectionately referred to as "women running from houses," is worthy of study in its own right, and in fact several websites and Pinterest boards are devoted to analyzing both the familiar tropes and the lives of the artists behind them.[5] There, collectors, fans, and researchers discuss (and sometimes poke gentle fun at) their favorites.[6] In most cases, a lush painting would depict a richly hued sky, a running woman and a large, imposing manor or castle. In addition to the requisite Usher-like structure and the fleeing ingénue dressed in a diaphanous gown (or occasionally a more flamboyant example of 1970s fashion), the cover might also depict a mysterious male figure in the background, pursuing the heroine (though at a decidedly relaxed pace). His identity is usually concealed by a hat or a shadow, leading the viewer (and likely the heroine) to wonder if his intentions are protective or deadly (and this, at least, reflected the usual storyline found in the books).

The central position of the female figure, and the relative unimportance of the man, clearly distinguished the gothics from the more traditional romances available at the time. Contemporary and medical romances, both popular in the early 1960s, tended to show the man in the foreground, perhaps even embracing (though never actually kissing) the heroine. This format, along with a woman's pseudonym under the title, reinforced the mass market gothic's almost exclusive focus on the female perspective.

Behind the frightened woman, a single light burns in a tower or upper window. This light was perceived to have a direct effect on the sales of any given title.[7] Many readers have speculated on the symbolic significance of the glow in the window—does it imply a haunted room, an abandoned lover inside, nefarious deeds in progress on the upper floors, or that the house itself is a sentient being observing her flight (and if so, is the house a benign or evil entity)? This last supposition is not as farfetched as it might seem. After all, every gothic manor or castle has a name (unlike, say, the heroine of *Rebecca*), and in many cases its peculiar architectural features play a role in either impeding or facilitating the heroine's progress through the plot. The proliferation of phallic towers, twisted underground tunnels, and burst gates and doorways likewise imbue many a gothic structure with Freudian symbolism. Some fans have joked that the real love story involves the heroine and the house rather than its master (interestingly, an irrational passion for the manor itself does indeed motivate the villain in Victoria Holt's *Mistress of Mellyn*).

Gothic romance cover art also tends to reflect the cheerful anachronism common to many of the novels, occasionally even depicting a woman in 19th-century clothing despite the story's modern setting. It seems likely that in many cases the artists did not (and did not need to) know any particulars about a novel's plot and setting. It seems likely that the ubiquitous, all-purpose flowing white nightgown remained a favorite costume choice because it could fit any time period, climate, or 20-year-old ingénue. Authors played along without (too much) complaint. As one anonymous gothic writer recalled, "Once, just to see what would happen, I wrote a story set in a suburban ranch house in a densely-populated valley, with every single scene taking place in broad daylight; the heroine was a short-haired redhead who wore jeans throughout the entire book. But when the paperback came out, sure enough,

1. The Gathering Mist

there on the cover was a long-haired blonde in a flowing white dress, haring away from some frightening mansion at the top of a lonely hill in the dead of night!"[8] As this passage suggests, part of the fun for both authors and readers was to tinker with the expected themes and devices, reassembling the familiar elements into new shapes as if playing a game of literary building blocks. Whatever the exact arrangement, though, every mass market gothic was certain to contain a standard set of ingredients.

First, and probably most important, is the heroine. Generally in her late teens or early 20s, she is naïve (or at least inexperienced in life) and usually alone in the world, she arrives at an imposing manor house as an employee, poor relation, or new bride. Though some members of the family may seem to welcome her, others are secretly plotting against her. She immediately feels that she is in danger, though she may have a hard time convincing others of this. Ultimately, she must survive various attempts on her life, unravel some mystery that will save both her and the hero, and win his love in order to become his wife—and usually, mistress of the manor—at the end.

Her counterpart, the hero, is sometimes the brooding master of the house and is wealthy and powerful. At other times, he is a foil character, such as the heroine's trusted platonic friend or another member of the family. The interplay between the heroine and the two (or, on occasion, three) male figures competing for her attention is central to the gothic romance plot. Suspense builds as she, along with the reader, struggles to figure out which man she can trust (and thus, which one can properly be identified as the hero). Many essays on the mass market gothic romance imply that every storyline begins with a woman marrying a husband whose motives and true feelings she suspects (for example, she fears he plans to kill her for her inheritance). While this was certainly a popular trope, it is not always the case. In some novels, the marriage of convenience is her idea, as a means of gaining economic or legal standing in order to advance some aspect of the plot (though she does so in the interest of restoring justice, never from greed).

Mass market gothic romances featuring a "boy next door" sort of hero rather than a neo-feudal lord or Rochester clone (along with a scaled-down house and fortune) are considered the forerunners of today's romantic suspense novel, a popular category that is still going strong. These novels are more like mysteries than they are either literary gothic novels or traditional romances, with heightened melodramatic situations and action sequences. The brave heroines of these stories seem to be constantly trying not to drown, freeze, topple off cliffs or fall into abandoned wells. Luckily, at least one of

The Gothic Romance Wave

the male characters is usually there to pull her to safety. What she must determine is whether he caused the danger in the first place.

In addition to the hero and heroine, a colorful supporting cast fills up the many spare rooms in the manor house or castle. This group consists of various troubled and dysfunctional family members and servants, much like a classic English manor house mystery. Some of these family members will become crime victims, and some may not turn out to be who they are supposed to be. At least one male outsider will arrive later in the story, such as a black sheep brother or cousin, though family lawyers and doctors are also popular choices. Slowly, the heroine begins to trust, confide in, and possibly fall in love with this man, which may or may not be a good (or safe) idea. The reader, along with the heroine, is caught up in the drama as both try to unravel the real relationships between the minor characters, the villain (whoever he or she turns out to be), and the hero.

Possibly in no other genre of popular fiction are setting and plot so thoroughly intertwined as they are in the gothic novel, no matter which century it hails from. The first gothics were the stepchildren of the Romantic writers, who recognized the inherent mystique of lofty architecture, while Ann Radcliffe understood the necessity of an action-filled storyline to keep readers entranced. At the center of the mass market gothic romance, therefore, stands the great house or castle with both a colorful history and a striking, almost poetic name. To this place the heroine comes either as an employee (such as a secretary or governess), a newly discovered heir, or as a bride or fiancée of its master. The house might be a castle, possibly located in continental Europe or the United Kingdom, or in at least one case transplanted brick by brick to the United States (as in the 1966 entry *Madness at the Castle* by William Johnston, writing as Susan Claudia). It might also be a manor home of some kind, usually a sprawling Victorian in a nod to *Jane Eyre*'s Thornfield. Once ensconced there, the characters rarely venture beyond the estate grounds and tend to spend most of their time indoors while domestic drama rages around them. As the story continues, the house becomes a microcosm in which the usual social order (including gender and class roles) can be inverted or dispensed with altogether.

In almost every case, the house has some sort of curse or cloud hanging over it, often due to past cruelties that took place within its walls, and as a result it is a loveless place inhabited by unhappy (and often homicidal) people. This gives rise to the major storyline that unfolds along with the romance, as the heroine begins to fear for her life. Yet the forces threatening her may not be supernatural in origin. As in Ann Radcliffe's novels, what the heroine

1. The Gathering Mist

thinks are ghosts or vampires often turn out to be illusions engineered by unsuspected enemies. In some cases, the hauntings are ambiguous. In others, they are real enough, but the heroine is able either to purify the house or flee it with the man she has chosen as her mate. Sometimes, if the evil inside is too great to be tamed by her goodness, the house implodes, Usher-like, behind her. It either goes up in flames or collapses under its own weight, burying its evil and its secrets in the rubble.

Along with the house, the time period in which the story is set also governs the trajectory of the plot. Today, historical romance is often associated with scorching scenes of pirate capture, lusty lords, and bodice-ripping. In early mass market gothics, as well as in the Zebra line of the 1990s, the 19th century remained the time period of choice, its fog-laden atmosphere fraught with meaning and foreshadowing (moors also made frequent appearances in homage to the Brontës). A historical backdrop could be used to comment on the changing role of women (a fact generally overlooked by feminist critics). Stories set in the Georgian or Victorian eras still relied on naïve governesses or innocent wards as protagonists; however, in Paulette Warren's *Lady Sinister* (1976), the Edwardian-era heroine is chosen as a companion to a difficult old woman because of her psychology degree, then a rarity for women. In a sequel, *I Take This Stranger* (1977), the heroine is widowed on the journey to her new husband's ancestral home and must instead accept the charity of his stepmother. However, to the heroine's surprise, the stepmother is no harridan but a forward-thinking, strong-willed activist in the suffragette movement, who soon converts the heroine to her cause.

Though the Romantics viewed the crumbling stones of Tintern Abbey and Coleridge's caves of ice as portals to the sublime, the storylines of mass market gothic romances may be closer to the productions of the 19th-century popular stage than to Coleridge's woman artist wailing for her demon lover. From the beginning, gothic tales had been enthusiastically adapted into plays (Polidori's *The Vampyr* being one obvious example). Theaters in 1820s London had even experimented with rudimentary special effects in order to heighten the gothic experience for the audience,[9] blending sentimental excess with a near-parody of natural transcendence. Stripped down, the plots of most mass market gothic romance novels are standard melodramatic fare: at first, the heroine is led to believe, largely through innuendo and circumstantial evidence, that the hero she has come to love is not only evil, but cruel and heartless. Various reversals and betrayals follow until she is nearly without hope. Then, in a final burst of determination, she is able to deduce whether or not her suspicions are correct or if, in fact, another character entirely (perhaps even another woman) is the one plotting against her. Her reward for solving the puzzle is marriage, while the punishment for her tormentors is ignoble death, literal or metaphoric. The pioneers of the genre, Holt, Coffman, and Whitney, offered their middle-class readers melodrama overlaid with the genteel veneer of an aristocratic life the morally upright heroine, as their surrogate, penetrates. Yet simmering below the surface of every story remained an undercurrent of self-conscious repression, vice, and even depravity. The combination proved as irresistible to 20th-century audiences as it had to those a century earlier. It is this far less progressive taste for "bourgeois sentiment" that Bloom sees as a mark of "Protestant unease … coupled … with nostalgia for a Catholic, monarchical, autocratic sentimentalism, that could be revisited to oppose modernity itself."[10] The same criticism, more or less, can and has been leveled at the Nixon-era gothic paperbacks and their fans.

In terms of their production history, mass market gothics also have much in common with pulp paperbacks and noir detective fiction of the 1940s and 1950s. Despite their lack of pretense to literary importance, the pulps represented more than just light entertainment to their earliest readers, who were overwhelmingly male. Geoffrey O'Brien suggests in *Hardboiled America* that men learned about sex from these tales,[11] just as women learned about adult relationships—at least the parts that could be expressed in written form in the 1950s—from romance novels (gothic or not). Put another way, early popular fiction for men taught them about the pleasures of the flesh. Books aimed at women instilled in them the primacy of marriage. In both cases, the mysteries the characters solve may very well stand in for the mysteries and fears that plague all erotic relationships. Male-centered pulps provided catharsis for their readers' pent-up lust, urban paranoia, and fluctuating perceptions of masculinity as social mores shifted rapidly after World War II. Things were changing for women, too, though popular fiction was slower to reflect that particular shift. Female readers (and writers) in the early 1960s were ready for a line of books that spoke directly to them. As women gained economic power and discretionary income, publishers decided to oblige.

When Dell Publishing brought out the paperback version of Victoria Holt's *Mistress of Mellyn* in 1960, retail bookshelves looked quite different than they do today. Romance and women-centered fiction had been a safe bet for publishers since the days of the dime novel,[12] the precursor to modern

1. The Gathering Mist

paperbacks. In 1921, Georgette Heyer released *The Black Moth*, which spawned today's Regency romance market, and in that same year Edith M. Hull's *The Sheik* shocked and captivated audiences with its melodramatic but highly sexual situations.[13] *Rebecca* appeared in 1938 (as did *Gone with the Wind*, another milestone in women's fiction) and went on to sell almost three million copies by 1965. The year 1944 offered two other seminal novels: *Forever Amber*, by Kathleen Winsor, which was not a romance in the current sense but nonetheless popularized the costume drama, and *Dragonwyck* by Anya Seton, a bestseller that, two years later, became a film starring Vincent Price.[14] With its fanciful title, villainous love interest, and plot of a sleuthing ingénue/bride, the book fits neatly between *Rebecca* and the countless imitators of both in the 1960s. Still, despite these successes, popular romance was not the booming industry it is today, with multiple shelves of beefcake-focused contemporary lines and sensual historicals featuring ecstatic ladies cavorting with shirtless rakes. Bookstores focused on hardcover volumes, expensive and literary, with paper dustjackets and forms too heavy and bulky to fit in a purse or a pocket. No one had yet thought to stock inexpensive books in supermarkets and pharmacies, where women shopped with just enough money left over to make small impulse buys. Cheap, light books that could be carried along on errands and discarded or given away without guilt turned out to be exactly what consumers wanted.

At the time, bookstores usually arranged sales racks by publisher, making it essential for covers to stand out and clearly indicate a book's genre to browsing shoppers. In 1939, Pocket Books had hit on the strategy of designing paperbacks to look like magazines, using bright colors, striking designs, and low prices to stand out.[15] Increasingly, as popular romances gained a foothold in the market, their covers utilized certain tones, fonts, and styles that identified their subject matter and appealed to the feminine readership. Yet romance models remained conservatively posed until the age of Fabio, with everyone clothed and clinches non-explicit (mass market gothics would continue to be especially chaste, not even showing an embrace or the couple within touching distance of one another). This marketing tactic would eventually be perfected by a small Canadian company that opened in 1949 and made the bulk of its sales via reprints imported from a U.K. publisher called Mills and Boons. By 1964, it stopped publishing other genres and focused strictly on romance, with which its name soon became synonymous.[16] That name, of course, was Harlequin. Its uniform covers and easily recognized branding are now considered a masterstroke of marketing savvy. After six

The Gothic Romance Wave

decades, they have become the largest and most influential romance publisher in the world.

In its early days, Harlequin, along with many other paperback presses, distributed a popular form of romance novel affectionately (and perhaps a bit condescendingly) known as the "nursie."[17] These short novels, combining light medical drama with a chaste love story, flourished from the mid-1940s through the 1960s. By today's standards, the nurse romance seems hopelessly dated, occasionally ludicrous, and driven by a casual sexism that makes even the most brutish gothic hero look progressive (which perhaps he did to 1960s readers). In some ways, though, the character of the nurse represented a step forward for women of the time. She was an independent career woman, professionally competent and dedicated to her patients and duties, and on rare occasions she worked as a physician herself. On the other hand, the heroine would always eventually defer to and marry a doctor (or some other suitably successful man), keeping her economically and socially in his thrall. There was usually a "bad girl" in the nursies who got what was coming to her, while the heroine was rewarded both for her moral nature (in particular her virginity) and her ultimate acceptance of male authority. "Nursies" were once as plentiful (and as easily recognizable) as mass market gothic romances, perhaps appealing to readers who preferred a less imaginative and more contemporary storyline, and many gothic writers, among them Dan Ross, Dorothy Fletcher, William Johnston, and Rachel Cosgrove Payes, got their start with that genre.

Dell, which had entered the paperback field in 1942, had published gothics before, experimenting with the packaging and pioneering the design that eventually became known as the "woman running from the house." In 1951, artist Robert Stanley created the cover for Lucille Emerick's *Web of Evil*, apparently using his wife as his model.[18] Though the colors are brighter than one generally finds on later examples, the illustration contains all the elements (eventually to become clichés) of the mass market gothic romance. A looming Victorian manor displays a single light in the tower window, a dark, storm-swept sky roils above, and a grotesquely twisted tree limb slashes at a woman in a flowing garment (in this case a chiffon-like wrap) running away in fear. It was with the acquisition of paperback reprint rights for the gothic novels of Victoria Holt that Dell made its permanent mark on the gothic landscape.

McKnight-Trontz credits the Dell editions of *Mistress of Mellyn* and other Holt novels with making romance a staple food in many women's reading diets and "solidifying the romance paperback habit"[19] throughout the

1. The Gathering Mist

1950s and 1960s. Just a few years earlier, Virginia Coffman's agent had told her not to use the word "gothic" for her novel *Moura* (eventually published by Crown in 1959), since it would decrease marketability.[20] Now, Dell's (and *Moura*'s) success inspired Gerald Gross to create a special line for Ace, which he decided to call "gothics." Phyllis Whitney's historical suspense novel, *The Quicksilver Pool*, had been popular in the mid–1950s, leading him to choose her new manuscript, *Thunder Heights*, to kick off the new line. Ace would continue to brand itself as "First in Gothics," the tagline appearing on every gothic it published, while the other paperback houses raced alongside in heated competition. Other lines developed recognizable labels for their own lines, such as Easy-Eye Gothics, Queen-Sized Gothics, Magnum Gothic Originals and Paperback Library Gothics (among many others). Joanna Russ reports that Gross described the gothics as sure to appeal to women because they would provide "all the excitement promised by marriage and career and seldom provided by either."[21]

Holt's *Mistress of Mellyn*, like *Jane Eyre*, is the story of a Victorian governess who falls in love with her employer, the brooding Rochesterian figure Connan TreMellyn, and sets about to solve the mystery of his first wife's murder while hoping to win his heart. Meanwhile, an unknown enemy attempts to kill her before she can uncover the truth. The story was so close to *Rebecca* in theme, tone, and setting that many readers and critics thought "Victoria Holt" might actually be a pen name for Daphne du Maurier.[22] Both Virginia Coffman and Phyllis Whitney released their own gothics around the same time. Coffman's *Moura*, still cited by many readers on gothic websites as a perennial favorite, follows the adventures of Anne Wicklow, a housekeeper in a Napoleonic-era girls' school. She receives a distressing letter from one of her former charges and travels to the mysterious French manor whose name supplies the novel's title.[23] There, she finds the girl dying and her imposing guardian suspiciously unconcerned about her condition. Whitney's *Thunder Heights* concerns an orphaned ingénue who travels to her grandfather's crumbling estate on the Hudson, where she attempts to solve the murder of her own mother many years earlier. There, she meets several young men who vie for her attention, but she suspects that one of them may actually be a killer. In each case, the author follows *Rebecca*'s example by combining a remote Brontë-esque manor house or estate with domestic mystery and passionate but non-sexual romance. These elements would undergo various permutations as the gothic era progressed, but the basic combination would remain unchanged. In these early entries, all published between 1959 and

The Gothic Romance Wave

1961, Holt, Coffman, and Whitney set the stage for almost every mass market gothic that came later.

By fusing mystery and romance, the genres most popular with women readers, and adding a heavy dollop of atmosphere and suspense, Dell, Ace, and their competitors struck gold. By 1972, Dean Koontz could advise would-be writers, "The inexpensive paperback book has become the most rewarding form of publication for the average category writer.... Gothics are booming, and editors are buying heavily."[24] In other words, low prices, availability, savvy marketing, and public taste all converged to create the perfect gothic storm—only this time, those gloomy black clouds were raining money. As time went on, publishers (and writers) sought to modernize and vary their offerings, hoping to attract the many fans of TV and film offerings like *Dark Shadows*, *Night Gallery*, *Rosemary's Baby*, and *The Exorcist*. Contemporary 1960s and early 1970s settings became more common, and the novels often referred to relevant elements of popular culture (in one amusing scene, a child in *The Silent Place* tries her nanny's patience by demanding to play her collection of Beatles and Monkees records).

The last evolution of the mass market gothic, probably inspired by the rising popularity of horror fiction and movies, was the Satanic or Occult Gothic. In these stories, which are often set in the modern era, the heroine arrives at the house or castle as a poor relation, employee, or new bride and finds that the house is headquarters to a sinister cult or genuinely malevolent entity (perhaps a vampire). In early gothics, the suspense arose from the strange behavior of the family members and the mystery revolved around run-of-the-mill motives for murder: economic greed, infidelity, or psychosis. Here, the murder may involve ritual sacrifice, vampire attacks, or the hunger of bloodthirsty monsters. The romance plot is far removed from the action here, though there will usually be the familiar suspicion of the new spouse and the intervention of a rival suitor. One of these men will generally turn out to be grooming the heroine to become a cult's sacrifice to ancient druids or demons.

Though the occult gothics definitely ratchet up the suspense and add a new element of "on camera" violence, it must be noted that the horror element in these books is not very strong, again tending toward melodrama and not gore (Phyllis Whitney once cautioned budding gothic writers to avoid "pea soup," alluding to the infamous and grotesque vomit scene in *The Exorcist*). Occult gothics are therefore neither romance, of which there is little, nor true horror. Readers seeking something stronger than the gothic heroine poking

1. The Gathering Mist

around in a dank castle probably branched off into the growing horror market, ignited by Stephen King's *Carrie* and others with more graphic content. Most contemporary gothics (and gothic authors like Susan Howatch and Phyllis Whitney) were rebranded as "romantic suspense" once the gothic craze had withered in the 1980s and subsided in the 1990s. The obligatory castle or manor house and suggestion of supernatural goings-on were gradually phased out as well or redirected into the paranormal romance lines that can still be found in bookstores today.

Ironically, the same uniformly styled covers that made the gothic popular also helped to trivialize the genre. The demise of the Zebra line in the early 1990s points to a failure of marketing more than any dissatisfaction with the content—after all, historical romance and romantic suspense were then and have continued to be popular. Instead, readers had begun to express dissatisfaction with the sameness of the covers and titles. *Gothic Journal* records their complaints about the strict packaging that even led to misleading blurbs, titles, and artwork. The 1960s publishers had at least presented a façade of earnestness. The Ace Cameo line, for instance, proclaimed on the back covers, "During the past fifteen years, the world's finest Gothic writers have appeared in Ace editions.... The Editorial Department, after a sincere and careful selection, decides which books will bear the Ace symbol.... This symbol distinguishes an elite collection of Gothic novels. It identifies for the reader those books that meet the unique Ace standard of excellence and optimum readability."[25]

In contrast, their 1990s counterparts made the mistake of condescending to the readers and turning both cover art and titles into near-parody. Annoyed and insulted, their customers ultimately turned away from the genre. Before long, Zebra was not selling enough to continue its gothic line, which soon went the way of Ace Gothic, Harlequin Mystique, Silhouette Shadows, and many others. Zebra continued to publish romances of other sorts, and is currently best known for its longer historical novels, particularly Regencies.

Popular gothic fiction never entirely died out, even if the jagged coasts of Maine and Cornwall did eventually run out of brooding eligible bachelors in need of a plucky governess or mail-order bride. Its elements still turn up in modern cozy mysteries and historical novels as well as a few specialized niche fiction territories as disparate as Christian fiction and same-sex erotic romance. Two 21st-century blockbuster movies, *Crimson Peak* and Johnny Depp's *Dark Shadows* reboot, celebrated the genre in all its glorious, histrionic excess. Fans continue to run websites, newsletters, and even a gothic

The Gothic Romance Wave

lending library that boasts some 3400 volumes.[26] Tracing the trajectory of the mass market gothic involves more than charting the rise and fall of a pop culture craze that enthralled readers from the mid–1960s to the late '70s. It allows us a peek at an amazing moment in American social and literary history, preserved between the yellowing covers showing a woman running from a house.

Today, the mass market gothic romance conjures the benevolent spirit of a simpler era, when heroine and reader, ordinary middle-class women, could triumph over the evils of both past and present, ensuring a more positive and egalitarian future. They were published at a time when men, and not just square-jawed heroes in mist-shrouded manor houses, were starting to realize that women were not helpless and useless. They could actually save the castle and the hero alike if only he would open his mind and heart enough to allow it. Once the walls had been stormed and breached with a minimum of bloodshed and mayhem, the conquering heroine was rewarded with wealth and power—including power over the hero, if she wanted it, though she always gave back just enough to ensure equality between them. Readers could hope for the same in real life, as they marched out into the changing world of the 1960s and early 1970s with a new purpose, outlook, and sense of strength. Gothic novels promised them that the suburban castle, with its mistress in compassionate control, really could transform and rule the land.

2

Shadowed Beginnings
The Mass Market Gothic, 1764–1840

> She released him and fluffed her blond curls. She shot a smug look at Clarissa. Then she widened her eyes. "Perhaps Lord Genvere is a deformed recluse," she said breathlessly. "He is so hideous he cannot go to London's parties. Even brothels would turn him away."
> Clarissa laughed. "You should write Minerva Press novels, darling. How debauched. Do you think he will also chain us up in the dungeon?"
> —*Deepest Desires of a Wicked Duke* by Sharon Page, 2016

The tale of the gothic novel is as dramatic as anything found between the covers of a dog-eared paperback. For two centuries the walls of the castle echoed with cutting slights and hissed accusations, the musty air stirred by the clash of strong personalities determined to malign each other's talent, impugn each other's motives, even question each other's very identity. Literary critics of various political persuasions, later joined by some modern successors professing feminist concerns, labored tirelessly to disparage and lampoon the genre, ostensibly for the intellectual and even moral good of the public. At the same time, authors and devoted fans worked feverishly to expand the gothic novel's cultural reach.

In the end, both sides could claim partial victory. The gothic achieved amazing popularity and changed both literature and society in myriad ways that can probably never be fully realized, much less catalogued. At the same time, critics succeeded in convincing the public that the genre was, at best, escapist fantasy not fit for serious study or readers, most useful as the butt of parody or the subject of campy humor. At worst, popular gothic novels were characterized as a threat to literary taste and possibly the mental stability of their readers.

Although the passages above may sound like a description of the critical milieu circa 1973, they could also apply, with a few changes only in the terminology used, to the waning of the gothic's popularity in the early 19th century. In the modern era, feminist critics vilified them as a threat to female self-esteem and the antithesis to what was then called "women's lib." In the 1820s, "serious" novelists and critics, almost all of them male, complained that such frivolous publications distracted readers from nobler forms of literature.

Eventually, to the critics' great relief, readers of both the 1820s and the 1970s grew weary of plucky ingénues threading their way through gloomy castles in search of true love, and sales declined. Yet, though the immediate threat had been neutralized, a strange yearning remained. Like Jane Eyre pining over Rochester after she has fled Thornfield, readers of both the 19th and 20th centuries held their memories of gothic adventures and forbidden love close to their secretly racing hearts. And, in slightly different forms that were no more palatable to the critics than the originals had been, the gothic romance continued, spreading outward like a dark vine that covered not only the castle itself but the neighboring village. Its dark tendrils crept over humble cottages and respectable manor houses alike, even extending to the austere walls of the local universities ... where some of the scholars not only took notice, but, squirreled away in library carrels and offices, began to write about the genre's history and significance. A few even wrote gothic novels of their own, adding various literary flourishes and other innovations. The tendrils— along with the gothic saga itself—stretched forward again, touching the next generation of readers, writers, and critics.

Of course, a disconnect between consumers (in this case, largely female) and those who claim to know what is best for them (usually, but not always, male) is not especially startling or unique; similar battles routinely rage around commercial products of all sorts, including television shows, comic books, and musical fare. What is striking is how closely the reading material as well as the controversy in 19th-century England resembles that of Nixon-era America. Even more striking is how little the participants' attitudes and genders have changed over the intervening centuries.

From the beginning, the gothic novel has been identified with a predominantly feminine sensibility. This was in keeping with 18th-century standards; the relatively new art form of the novel had appealed to women from its earliest incarnations, Samuel Richardson's *Pamela* (1740) and *Clarissa* (1748). These books had been written for the express purpose of instructing young women, who were slowly gaining greater social freedom, in proper sexual morality. Both stressed the importance and safety of conventional marriage in contrast to wild escapades with rakish lovers. Commercial publishing was, it turned out, an ideal manner of disseminating the code. Reasonably low prices ensured that the books would reach middle and lower classes, who could most benefit from the content, and high-volume printing ensured that the message would travel through many pairs of hands all across England (and even the New World).

Somewhat predictably, readers seemed to enjoy the sensationalism of *Pamela* and *Clarissa* more than they did the moral lessons. Later novels became less overtly instructive, and Richardson's stodgy absolutism even became the butt of parody in Fielding's *Shamela* (1741). Though gothics concerned themselves at least ostensibly with questions of good and evil, including the kind of evil represented by lecherous and inappropriate suitors, their purpose tended toward entertainment rather than instruction. How many women actually fantasized about attracting and taming a real-life Mr. Lovelace will never be known, but the current popularity of domineering millionaire Christian Grey suggests that women's erotic daydreams often run in unexpected directions. Whether their reading material fuels or merely reflects these secret tastes is a question men like Richardson did not and perhaps could not address. He confined himself to a didactic view of female sexual behavior, honed by male standards and imposed from the high perch of paternal authority.

For women readers, entertainment meant not just dungeons, avenging ghosts, and other medieval trappings, but an emphasis on romantic relationships. Horace Walpole's *The Castle of Otranto* (1764), like the many gothics that came after it, used marriage as its central plot component. The story opens with the betrothal of Prince Manfred's ineffectual son to Isabella, one of the novel's two heroines. When the son is unexpectedly killed by a giant falling helmet, Manfred decides he ought to marry Isabella himself, despite the fact that he is much older and already married. After a series of melodramatic adventures, the story ends with the marriage of Isabella to the dull but good-natured Theodore, the rightful heir to the castle. Even Matthew Lewis's *The Monk* (1796), with its lurid scenes of torture and perversion, revolved around the efforts of an earnest young suitor, Raymond, to rescue his beloved, Agnes, from the clutches of the evil Ambrosio. If necessary, readers could cite their anxiety over the young lovers' fate to justify their excursion through, and no doubt their unspoken fascination with, the plot's debaucheries.

Both *Otranto* and *The Monk* were written by male authors and feature male protagonists. Women readers may have thrilled to the improbable plot

The Gothic Romance Wave

devices and shivered on behalf of the imperiled heroines, but the viewpoint was not their own. As with the earliest novels by authors like Samuel Richardson, Henry Fielding, and Daniel Defoe, they were spectators who viewed Isabella and Agnes, along with Pamela, Clarissa, Shamela, Moll Flanders, and many others through a lens of masculine design. Even Clara Reeve's popular 1778 gothic, *The Old English Baron* (the second edition of which was published with the assistance of Samuel Richardson's daughter), took its inspiration from *Otranto* and focused on the adventures of Sir Phillip Harclay, rather than the primary female character, Emma. It would take the genre's first genuine superstar, a woman who was for a time considered the most popular novelist in England, to create a genuinely female-centered narrative told in a genuinely female voice.

To readers of the 1790s, Ann Ward Radcliffe cast an appealingly mysterious shadow. She was not the first successful female novelist, following instead a trail blazed by earlier women such as Aphra Behn, Fanny Burney, and Clara Reeve herself. However, she captivated readers with her highly imaginative and almost theatrically emotional tales, and her adoring public delighted in titillating gossip about her private life. Rumors proclaimed her insane, a spy, and an eater of raw meat who courted nightmares for inspiration. Rather like a character in a lurid gothic, she was consigned to her tomb more than once, only to spring up alive again.[1] Her first gothic, *The Castles of Athlin and Dunbayne, A Highland Story*, appeared in 1789, with both the title and the plot clearly indebted to Walpole. The story concerns the attempts of the hero, Osbert, to avenge his father's murder and marry the gentle Laura, a lady taken hostage by Malcolm, the villain. The tale ended happily, with a double wedding, as Osbert's sister also marries Alleyn. He, like Otranto's Theodore, is a supposed peasant who is actually of noble stock. Her follow-up novel, *A Sicilian Romance* (1790), transfers the action to the Mediterranean but keeps the castle setting and the theme of the ingénue resisting the advances of a wicked, unwanted suitor and instead choosing a more compliant and suitable mate for herself. *The Romance of the Forest* (1791) added scenic landscapes to medieval stone labyrinths but again threatened a naïve young heroine with the decadent aristocrat's sexual advances.

Unlike Clarissa, she is able to outwit him and gain not only the husband she prefers, but considerable wealth as a newly recognized heiress. Radcliffe would soon use this trope again. In 1794 she published her masterpiece, a novel in four volumes that would make her fortune, inspire a young Jane Austen, and create the modern gothic romance as we know it today: *The*

2. Shadowed Beginnings

Mysteries of Udolpho, A Romance. Udolpho is now acknowledged as the book that, as Daphne Clair puts it, "changed the course of women's fiction and made the Gothic novel a peculiarly female genre. [It] is the direct ancestor of the Brontës' novels, of du Maurier's *Rebecca*, Holt's *Mistress of Mellyn*, and every modern Gothic thriller."[2] Most modern readers come to it from a sort of reverse direction, as it is most often excerpted or bundled with the delightful pastiche it birthed, Austen's *Northanger Abbey* (1818). Yet its popularity and influence in its own day was virtually unsurpassed. Even Austen's cynical Henry Tilney has nothing but praise for it, correcting Catherine Morland when she protests that surely "gentlemen read better books":

> "The person, be it gentleman or lady, who has not pleasure in a good novel, must be intolerably stupid. I have read all Mrs. Radcliffe's works, and most of them with great pleasure. *The Mysteries of Udolpho*, when I had once begun it, I could not lay down again; I remember finishing it in two days—my hair standing on end the whole time."
>
> "Yes," added Miss Tilney, "and I remember that you undertook to read it aloud to me, and that when I was called away for only five minutes to answer a note, instead of waiting for me, you took the volume into the Hermitage Walk, and I was obliged to stay till you had finished it."[3]

When they discuss the book, Austen's characters focus on the "thriller" aspects of the plot: kidnappings, haunted rooms, the black veil, the wax figure the heroine at first mistakes for a dead body. Today, readers and critics are more apt to discuss the psychological aspects of Radcliffe's work—both with respect to the characters and to the author and her real-life audience. The castle and forest settings have been scoured for Freudian symbolism, the gender roles dissected for proto- (or anti-) feminist sentiment, British readers' gleeful *frisson* analyzed for latent Catholic nostalgia, and the like. To be sure, *Udolpho* is long and vast enough to support a variety of critical approaches, even if its original purpose has been forgotten and almost no one reads it strictly for pleasure anymore. Structurally, its contribution to the gothic romances of the next two centuries—and to the romance novel in general—cannot be overestimated.

Walpole and Reeve had delighted audiences by stocking their castles and abbeys with fetid dungeons, corrupt aristocrats, and supernatural interventions of every sort imaginable. These features, combined with the medieval settings, gave their stories a surreal quality reminiscent of fairy tales. Radcliffe's contribution to the formula was to inject an Age of Reason–style corrective: what appeared to be the result of other-world visitations or evidence for paranormal activity was actually a ruse engineered by the heroine's enemies or her own overactive indulgence in what was then called "sensibility."[4] The shift helped mark the point at which gothic romance separated from gothic horror. It also separated the two strains that modern critics like Ellen Moers would call Male and Female Gothic.[5] This single adjustment, perhaps more than any other, would have the greatest effect on the modern gothic romance, and perhaps in all the popular romances to follow. By removing the influence of ghosts, fate, and curses and giving the heroine, Emily St. Aubert, the ultimate responsibility for what she both perceives and does, Radcliffe centers her story on feminine agency. The heroine may still live within a patriarchal (even feudal) system, but at the same time her will and spirit remain her own. She is free to resist and define herself and her future as she sees fit. Central to this idea in the 18th century is her ability to engineer her own marriage.

In keeping with the medieval (or at least pseudo-medieval) setting of early gothics, arranged marriage is a frequently employed motif. In fact, a contracted betrothal is the catalyst for the plot of *Otranto*; Conrad, the prince and potential bridegroom, is described as "a homely youth, sickly, and of no promising disposition," not to mention possessed of a father, Manfred, who will make a singularly unappealing in-law. Nonetheless, the intended bride, Isabella, raises no strenuous objection to the marriage, though Walpole notes that "she had conceived little affection" for her fiancé. When Conrad is killed by the falling helmet, her relief is mentioned almost in passing: "she was not sorry to be delivered from a marriage which had promised her little felicity."[6] When Manfred decides to substitute himself for his dead son in the matrimonial bed, Isabella's main objection is to the fact that he is already married, not to the fact that the union will be loveless and distasteful. Eventually, the restored prince Theodore steps into the role and Isabella accepts him without any particular enthusiasm. *Castle*'s end is only guardedly happy; the couple seems less in love with one another than they are with the idea of joining forces to mourn Mathilda, Manfred's daughter, whom both of them loved. Reeve's *Old English Baron* likewise uses the device of an arranged marriage to heal old wounds: "When time had worn out the prejudices of Sir Robert Fitz-Owen, the good old baron of that name proposed a marriage between his eldest son and heir, and the daughter of Edmund Lord Lovel, which was happily concluded. The nuptials were honored with the presence of both families; and the old baron was so elevated with this happy union of his descendants that he cried out—Now I am ready to die!" Sure enough, Reeve tells us, "[h]e did not long survive this happy event."[7] In this case, the bride's

2. Shadowed Beginnings

feelings are not even mentioned (though, in fairness, neither are the groom's). Both *Otranto* and *The Old English Baron*, however popular they might have been with female readers, were the stories of men and political conflicts; who marries whom is of interest mostly because these matches affect who inherits the title and the power that goes with it.

For Emily St. Aubert, orphaned and adrift in the mountains of Europe, the question of whom she will marry is less one of securing political advantage than of avoiding complete disenfranchisement and perhaps even death. During the course of the story, Emily's own aunt serves as a dire warning, marrying the villainous Montoni and then losing her independence, her property, and ultimately her life. Seeing the danger even before her aunt fully understands it, Emily struggles against Montoni's insistence that she marry his friend, Morano. Unlike Isabella, she raises her objections at once, only to meet with a chillingly logical assessment of her own powerless state as a woman, far from home, in a patriarchal culture:

> Emily, who had hitherto tried remonstrance, had now recourse to supplication, for distress prevented her from foreseeing, that, with a man of Montoni's disposition, supplication would be equally useless. She afterwards enquired by what right he exerted this unlimited authority over her? a question, which her better judgment would have with-held her, in a calmer moment, from making, since it could avail her nothing, and would afford Montoni another opportunity of triumphing over her defenceless condition.
>
> "By what right!" cried Montoni, with a malicious smile, "by the right of my will; if you can elude that, I will not inquire by what right you do so. I now remind you, for the last time, that you are a stranger, in a foreign country, and that it is your interest to make me your friend; you know the means; if you compel me to become your enemy—I will venture to tell you, that the punishment shall exceed your expectation. You may know I am not to be trifled with."
>
> Emily continued, for some time after Montoni had left her, in a state of despair, or rather stupefaction; a consciousness of misery was all that remained in her mind.

Though shocked into silence, at least for the moment, she quickly forms an alternative plan involving the sort of passive resistance she sees as her only hope. "When her mind, however, had recovered from the first shock of this behaviour, she considered, that it would be impossible for him to compel her alliance with Morano, if she persisted in refusing to repeat any part of the marriage ceremony; and she persevered in her resolution to await Montoni's threatened vengeance rather than give herself for life to a man, whom she must have despised for his present conduct, had she never even loved Valancourt; yet she trembled at the revenge she thus resolved to brave."[8]

The Gothic Romance Wave

At the heart of Emily's desperation, of course, is her desire to make a match for herself that will ensure both financial and personal autonomy. Valancourt, though a less exciting prospect to modern readers than Mr. Rochester or Max de Winter, represents through his good-natured passivity a path to the kind of liberation that eludes both single women of Emily's era as well as those trapped with domineering husbands like Montoni. At the end of the story, Emily achieves her goals by marrying the man she loves and sharing her newfound economic security with him after he loses his own wealth.

Udolpho set the tone and the standard for many a tale of a solitary orphaned girl who explores a fearsome castle while avoiding an unwanted marriage, and Emily's triumph must have resonated with audiences who recalled Pamela's ineffectual struggles against Mr. B. and Clarissa's tragic imprisonment by Mr. Lovelace. As Pamela Regis points out, modern critics who believe that romance novels (gothic or otherwise) revolve around men conspiring to capture and rape passively victimized women fail to notice the genre's shift from a mode of patriarchal discourse warning innocent young females against wicked sexual temptations to a sort of communal mythmaking among women, sharing strategies and templates for satisfying marriages. In other ways, too, she shows that the feminine (though obviously not always feminist) vision of heterosexual love presented in romance novels differs significantly from that favored by male writers. Love at first sight with little attention to the social ramifications of a match, for example, is generally the product of masculine fantasy,[9] while women (of necessity) tend to focus on the details of courtship in order to make sure a potential mate can be trusted and relied upon.

Though *Northanger Abbey*'s male leads, John Thorpe and Henry Tilney, have both read and enjoyed *The Mysteries of Udolpho*, Ann Radcliffe was regarded primarily as a writer who appealed to women, and her message must have commanded attention at a time when women's issues rose to the forefront of intellectual conversation. Wollstonecraft's *Vindication of the Rights of Woman* had appeared only two years earlier; even those readers who might have found her rhetoric a bit too strong must have smiled and nodded approvingly when Emily claimed her man and her birthright, settling not only into "domestic blessedness" but "to the securest felicity of this life, that of aspiring to moral and labouring for intellectual improvement."[10] For Diana Wallace, this convergence of ideals is no accident. She points out that "[t]he major peaks within the Female Gothic tradition are closely connected with the waves of feminism," starting with Wollstonecraft and most certainly including the mass market gothic romance of the late 1960s.[11] The gothic novel, especially books with historical settings, may even provide a safe space for feminine (or feminist) protest. The heroine's journey from the dangers of the patriarchal castle to the domestic comforts of a feminized pastoral haven is in one important sense a metaphor for women's social progress.

In fact, Emily St. Aubert's quest may provide the first and best example of gothic female independence. One of Radcliffe's innovations in *Udolpho* was to dispense with the second heroine and send Emily off into the world alone. Even Valancourt is absent from the story for long stretches of time. Whatever friendships she may cultivate along the long path to her happy ending, Emily is usually left to her own devices and must live and survive by her own wits. Radcliffe herself set a real-life example of female autonomy: though happily married to a journalist who encouraged her writing, Radcliffe made her mark as a highly successful female author at a time when women generally did not earn fortunes of their own. *Udolpho*, for example, earned her £500 in 1794, worth some £65,000 (or nearly $95,000) in 2017.[12] It seems probable that economic envy spawned at least some of the invective against the popular gothic, much as it became *de rigeur* for pundits to disparage Stephenie Meyer's vampire romance *Twilight* after it earned the author millions of dollars, film deals, and bestseller status, whether those denigrating her books had actually read them or not. It is not hard to find an echo of this in modern feminist critics like Russ, who railed against *Udolpho*'s descendant, the mass market gothic, in 1973. "What are women reading today? God knows…" she laments,[13] before going on to vilify examples of what she considers paperback gothic pablum.

The deplorable decline of public taste, and perhaps even civilization itself, was soon associated with increasing female leisure time, especially the penchant of female readers to snap up fashionable but frivolous books.[14] By the year 1800, England's increasingly literate population, burgeoning novel trade, and female readers and writers, provided an ideal hothouse for the gothic thriller and its close cousin, the domestic romance novel. The improved printing technology of the time and a steady supply of eager authors enabled publishers to churn out hastily composed castle-dramas by the score. Franz Potter notes that "[b]y the nineteenth century the Gothic trade was expanding at a tremendous rate with the production of novels continually on the increase: 1800–1809 were the most productive years for novel production with 199 titles appearing, compared to 109 for the period 1790–1799 and

89 for 1811–1820."[15] Even Percy Bysshe Shelley longed for a piece of the gothic action, penning and publishing two forgettable (and largely forgotten) short novels, *Zastrozzi* in 1810 and *St. Irvyne* in 1811. Neither found critical or popular success, and the disappointed author fatefully turned his attentions back to poetry.

The most prolific of the gothic publishers was William Lane, owner of Minerva Press, whom Martin Tropp identifies as "the first to apply mass marketing techniques to the creation and distribution of literature."[16] Minerva's success inspired other publishers to adopt his model and prompted Lane to create a fee-based lending library Tropp likens to a modern franchise "supplying the literary equivalent of fast food." The metaphor is fitting, since this explosion of wailing ghosts and rattling chains provoked as much outrage as the proliferation of greasy fries and burgers sometimes does today. Just as the original Goths and Vandals were said to have destroyed Classical society and art, the new gothics were lamented as crude and barbaric, a threat to serious literature and public taste.[17] These books, much like mass-produced genre novels today, were "instantly condemned in reviews for their overall shoddiness"[18] and recognized as repositories of "simply bad writing."[19] Sir Walter Scott, despite his admiration for Ann Radcliffe's art, decried "the overstocked hamper of imitations and common Gothic novels."[20] Yet the new reading public, many of them women (as were many of the authors Lane employed) cared little that the books he offered were "the most unreadable ever produced.... Full of typographical errors, printed on coarse yellowish or gray paper in miniscule type."[21] What mattered was that the plots were thrilling and the prices affordable.

This flurry of substandard trade publishing, according to Franz Potter, thwarted any real chance of advancing the gothic novel as an art form by 1820.[22] Instead, the gothic took on a permanent identity as a mass market commodity, a disposable and self-referential form of entertainment that created its own standards of quality and seemed to delight in its own crassness. Clive Bloom might almost be talking about the authors of 1960s gothic romances when he describes the authors who churned out endless cheaply-bound tales to satisfy a hungry audience well into the Victorian era: "it would be wrong to think that all their productive life was dedicated to producing second-rate hack work. Such writers remained directly in touch with public taste and demands and worked tirelessly to satisfy it. Although most were forgotten almost immediately after they died (if their true names were made public at all), they were often talented writers of melodramatic thrills and

2. Shadowed Beginnings

were adept at witty dialogue and clever plotting. They were also excellent at reinventing stock situations,"[23] paving the way for the penny bloods (also called penny dreadfuls) of the 1840s as well as, much later, American pulp fiction.

Across the Atlantic, American readers likewise found themselves captivated by gothic romances. British imports dominated the market, though homegrown tales set in Puritan New England and the antebellum South soon took their places alongside those staged in medieval Europe. By 1798, America had a bestselling gothicist of its own, Charles Brockden Brown, whose stories were light on romance but resembled Radcliffe's in their use of psychology and rational explanations for supernatural occurrences.[24] As in England, readers devoured the lurid tales in great numbers. Gothics and sentimental novels written by and marketed toward women were so successful in America that as late as 1855, Nathaniel Hawthorne famously erupted against the "d—d mob of scribbling women" whose work eclipsed, at least temporarily, his earnest literary effort, *The Scarlet Letter*.[25]

Literary history, of course, has been less charitable than Bloom toward the popular gothicists and more sympathetic toward Hawthorne and two British authors who shared his exasperation with their excesses. Early 19th-century British prose is now recognized as the domain of two novelists who voiced their own disdain for the genre. One of them, Sir Walter Scott, is credited with elevating the historical novel to a recognized and respectable art form. The other, Jane Austen, is acknowledged as having perfected the novel of manners and for creating what is probably the first and best modern romance novel, *Pride and Prejudice*. She also wrote the only 18th-century gothic that is still read for pleasure today, *Northanger Abbey*.

Northanger Abbey presents a curious interlude in the history of the gothic novel. The novel itself both is and is not a gothic, but has attained a classic status that eluded the novels that inspired it. Most readers come to *Northanger* after reading and enjoying some of Austen's more mature works, especially *Pride and Prejudice* and *Emma*, and it is probably the main reason anyone still picks up *The Mysteries of Udolpho* today.[26] Many readers and critics mischaracterize *Northanger Abbey* as an expression of haughty disdain for the typical gothic novel of the time. In fact, Austen's take on the gothic is playful and even affectionate. Her heroine, Catherine Morland (whom Tropp characterizes as a "representative of the new middle class reading public"[27]), undertakes a less dangerous but no less character-building journey than Emily St. Aubert as she journeys to Bath, then Northanger, and then home again, alone, in the humbling confines of a public stage coach. And, in the end, even Henry Tilney acknowledges that Catherine was correct in her gothic-inspired suspicions of General Tilney's villainy and the toxic nature of repressed familial dysfunction. In fact, the elder Tilney did kill his wife, but in a way English law neither recognizes nor prohibits—by grinding her down, Montoni-style, with his greed and his coldness.

By rejecting his father's questionable (and traditionally patriarchal) values, Henry will avoid making the same mistake in his own marriage. Catherine understands Radcliffe's message in the best and most useful way possible: she uses fiction to improve her own understanding of society and her place in it as a woman. The naïve Catherine who was so easily fooled by the Thorpes' shallow fibs no longer exists at the end of the novel. By then she is a married woman, truly the heroine of her own story. Austen may have poked gentle fun at the sensational histrionics of the gothic of her day but reaffirmed its essential metaphoric (some might say psychological) truth.

Since readers sometimes miss this sly affirmation of gothic insight, they may also mistakenly assume *Northanger Abbey* helped dampen the public's enthusiasm for the genre. In fact, Austen's novel was begun in 1799, not published until after her death in 1818, and was apparently lost in the still-surging gothic tide that continued unabated until about 1830. Austen's wry take on the genre seems to put a definitive period on its trajectory only in hindsight.[28] Readers of her own era remained unchastised and continued to buy, read, and even write their own gothic novels in impressive numbers. Instead, the demise of the gothic may be more accurately attributed to the arrival of a new author—university-educated, titled, and male—whose serious historical novels eventually sandbagged the gothic flood.

As Diana Wallace points out, during the 18th century, historical fiction of all types was in its infancy. Novelists, including Horace Walpole and Ann Radcliffe, chose medieval settings and used them mostly for atmosphere or symbolic effect, but without any particular concern for accuracy. In contrast to this "cheerfully anachronistic" style,[29] Scott emphasized military adventure and the recorded past over the internal discovery of emotional truths and the small dramas of domestic experience. This masculine-centered approach attempted to reclaim the historical fiction genre from women writers like Radcliffe and Sophia Lee, among others. Depictions of medieval castles soon became exercises in historical verisimilitude rather than scenes of spine-tingling terror (or feminine rebellion). The stolid male protagonist forging his way in the world of real-life politics and war displaced the female ingénue

2. Shadowed Beginnings

poking her way through labyrinthine hidden chambers. Reading and literature became a serious business, the province of men. Women were admitted only so long as they recognized and capitulated to masculine taste and authority. The rest could indulge themselves with popular romances and penny dreadfuls, still available by the barrelful, while the intelligentsia looked on with pity, scorn, or patrician indifference. Astonishingly, this divide has endured until the present day. Only recently have scholars like Pamela Regis, Joanna Gregson, and Jen Lois, among others, begun to challenge these assumptions.

It is reasonable to ask what it is about the gothic, and specifically the gothic romance, that has managed to attract a steady stream of readers from the 18th century well into our own. Victoria Nelson identifies two elements that kept readers coming back for more. One, she believes, is the continued and ever-unsatisfied longing for the divine. Though the peculiar comfort of superstition is largely absent from modern secular culture, it lives on, in mutated form, through tales fraught with ghosts, vampires, psychics, and various elements that bridge some undefined but lurking "other side." Whether people's religious beliefs are unconventional, mainstream, or entirely absent, Nelson suggests, readers are drawn to numinous mysteries either as a matter of spiritual inquiry or as role-playing that entertains while salving a deeper need. This likely accounts for everything from gruesome tales involving monks and nuns (such as *The Awful Disclosures of Maria Monk* in 1836 and, of course, Matthew Lewis's 1796 sensation *The Monk*) to the current popularity of horror movies and supernaturally themed computer games.

In all these ostensibly casual pastimes, she notes, "a certain kind of low-level but potent theological rumination is constantly taking place."[30] It is true that most gothics, both then and now, contain at least one ruined chapel or abbey and perhaps even a spiritual leader whose motives are suspect. One self-published effort from 2012, Lisa Greer's *Come to the Tower, Love*, earned praise from an Amazon reader for fulfilling her fantasies involving "sexy priests,"[31] namely one with the evocatively sanguineous name of Noel Crimson. The howling spirits, rattling chains, and terrifying curses that populate gothics are, from this perspective, more than just a woman wailing for her demon lover, as Coleridge put it. It is the collective wail of humanity, forced into maturity by the rigors of an increasingly scientific world, clinging to the tattered props of its lost collective childhood.

The second common factor Nelson identifies is the presence of a high emotionality, a mood of "high pitched and unremitting anxiety"[32] in almost

The Gothic Romance Wave

every early gothic. Critics of later gothics and women's fiction of the 1960s and 1970s noted, as does Nelson, the deceptive nature of the happy ending in such books. The plot appears to be resolved, the lovers united and the villain punished, and yet there remains a little frisson of unease, a sense of greater issues left unresolved. This creates an addictive lacuna in the psyche of the (female) reader[33] and leads to the mass consumption of gothics and modern Harlequin-style formula romances. Yet, as epistemologically fashionable as such a reading may be, there may be a simpler and equally persuasive explanation. Despite what critics would like to believe about themselves or those they would consider appropriately serious readers, melodrama has and probably always will appeal to human nature. This may be especially true during times of great social change or cultural paradigm shifts, which could explain why gothic romances surged in popularity when feminism gained public momentum both in the 1790s and the 1960s. Gothics have never apologized for lapsing into melodrama (or, as the more jaded 1960s preferred to call it, camp), and its audiences have seen no need to apologize for enjoying their excesses.

Nor, perhaps, should they. Melodrama, as Eric Bentley has noted, has always served a real and valuable purpose as an outlet for the subconscious, and we eliminate it from our lives and our artistic diet at our peril.[34] The gothic setting frees the subconscious to wallow in the primal settings of dungeons, locked rooms, and towers, bewailing the disappointments and dangers of adulthood (for example, frustratingly inadequate employment prospects or a taciturn, distant spouse) along with the near-constant *mementi mori* that accompany age and (sometimes reluctant) maturity. Gothic romances celebrate the hard-won satisfaction of confronting and banishing fear, claiming a forbidden lover, and examining life on a grand scale. The adventure, and the eventual triumph over darkness, is always vicarious: the reader has no genuine fear of being bitten by a vampire or trapped in a tomb (not even Catherine Morland's fantasies went that far).

As noted earlier, the gothic novel's connection to stage melodrama was forged early on, when "Monk" Lewis presented a stage play called *The Castle Spectre* in 1797. Clive Bloom notes that this play "set the standard for the sensational.... The stage directions are filled with expansive gestures, swoons, and of course the looming spectral title figure."[35] The play issued a sort of challenge, Bloom believes, for stage melodramas to go ever further in finding ways to titillate and horrify their rapt audiences. One reason melodrama works so well is because a certain cynical humor is always bubbling under

2. Shadowed Beginnings

the surface for those who care to see it. The 19th century was well aware of this, and many gothic theater productions mixed comedy in with the thrills,[36] much as Jane Austen and Thomas Love Peacock do in *Northanger Abbey* and *Nightmare Abbey*, respectively. The temptation to do the same in a novel must have tugged at many a 20th-century gothicist's conscience. In a "how to" article aimed at would-be gothic authors, novelist Virginia Coffman warned against attempting to simultaneously exploit and subvert the genre by imbedding satire into their narratives. "I wouldn't advise you to put your heart into writing an expose of the gothic romance," she writes, "because these always turn into genuine gothics with a little humor, not an expose at all. And if it fails, no one will care." Real gothics, she says, are skilled at using "a little humor that laughs at the absurdity just before the absurd danger becomes all too real."[37] Phyllis Whitney agreed: "I doubt you can write Gothic novels unless you like reading them. You must be able to throw yourself genuinely into your performance as you write."[38]

Whitney's characterization of writing a gothic as putting on a performance is telling. The writer becomes a sort of ham actor, strutting and tearing out his hair and declaiming on an imaginary stage. In 1964, Bentley had used the same metaphor to describe the subconscious need for melodrama:

> If you have dismissed tears and loud lamentation from your daily life, you might check whether they are equally absent from your dreams at night. You may be no more sentimental than the next man, and yet find you have many dreams in which you weep profusely and at the same time disport yourself like an actor in the old melodrama: throwing yourself on your knees, raising your arms plaintively to heaven, and so forth. For you, in that case, grandiose self-pity is a fact of life. As it can only be copied by the use of grandiose style, the grandiosity of melodrama would seem to be a necessity.[39]

Bentley's tormented dreamer is a male, one who shuns sentimentality; after Radcliffe the reader of the gothic novel, increasingly, is envisioned as a female who can be expected to identify, at least symbolically, with the struggles of the lonely, castle-bound heroine. Of course, such titanic passions seemed wasted on upstanding but placid suitors like Valancourt and Henry Tilney. What women longed to read (and write) about, it seemed, were love interests with fevered hearts and temperaments as wild as a storm over the windswept English moors.

The moors of Haworth, Yorkshire, to be exact.

3

A Dark Blossom
Gothic Novels, 1840–1960

> I pictured myself as I must appear to my fellow travelers if they bothered to glance my way, which was not very likely: a young woman of medium height, already past her first youth, being twenty-four years old, in a brown merino dress with cream lace collar and little tufts of lace at the cuffs. (Cream being so much more serviceable than white, as Aunt Adelaide told me.) My black cape was unbuttoned at the throat because it was hot in the carriage, and my brown velvet bonnet, tied with brown velvet ribbons under my chin, was of the sort which was so becoming to feminine people like my sister Phillida but, I always felt, sat a little incongruously on heads like mine. My hair was thick with a coppery tinge, parted in the center, bought down at the sides of my too-long face, and made into a cumbersome knot to project behind the bonnet. My eyes were large, in some lights the color of amber, and were my best feature; but they were too bold—so said Aunt Adelaide; which meant that they had learned none of the feminine graces which were so becoming to a woman. My nose was too short, my mouth too wide. In fact, I thought, nothing seemed to fit; and I must resign myself to journeys such as this when I travel to and from the various posts which I shall occupy for the rest of my life, since it is necessary for me to earn a living, and I shall never achieve the first of those alternatives: a husband.
> —*Mistress of Mellyn* by Victoria Holt, 1960

Nineteenth-century England and the gothic novel have long maintained a complex and close relationship. The Victorian period, with its reputation for overdone décor, repressed sexuality, and decorous manners masking secret perversities, remains the go-to setting for period gothics in both print and film.[1] Any discussion of Victorian literature is peppered with the names of

3. A Dark Blossom

towering gothic figures such as Heathcliff, Rochester, Dorian Gray, and Dracula. None is the hero of his story in the manner of, say, Fitzwilliam Darcy or Ivanhoe. Each of these men, and many derivative characters, is responsible for villainous acts of all descriptions, but all remain reader favorites into the 21st century. Along with enticing visions of foggy London back streets and vast, windswept moors, the peculiar conflation of hero and villain is the Victorian gothic's lasting legacy to the genre. It is no exaggeration to say that without these literary contributions and those of Charlotte and Emily Brontë in particular, the mass market gothic romance, and perhaps the paperback romance in general, as we now know it would never have existed.

The fondness of modern readers (and writers) for a hyperbolic version of the past was one that infected early gothicists as well. The word "gothic" had, of course, traditionally been associated with both a barbarian tribe and the hulking stone edifices of the Middle Ages. Walpole, Clara Reeve, and Radcliffe, along with the majority of their successors and imitators, made the reference literal, finding medieval settings ideal for their lurid tales of dungeon imprisonments and animated suits of armor. Historical fidelity was of no concern, and audiences cheerfully tolerated more than a few anachronisms in the service of atmosphere and suspense. Many authors followed the lead of Walpole and Reeve by adding prefaces that claimed their novels were translations of manuscripts that had been newly discovered after hundreds of years. This transparent ruse probably fooled no one and displeased even fewer.

The late 18th- and early 19th-century public's fascination with the lost medieval world is not difficult to understand. The old order, with its legendary faith and chivalry, had withered in the light of modern science, technology, and freedom from religious orthodoxy. Left in the wake of what Matthew Arnold would call in 1867 "its melancholy, long withdrawing roar" were the ruins of feudal castles and pre–Reformation abbeys, which provided fertile soil for the English Romantic imagination. Scholars like Victoria Nelson associate this fascination with Pre-Reformation culture with a subconscious yearning for the numinous, which modern rationalism banished to supernatural fiction. Ghosts, vampires, and other revenants, not to mention martyrs, monks, and nuns, represent a link with another world the Middle Ages seemed to respect and commune with almost effortlessly. Yet along with images of gleaming knights and courtly love come darker cultural memories of bizarre tortures and petty tyrannies carried out beneath the leer of sinister gargoyles. Denizens of the Age of Reason were equally eager to experience

The Gothic Romance Wave

medieval barbarity at a safe distance. Gothic novels, read in the safe spaces of their middle-class homes in a more enlightened era, turned forbidden thrills into acceptable titillation. The reading of gothics has often been interpreted as a way of confronting the fear of death (or, for some feminist scholars, the fear of rape). If so, the medieval castle may be as close to the charnel house as early gothic readers cared to go (or were able to imagine). Vicarious escape provided subconscious balm: no matter how many times the heroine found herself trapped behind fearsome castle walls, the reader knew she would eventually escape to the safety of the hero's embrace.

By the end of the Victorian era, however, the Middle Ages had been supplanted by the modern world as the setting of choice. To be sure, its shadow lingers over hybrid spaces like Dracula's Transylvanian castle and Wuthering Heights, which bears a curious inscription over the door: "Hareton Earnshaw, 1500." Yet, though allusions to the distant past would continue as a staple of the mass market gothic romances (after all, every book featuring a castle or abbey must contain at least one scene involving a dungeon, oubliette, or newly unearthed skeleton), stories set entirely before 1790 are almost nonexistent.[2] The shift had artistic as well as aesthetic implications. By setting their novels, gothic and otherwise, in their own era, Victorian authors were able to offer social critique along with the requisite drama (or even melodrama). Increasing attention to psychological realism, with well-developed voices and a connection between childhood experience and adult personality, expose earlier gothic characters like Walpole's for the cardboard cutouts they really were.

Carol A. Senf has identified gothic (specifically vampiric) elements in serious novels like *Bleak House* and *Middlemarch* (not to mention the political writings of Marx and Engels), demonstrating their application to the depiction of Victorian social problems. Thus Emily Brontë "uses gothic materials as metaphors to focus on certain aspects of reality"[3] and even the most realistic and rational storytellers like George Eliot reinforce for readers that "awe and dread—in many cases, even horror—are present in the most mundane social situations."[4] For example, aristocratic vampires like Lord Ruthven morph into wealthy, arrogant industrialists or titled landowners who act as figurative bloodsuckers to economically oppressed characters; women trapped in gloomy castles stand in for proto-feminists stifled by enforced domesticity, and so on. This new artistic maturity served the gothic well, elevating it to the level of high art. Today, any survey of the greatest Victorian literature will inevitably contain what are also considered the great gothic classics: *Jane Eyre, Wuthering Heights, The Picture of Dorian Gray*, and *The*

3. A Dark Blossom

Turn of the Screw, among others. Even gothic-inspired horror novels like *Frankenstein* and *Dracula*, while not always championed as great literature, hold an indisputably important place in the history of popular culture, and the titular characters are universally recognized.

This familiarity, along with the genuine enduring popularity of these stories, may be why 20th-century gothic readers (and beyond) have enjoyed returning to the Yorkshire moors or gaslit London; it is also likely that the types of conflict encountered by the heroine in a Victorian setting speak to the modern reader from the same safe distance that shielded Mrs. Radcliffe's fans from Montoni's Old World wrath. Despite enormous progress, it would be disingenuous to suggest that the era of Queen Elizabeth II has resolved the issues confronting Queen Victoria—social and gender oppression, economic insecurity, mental illness, criminal pathologies, and so on. Finally, Victorian settings may provide just enough verisimilitude to make melodramatic plot devices, such as the feisty orphan and the virtuous governess, not to mention the occasional appearance of a ghost, werewolf, or vampire, more plausible within the fictional framework. And since sinister housekeepers or secretive butlers are generally necessary to torment (or sometimes rescue) the heroine, a manor house of old provides a suitable environment for some upstairs/downstairs intrigue.

Obviously, setting's primary function is to immerse readers in a book's fictional world, and a novel's themes may, consciously or subconsciously, resonate in a way that drives them to similar texts. Yet the majority of readers would probably identify a novel's characters as the fictional element they care most about. Since gothic novels had maintained a substantial female audience since the late 18th century, the relationships between those characters took on greater significance than in novels aimed at men. Pamela Regis identifies the birth of the romance novel in the early 18th century with the publication of Samuel Richardson's *Pamela*. Enthusiastic fans (presumably of both genders) became so caught up in the relationship between Pamela and Mr. B., she reports, that they actually celebrated the fictional couple's wedding day.[5] At the same time, Richardson's didactic novel bears little resemblance to romances that came later, either in style or substance. The epistolary structure fell out of fashion, and Mr. B.'s putative courtship of Pamela can only be described as bizarre at best and sadistic at worst. Later romantic heroes, like *Udolpho*'s Valancourt and *Northanger Abbey*'s Henry Tilney, represented a softer and more egalitarian approach. In fact, Emily appears to be the dominant partner at the conclusion of *Udolpho*, and despite his occasional sarcasm

The Gothic Romance Wave

Henry has no problem discussing the quality of muslin with ladies and eventually humbling himself to beg Catherine's forgiveness for his father's cruelty. If Mr. B. has any counterpart in these later productions, it would be the arrogant General Tilney or the wicked abductor Montoni. By the end of the 19th century, a curious conflation has occurred. The gothic novel's villain, with his sardonic manner, mercurial temper, and domineering (even overbearing) personality has become instead its hero.

The Castle of Otranto had established the trope of using two suitors, one desirable and one evil, to harass the heroine. *Castle* ended much as one might expect, with the ill-tempered Manfred losing both his kingdom and the heroine to Theodore, a gentle and honorable man later revealed as the true heir to the principality. *Udolpho* contrasted Valancourt with Montoni and even *Northanger Abbey* included brash John Thorpe as the docile Henry's rival. However, things would change greatly for gothic heroines between the 1760s and the 1960s: in modern gothic romances, the more villainous-seeming of the two would turn out to be the heroine's ideal mate, while the ostensibly insipid, safe choice would be revealed as a wolf in sheep's clothing. Had either *Otranto* or *Udolpho* been written in the 1960s, their heroines would undoubtedly have ended up happily wed to different grooms. As Victoria Nelson puts it,

> It's as if Isabella in *The Castle of Otranto* found herself against all reason attracted to the tyrant Manfred, learned he had not done any bad things after all but was merely the victim of jealous gossip, and dropped the insipid Theodore/Frederic as her dreaded arranged marriage to Manfred is revealed to be the hoped-for happy ending. Or that Emily in *The Mysteries of Udolpho* discards her own blandly upright Valancourt in favor of the charismatic Montoni.... [In modern romance novels] The darkly attractive character is always suspected of all sorts of crimes and sexual profligacies (the structural echo of his former role as villain), but in the end he is proven innocent (explained wickedness) and pledges lifelong domestic fealty to the heroine.[6]

Alluring Byronic figures in gothic fiction were nothing new; Polidori's Lord Ruthven, modeled on the living Byron, had charmed his fictional social circle and readers alike in 1819. Yet even though Miss Aubrey presumably considered herself fortunate to have won his hand, the text implies that her wedding night ended in her horrific death as he glutted his vampire thirst on his bride. A generation later, Heathcliff would exhibit behavior toward his new wife, Isabella Linton, that dwarfs Mr. B.'s manipulation of Pamela, and surly Edward Rochester's attempt to trick Jane Eyre into bigamy would lead not to disgrace and death but to the couple's eventual happy union. By now, especially in mass market romance novels, the domineering hero as a lust

3. A Dark Blossom

object for the heroine, as well as the female reader, has become something of a cliché (even fans of the genre refer to more egregious examples of these so-called "alpha heroes" as "alphaholes"). The villain repurposed as hero was the Victorian gothic's most significant and lasting contribution to popular women's fiction up to and including the early 21st century. The genesis of this innovation can be traced directly to the doorstep of the Haworth parsonage in the late 1840s.

Committing wildly imaginative fantasies to paper had been a pastime for all three Brontë sisters since their childhood, when they created tiny handmade magazines reporting on various intrigues in their imaginary kingdoms, Gondal and Angria. Their father, the Reverend Patrick Brontë, introduced his children to Milton's *Paradise Lost*, and this work, along with the poetry of Byron, took deep root in their creative psyches.[7] Milton's Satan had a profound influence on Romantics in general and gothic writers in particular,[8] and the explosive combination of dissipated aristocrat and demonic tempter proved irresistible to all three Brontës. From this potent cauldron came what Harold Bloom has called "a relatively new genre, a kind of northern romance."[9] Charlotte and Emily, in particular, introduced a combination of fictional elements to which all modern romance novels, especially the mass market gothic, are indebted.

Wuthering Heights and *Jane Eyre* inverted reader expectations by presenting demure, socially acceptable suitors like Edgar Linton and St. John Rivers (a clergyman like *Northanger Abbey*'s Henry Tilney) as poor matches for the feisty heroines. Jane realizes this in time and refuses St. John's loveless proposal; the second Catherine, however, relives her mother's fatal error in her horrifying forced marriage to the sickly Linton Heathcliff. Only when she civilizes and marries the rough-edged Hareton, a less savage version of his adoptive father, Heathcliff, does the younger Catherine atone for the elder Cathy's action. Though a legal, socially sanctioned union is denied Heathcliff and his Cathy, in good gothic fashion their spirits are thought to walk the moors together after their deaths. Heathcliff is even more closely connected than Rochester to demonic precursors like Lord Ruthven: at one point, Nellie Dean actually refers to him as "a vampire," and Twitchell has suggested[10] that Brontë's original readers would have had no trouble identifying the significance of his pale, bloodless skin and exposed sharp teeth when his body is discovered. Quintessentially Byronic with his dark allure,[11] tortured psyche, and uncontrollable passion for the heroine, Heathcliff provided the blueprint for almost every hero found in current bookstores' romance section.

The Gothic Romance Wave

Meanwhile, the cynical and domineering Rochester, a would-be adulterer and almost-bigamist who imprisons his first wife in the tower Montoni-style, is revealed as Jane's heart's desire, her true soul mate, and eventually her husband. For many readers, the lighter domestic drama of *Jane Eyre* proved more palatable than the violence, abuse, and morbidity (even extending to necrophilia) of *Wuthering Heights*. It was also more easily imitated. If Heathcliff served as the prototype of the demon lover who populates today's mass market romance fiction, Jane and Rochester's story provided the structure that would become a staple in paperback gothics and a good many popular mysteries as well: a young woman, destitute and alone in the world, moves into a gloomy manor house where she must unravel the source of ghostly shrieks, foil murder attempts, and fall hopelessly in love with its emotionally aloof master.

Curiously, the only Brontë sister to adhere to the traditional concept of the romantic hero has remained the least celebrated. Anne Brontë's *Agnes Grey* featured a solid but unremarkable clergyman hero, Edward Weston, whose relationship with the governess Agnes seems socially appropriate and morally above reproach but strikes none of the (literal) sparks as that other Brontë governess and her own Edward. Her second novel, *The Tenant of Wildfell Hall*, features a determined heroine, Helen, who leaves her rich but brutish husband, Arthur Huntingdon, and later marries Gilbert, a gentle farmer who cherishes her and is kind to her son. Published in June 1848, *Tenant* shocked Anne's contemporaries with its frank scenes of alcohol abuse and adultery, but modern readers have (at least so far) failed to embrace it with the enthusiasm they have shown Charlotte and Emily's work. *Tenant* rejects literary gothicism in favor of feminist politics; though Arthur is as Byronically loutish as Heathcliff and Rochester, he seems to prefer his mistress to Helen, while she prefers the more respectful Gilbert. Anne's message seems to be that a sensible woman should reject cads like Arthur (or Rochester) and embrace relative dullards like Gilbert. One wonders if, had Anne reversed the characters and let the dynamic Arthur rescue Helen from a dreary courtship with the overly respectable Gilbert, the novel would now be as revered as *Wuthering Heights* and *Jane Eyre*.[12] Female readers, then and now, tend to forgive Heathcliff and Rochester (as well as their literary descendants) a great variety of sins because of their all-consuming love for the heroines. Arthur's indifference to his bride is the one transgression they cannot overlook.

Charlotte, the last surviving Brontë sister, died in March 1855. Her last

3. A Dark Blossom

two novels, *Shirley* and *Villette*, contain nothing explicitly gothic and feature relatively forgettable characters and couples. Like Charlotte, Victorian literary culture had apparently outgrown the gothic, though some of its elements retained their usefulness as metaphors. In 1890, *The Picture of Dorian Gray* would employ gothic tropes to examine aesthetic philosophy and, from a safely symbolic distance, sexuality. Henry James' 1898 *The Turn of the Screw* brought Victorian gothic into literary adulthood, exploring aberrant psychology and forbidden sexuality with a touch so fine that critics have never been able to solve its central mystery or agree on exactly what sort of demons the nameless governess faced. Still, not every author enjoyed writing high-minded tomes filled with social critique, and not every reader found contentment in sentimental domestic dramas. Literacy rates were growing steadily, while printing technology continued to evolve. A vast public with diverse interests and various degrees of sophistication clamored for inexpensive, entertaining reading material. Like their counterparts a hundred years earlier, they clamored for gothic fiction.

The year 1847 saw not only the publication of both *Jane Eyre* and *Wuthering Heights*, but another gothic-themed work that has stood the test of time for slightly different reasons. *Varney the Vampire or The Feast of Blood*, a popular serial that had been running in installments since 1845, was released in a single volume that filled some 868 pages. Though lacking in artistic finesse and sometimes in coherence, *Varney* has become the best-known of the penny bloods (referred to after 1860 as penny dreadfuls), inexpensive editions of lurid fiction, often hastily composed, that intentionally echoed (and borrowed from) the melodramatic 18th-century gothics[13] published by Lane and his competitors. *Varney*, thought to be the work of James Malcolm Rymer, seems to take its chief inspiration from Polidori's *Vampyre*, published nearly 30 years earlier (in fact, a character named Polidori appears in the text). Like Ruthven, Varney seeks not only female victims, but a bride. This poses some difficulty because there is nothing romantically appealing about him and he is described as physically repulsive. His attacks on various maidens are just that, with none of the erotic innuendo that would accompany the vampire bites in later works (and would transform vampire mythology in the late 1960s).

Literary gothics like *Wuthering Heights* and, later, *The Turn of the Screw* would straddle the line between gothic metaphor and the actual depiction of supernatural activity, but the author and audience of *Varney* had no time for such delicate artistic maneuvers. Varney's exploits were unabashedly constructed as entertainment for the newly literate middle class, complete with occasional jabs at the aristocracy and peasantry alike. *Varney* also featured an abundance of melodramatic conventions that made the story a natural candidate for the stage, where it also enjoyed a successful run[14] in the manner of its precursor, Polidori's *The Vampyre*. Rymer followed *Varney* with another lurid tale that is still well known today, *String of Pearls* (now better known by the name of its main character, Sweeney Todd). Along with other penny bloods, some bearing intriguing gothic titles like *The Spectre at the Hall*, the coarse but inventive *Varney* captured the public imagination to such an extent that at least one moralizing publication lashed out against its excesses, only to recapitulate and start writing its own brand of didactic vampire tales.[15]

Varney is especially interesting to modern aficionados of the gothic because of its obvious influence on Stoker's *Dracula* (1897) and, by extension, all the gothic vampire literature that came afterward. Though it contained scenes of domestic drama, vampire courtship, and a few thwarted weddings, *Varney* does not seem to have been aimed at female readers and has little in common with the novels of Radcliffe or the Brontës. The viewpoint throughout is essentially masculine, and there is no interest in topical issues like women's rights or economic inequality (though class issues do impact the plot). Its forthright use of supernatural trappings, with the author providing no rational explanation in the manner of Ann Radcliffe, would seem to ally it with the horror fiction of Walpole and Monk Lewis rather than popular romance. At the end of the story, Varney casts himself into a live volcano to end his tormented and lonely existence instead of finding a patient heroine willing to accept and manage his considerable flaws. However, its success demonstrated ongoing public interest in the gothic genre, and its distribution by means of inexpensive, mass-produced copies prefigures the marketing strategy of the 20th-century paperback purveyors.

During the 19th century, the manufacture and distribution of popular fiction became an established commercial enterprise both in England and America. Printing technology, along with increased literacy and economic opportunity, enabled authors and publishers to target a new and potentially lucrative market: fiction aimed primarily at women. Though post–*Varney* penny dreadfuls shifted toward a young male audience, with tales of wayward boys and sensational crimes replacing romance and heroines in peril, other forms of fiction took up the slack on both sides of the Atlantic. Female readers were proliferating as education and literacy expanded exponentially, and respectable ladies of the leisured class were eager for vicarious adventure.

3. A Dark Blossom

Kay Mussell has traced the expansion of this specialized trade and notes that the novel as an art form and an economic commodity gained traction in America just as the 18th-century gothic peaked in England[16]; this had important ramifications for the development of American reading habits and tastes. Fittingly enough, Walpole's *Castle of Otranto* was one of the first novels imported to the United States, where it enjoyed immense popularity along with the works of Monk Lewis, Clara Reeve, and Ann Radcliffe. By studying bestseller lists and lending library inventories, Mussell found that by the 1840s, gothic romances were staple reading material for ladies in America as well as England, with many successful titles also penned by women.[17]

Though many of these authors are now forgotten and their works lost to posterity, American influence changed the gothic in several important ways. First, American authors, perhaps for cultural reasons, tended to be less interested in medieval trappings than their European counterparts, and some substituted Puritan New England as a suitably oppressive backdrop,[18] prefiguring Hawthorne's 1850 novel, *The Scarlet Letter*. Others located their fiction in warmer climates and sowed the seeds of the Southern Gothic, which would eventually become a genre in its own right. Second, American readers tended to prefer gothics in the vein of Mrs. Radcliffe, with apparently supernatural occurrences later revealed to have logical explanations.[19] These types of plots, moving steadily away from the sort of lurid horror represented by *The Monk* and *Varney*, would result in the creation of one of the most lasting and popular fictional genres, the mystery. The tale of detection had of course started with another well-known American writer in the gothic tradition, Poe. Gothics already had much in common with another popular genre at the time, the domestic sentimental novel, so grafting on a few elements of the mystery novel afforded several new avenues for development.

The first three decades of the 20th century represented a boom period for the production and consumption of popular fiction. Advances in the technology of printing, binding, and transporting books, as well as the spread of accessible retail outlets,[20] made books an affordable and even disposable commodity. Penguin Books had released its first paperbacks in the United Kingdom in 1935, though they were simple affairs without cover art. In 1939, the first recognizably modern paperbacks made their way into the American marketplace. The brainchild of Pocket Books' founder, Robert DeGraff, these new paperbacks offered readers something new and irresistible. Brightly colored, portable, and inexpensive, the books were marketed aggressively, displayed and sold like periodicals, and soon became a cornerstone of popular

The Gothic Romance Wave

culture.[21] Most early paperbacks reprinted books that had originally appeared in hardcover, with detective fiction immediately seizing a sizable market share. Eventually, paperback publishers began hiring writers to create stories that would go directly to press. Writers like Dashiell Hammet and James M. Cain were soon turning out "pulp fiction"—stories that could be written quickly, tightly, and to a recognizable formula. Mass-produced science fiction, westerns, and adventure novels followed. These stories, particularly the "hard-boiled" detective tales, were mostly written by men for a male audience. Women's fiction certainly existed, including some that remains popular today, such as the Regency romances of Georgette Heyer, which spawned another mass market genre. Much of this output is so dated and generic that it has not survived the test of time and is now considered mainly as ephemera. A line of paperbacks pitched directly at female readers had yet to appear. All that would soon change.

In August 1938, nearly two centuries after Richardson's *Pamela* and just shy of one hundred years after *Jane Eyre*, Daphne du Maurier's *Rebecca* appeared to immediate critical and public success. Du Maurier was the product of a theatrical and literary family, with an actor father and a grandfather, George du Maurier, who created another iconic character whose name has passed into common parlance, Svengali.[22] *Rebecca* was the 31-year-old author's fifth novel; her first, *The Loving Spirit*, had taken its title and theme from an Emily Brontë poem. Legend has it that du Maurier struggled with the first draft of *Rebecca* but eventually isolated herself from her family and completed the manuscript in four months.[23] This time, she turned to Emily's sister Charlotte for inspiration.

Rebecca expands on many of *Jane Eyre*'s situations and themes, not to mention the basic setup for the plot: a naïve young woman without family or prospects moves into an imposing English manor house (which has a name even though *Rebecca*'s heroine does not) and tries to overcome her status as an outsider in a hostile atmosphere. There she endures a series of unsettling adventures and romantic disappointments, even a threat to her life. She only reaches a point of personal validation and strength when she becomes indispensable to the hero, whose own sins and legal transgressions have broken him physically and mentally. The two declare their love for each other and embark on a real marriage, though the union is haunted by the tragic events that have befallen them during the course of the story. The heroine's love redeems the hero and enables the couple to start a new life free of the past's ugly specter. In both novels, the couple leaves the original site of their troubled courtship, which burns to the ground in a kind of purging ritual. Though many critics have debated the passive role of the gothic heroine, Mrs. DeWinter, like Jane Eyre before her, ultimately emerges as the stronger of the two main characters. Meanwhile, her flawed male counterpart is punished with physical maiming and at least some degree of economic deprivation: Rochester is temporarily blinded and loses a hand in the destruction of Thornfield, while Maxim loses Manderley and becomes an exiled, aging shadow of his former self. Jane and the nameless heroine of *Rebecca* finish their narratives with their once-dominant (perhaps even domineering) husbands more or less at their mercy.

Rather than simply modernizing the plot of *Jane Eyre*, du Maurier inverts it. The wedding of the nameless narrator and the hero, Maxim de Winter, comes not at the end of the novel but at the beginning, and the antagonist is not a shrieking madwoman imprisoned in the attic, but the aristocratic Maxim's deceased wife, beautiful and socially accomplished in a way the middle-class narrator knows she never will be. The novel climaxes not with a declaration of love between Maxim and the narrator, but with a revelation about Rebecca's death. For these reasons *Rebecca*, like the many paperback gothics that followed it, has less in common with romance novels than it does with mysteries. The fusion of the two genres, handled with consummate skill, proved irresistible to readers. Since 1938, *Rebecca* has sold millions of copies and has never been out of print.

Along with *Jane Eyre* itself, *Rebecca* provided the soil from which all subsequent mass market gothics and romantic suspense novels have sprung. In the 1940s, Joan Fontaine starred in movie versions of both books, further connecting the two in the public's mind. The covers of many early gothics touted these new stories as "in the tradition of" or "influenced by" one or both of these two books. Joanna Russ even claimed to find one chronologically challenged edition of *Jane Eyre* being "promoted as 'in the tradition of *Rebecca*.'"[24] Later gothics would generally follow one of these two novels in setting up the basic plot, bringing a naïve young woman to a sinister house either as an employee or as a new bride who soon realizes she knows almost nothing about her husband's past or true motives (this "frightened bride" trope gave Russ the title for her classic essay on the genre as well as arousing her feminist ire). Du Maurier is also credited with creating the archetype of the sinister housekeeper[25] who secretly plots the heroine's demise, later (with a few variations) to become a staple in mass market gothic romances.

Rebecca's success inspired many imitators both in print and in theaters,

The Gothic Romance Wave

where the film version made a splash in 1940. Among gothic-themed book/movie pairings were Lady Eleanor Smith's *The Man in Grey* (also known as *A Dark and Splendid Passion*, the novel was a 1942 bestseller), featuring a brutal Heathcliffesque male lead, *Dragonwyck* (published in 1944), a sort of American *Jane Eyre* by Anya Seton, and the 1946 film *The Spiral Staircase*, based on Ethel Lina White's 1933 novel *Some Must Watch*. Victorian classics by Hawthorne, Poe, Wilkie Collins, Wilde, and of course the Brontës were pressed into service as movie premises as well. These "gaslight melodramas," which have been examined and catalogued by Guy Barefoot,[26] provided an alternative to the hypermasculine pulps that many women no doubt found distasteful. Rough urban settings were replaced with lush Victorian and Edwardian domestic interiors; dramatic tension came from psychological conflict rather than ham-fisted violence. While the storylines might not have been recognizably feminist, female characters and women's concerns were central to the plots.

The 1950s saw a steady increase in what were then known as novels of suspense, many of which contained gothic and romantic elements. Mystery writer Val McDermid describes her own reaction when, as an undergraduate in Oxford, she discovered this female-dominated field in second-hand bookstores:

> I read everything I could get my hands on, from decorous English country house mysteries of the Golden Age to American pulp fiction with its vamps, vixens and victims.
>
> I knew instinctively that these books were a key element in my education as an aspiring writer. They were absorbing and page-turning, but that wasn't unusual in the mystery genre. What was unusual was their methods. They kept me on the edge of my seat neither because of constant fast-moving action nor because of the judicious scattering of puzzling clues. Often there was little action, fewer clues and not so much a case of "whodunit" as "Oh my God, what's going to happen next?"[27]

Many of the authors McDermid found are little-known today; others, like Charlotte Armstrong and Patricia Highsmith (the creator of Ripley), are remembered as pioneers of the suspense genre, which is still going strong in the 21st century. By the 1950s, with the paperback trade booming, readers hungry for new material, and women writers gaining respect and economic traction, the market was ripe for a new development that would change publishing history and countless women's lives.

In 1960, a determined British novelist named Eleanor Hibbert was trying her hand at a suspense-laden romance containing elements of *Jane Eyre* and *Rebecca*. Though the prolific Hibbert had found modest success with a series

3. A Dark Blossom

of romances and historical novels written under various pseudonyms, her new novel also resembled *Nine Coaches Waiting* (1958), the third novel of an established writer of women's suspense, Mary Stewart. For her new effort, Hibbert chose a fresh pen name: Victoria Holt, a nod to England's great queen as well as, providentially, the name of Hibbert's bank.[28] Set in Cornwall, as *Rebecca* had been, Holt's *Mistress of Mellyn* told the story of a governess who simultaneously tried to solve a murder and win the heart of her brooding employer. The book was an international success, finally bringing Hibbert wealth and worldwide fame. The book invoked the spirit of *Rebecca* so completely that many speculated Daphne du Maurier had written it under a pseudonym.[29] Not only the theme and style, but also the cover of the first edition of *Mistress of Mellyn* set the pace for the many popular gothics that followed. A young woman in bare feet and a billowing white nightgown runs down a winding stone staircase, fleeing a castle with a single light blazing in the turret.[30] After 1960, *Rebecca* would retroactively be labeled a gothic novel, as would *Jane Eyre* and a good many other, older novels that were reissued with the now-familiar blurbs and the "woman running from the house" cover.[31] Holt's name would eventually become synonymous with the style of gothic romance that would come to dominate the paperback market. As "Victoria Holt," Hibbert would publish 31 highly successful novels in this vein, the last in 1993, the year of her death.

Meanwhile, on the other side of the pond, American author Phyllis Whitney was struggling to find a niche for her fiction. Whitney had become a full-time writer at the relatively late age of 48, writing light mysteries and "career novels" aimed at young women setting out for the workplace. Early on, she experimented with what would later be called the mass market gothic romance and managed to sell a few to hardback publishers. When it came to finding mass commercial distribution for her work, she ran into an obstacle. "The men editors of softcover books said there was no market for the sort of thing I was writing," she recalled in 1980, "so not one of my romantic suspense novels was brought out in paper." Eventually an editor told her "they were looking for 'entertaining novels for women, which would be both romantic and suspenseful.'"[32] Whitney quickly offered the paperback rights to her latest manuscript, *The Quicksilver Pool* (the hardback version of which had been published in 1955). Aimed specifically at this particular cross-section of readers, *Quicksilver* proved instantly profitable and remained in print until 1992. Copies of the novel in several different editions were numerous and are still easily obtained today. Whitney noted the importance of packaging and what

The Gothic Romance Wave

we would now call "branding" the novels: "It wasn't that other such books weren't already being published here and there, and even in paper by one perceptive woman editor, but until that moment no one had pulled them together and given them a 'category' label."[33]

The idea to pitch suspense novels specifically at women readers soon proved successful beyond anything the publisher had probably imagined, and his next step was, like so many of the novels themselves, inspired by Daphne du Maurier's bestseller. As Whitney recalls, "One of the paperback editors noticed that his mother's favorite novel was *Rebecca*.... He was thinking of trying a series of such books for women readers, and he cast around for possible titles. The first one he decided to publish was my *Thunder Heights*. The publisher called the new series 'Gothics,' and the run was on." This publisher was Gerald Gross at Ace Books, which would proudly style itself "First in Gothics" and dominate the field for the next two decades. Ace's marketing strategy deliberately and insightfully positioned the new paperback series as the favorite reading material of middle-class female consumers.

Whitney's title, which fittingly echoed *Wuthering Heights*, appeared in 1960. This atmospheric domestic drama borrowed *Dragonwyck*'s setup of the poor relation who moves into her estranged family's Hudson Valley manor and wove in stands of the Brontës, Holt, and du Maurier. The Ace edition boasted this connection on the cover of the 1960 edition, touting it as "like *Rebecca* and *Wuthering Heights*." Whitney became the first American author to achieve success with her books, now officially known as "gothics." For several decades, she, Holt, and Stewart would rule the bookshelves as the three queens of the gothic suspense. Their combined success reinvigorated the novels that had originally inspired them and in turn generated countless clones and variations in an ongoing literary cross-pollination. Whitney would eventually publish 74 novels, two books on writing, and countless articles on the techniques of gothic romance and suspense fiction. She released her final book in the genre once again called "romantic suspense," in 1997 at the impressive age of 94 before her death ten years later.

Ironically, the split between male and female modes of gothic[34] in the 19th century set the stage for the genre's modern incarnation. During the 18th and 19th centuries, male readers and authors helped shape the gothics, but in the 20th, women would come to dominate the field on both sides of the book covers. In a reversal of the tradition that once forced the Brontë sisters to take on the male pseudonyms Currer, Ellis, and Acton Bell, men writing gothics would now assume feminine pen names and court an almost

3. A Dark Blossom

entirely female audience. The mass market gothic of the 1960s and '70s would have little in common with *The Castle of Otranto*, *The Monk*, or the sort of gothics Jane Austen knew and parodied in *Northanger Abbey*. Instead, they would resemble a hybrid of women's suspense novels and category romances of the sort published by Mills and Boon in the United Kingdom and their sister company, Harlequin, in the United States.

From a 21st-century perspective, the growth and decline of the mass market gothic romance forms a curious parallel to the trajectory of its earlier 18th-century incarnation. In both cases, early gothics, rough-hewn but earnest, established a loyal audience who clamored for more stories in the same vein. Consumer demand gave rise to a second wave of imitators, ranging from those sincerely inspired by the genre to those like William Lane in the 18th century and the modern author Dean Koontz, whose primary purpose was to cash in despite an apparent disdain for the form and its readers. Eventually, parodists reclaimed and reshaped the material, while a competing genre lured away erstwhile fans who had become bored by a market glut of substandard material.

But before that happened, the paperback gothic romance was to experience a surge of unprecedented mass popularity and enter its golden era.

4

Gothic Flower Power
The Gothic Explosion, 1960–1970

> She stood there dazed, then her eyes wandered to the body of the chapel, and she saw the blurred outlines of a figure standing stock still at the back of the center aisle and regarding her silently.
> It was another shock and she gasped out once more. As she did so, the somber figure advanced towards her. In the light from the single bulb, she was able to make out something of the silent bystander. He was a tall man, wearing a dark, caped coat and carrying a cane. It took her only a moment to guess that this must be the cousin from England, Barnabas Collins.
> "Mr. Collins?" she asked nervously.
> The man nodded. "I am Barnabas Collins," he said in a deep, mellow voice.
> "I couldn't see you clearly for a moment," she apologized.
> "And I fear that I frightened you." Barnabas Collins said, coming close to the front of the stage so that she could see him clearly. He had a handsome, rather melancholy face with deep-set burning eyes, a Byronic face. His thick black hair was loosely brushed across his forehead, and his skin had an unusual sallow tint.
> Diana was embarrassed at having made herself ridiculous before this self-assured man, and said, "I guess I was determined to see phantoms. But I just had a strange experience."
> —*Barnabas Collins and the Mysterious Ghost* by Marilyn [William Edward Daniel] Ross, 1970

By 1960, the American paperback trade was flourishing. The pulps of the 1940s and 1950s had established what Geoffrey O'Brien calls the "big-city narrative,"[1] a kind of mythologizing realism populated by tough-guy noir detectives and juvenile delinquents pummeling their way across a seedy urban backdrop. Simultaneously titillated and horrified, readers gorged on these

4. Gothic Flower Power

novels in great quantities. Soon colorful yarns featuring crime, adultery, and drug abuse began to displace classics and literary fiction on sales racks.

The mean streets of the pulps, like the offices of their publishers, were by and large a masculine landscape. The creation of V.I. Warshawski was decades in the future, and the few women (or "dames," as they were often referred to) who did venture through the pages of the pulps were victims, molls, or double-dealing temptresses (best exemplified by Dashiell Hammett's Brigid O'Shaughnessy). The other side of the typewriter proved just as testosterone-soaked. The writers most associated with pulp fiction, such as Hammett, Raymond Chandler, James M. Cain, Mickey Spillane, and John D. MacDonald, were males who favored a particularly hard-bitten style modeled on Hemingway.[2] Women readers who sought accurate representation, or at least relatable characters, were left with nurse romances, domestic dramas, or cozy mysteries modeled on Golden Age crime authors like Agatha Christie and Dorothy Sayers. Though some of these novels flirted with hardboiled themes, female sleuths tended to avoid knuckle-bruising forays into the world of gangs and gruesome murders, and nurses who confronted junkies tended to do so in the safety and sterility of an examining room with at least one protective male doctor around. For the most part, novels with female protagonists stuck to themes intended to appeal to their expected female readership. Plots revolved around dysfunctional families, small-scale domestic treachery, and the ever-pressing quest for a suitable long-term mate. Quiet and low-key, these novels filled an obvious need and brought in steady sales, though none attracted much critical notice or attained mainstream bestseller status.

The success of Victoria Holt's *Mistress of Mellyn* in 1960 changed all that. Holt, then still known only as Eleanor Hibbert, had long been angling to hit the bestseller lists and deliberately set out to combine elements she thought would sell.[3] After earning its author a small fortune, the book opened the floodgates for a new trend in fiction aimed at women, combining light mystery with romance and Victorian costume drama. The formula was both flexible and imitable, allowing seemingly endless permutations and imitations. Publishers were quick to cash in on Holt's popularity, scrabbling to find more gothics—then still known as "novels of romantic suspense"—to feed suddenly hungry female audiences. The standardized cover grew from the original design on *Mellyn*'s first edition, which depicted a woman in Victorian dress facing an imposing castle. The subsequent paperback edition changed the scene to that of a barefoot woman in a nightdress hurrying down the steps

The Gothic Romance Wave

of a gloomy castle. In the central round tower, a burning light reveals the hint of a silhouetted figure watching her. This trope, the famous "woman running from a house" would become homogeneous to the point of parody by the mid-60s. The "gothic" label, created by Gerald Gross at Ace (thus allowing Ace to style itself "First in Gothics" on its covers), gave the new genre—a hybrid of cozy mysteries, light horror, and romance—a literary flavor, aligning it with the beloved classics of the 19th century.

Along with Phyllis Whitney, another American author, Virginia Coffman, found her sea legs with the advent of the gothics. At first, like Whitney, Coffman found herself stymied by a publishing industry that claimed there was no market for her novel, the story of a brassy Irishwoman who hires on as housekeeper at a French castle to investigate a friend's disappearance. "I wrote *Moura* in the 1950s," Coffman recalled 30 years later, "and my publisher said, 'Don't call it a gothic. No one today ever heard of the word.'"[4] Undaunted, Coffman persisted, and *Moura* was eventually published by Crown Publishing in 1959. Though it did not sell in the same numbers as *Mistress of Mellyn*, it proved popular enough that it enabled her to become a full-time writer by 1965. After the unexpected success of *Moura*, retroactively labeled a gothic, Coffman reworked another of her novels, *The Devil Vicar* (1966), into a sequel called *The Vicar of Moura*. Along with the retooled title, *Vicar*'s original heroine, Estelle Varney (the last name recalling the famous vampire), morphed into Anne Wicklow, the now-widowed protagonist of the original *Moura*. Set in Yorkshire in a town reminiscent of the Brontës' Haworth, the novel is rife with vicious dogs, a maniac stalking the moors, and a near live-burial, while her hero, Marc Branshaw, bears more than a passing resemblance to Heathcliff (as well as a name echoing *Wuthering Heights*' Earnshaw family) as he trods the moors with long-simmering revenge on his mind. Another entry, *The Vampire of Moura*, published in 1970, may have been an attempt to attract fans of *Dark Shadows*, as was her *Lucifer's Cove* series in 1971. Coffman went on to write more than 50 gothics and other novels under several pseudonyms before she died in 2005. The Nevada Writers Hall of Fame noted that "by the 1980s, Coffman was recognized as the author largely responsible for setting off the Gothics craze of the 1960s, earning her the reputation of 'Queen of the Gothics.'"[5]

There could be no question of the intended audience for the new product: plot, tone, and style were feminized as ardently as the pulps had once promoted a particular loutish version of masculinity. Coarse descriptions of brutal violence and metropolitan mayhem had no place in these new novels.

4. Gothic Flower Power

Set in genteel manor houses and discreetly modernized castles, the tales would emphasize terror over horror, as Ann Radcliffe once described her own method.[6] Feisty but sexually innocent heroines would replace gun-toting dames, their kind hearts captivated by taciturn but noble aristocrats. If swaggering, street-smart palookas appeared at all, it was in the role of the villain—though not even the villain swears or uses street drugs in a gothic. Sex, if mentioned at all, was at most euphemistic and in many cases avoided altogether, at least in the early gothics. Not even the most liberated heroine mentions The Pill or invites the hero for bedroom romps before marriage. Tame, chaste, and virtually devoid of anything more violent than a fall down a staircase or a tumble from a horse, the gothics would provide suitable entertainment for teen girls and dowagers alike, with their biggest audience coming from the vast group in between.

In order to attract buyers and encourage serial purchasing of gothics, pricing was set competitively low. The 1950s pulps had generally sold for a quarter (worth about $2 in 2017 money); early 1960s gothics ranged from 50 to 75 cents, with 60 cents as the most common price (equivalent to about $5 in 2017, roughly the price of a category Harlequin romance). By the late 1960s, gothics would rise to 95 cents and, in the '70s, $1.25 to $1.50. From the beginning, the novels, like the pulps before them, were regarded as near-disposable. Mass market gothic romances were riddled with typographical errors and sometimes bound with pages or entire sections missing. In one case, a novel called *House of Strangers* by Meg Padget was glued into a cover flat meant for *House of Strangers* by Jennifer Hale.[7] Twenty-first-century collectors of gothics have only to flip through the brittle, yellowed pages and taped-together covers to see that these books were not meant to be saved for posterity. In some ways, mass market gothic romances were like television shows before the advent of home recording devices, meant to be watched and enjoyed once and then set aside in favor of a new installment.

As the new decade got underway, Ace, Dell, Lancer, and others readied themselves for a brisk and profitable trade in gothics. All that remained was to fill the waiting stable with authors and the editors' shelves with manuscripts. One obvious source tapped by editors was their existing pool of "nursie" writers, who had proven they could produce formulaic stories quickly. Rachel Cosgrove Payes once recalled how she was wooed by an editor from DAW Books in 1967. The editor assured her that if she "could stand" writing nurse romances, she "could stand to write anything!" Eventually, after studying a few current gothic paperbacks, Payes discovered "they were just con-

The Gothic Romance Wave

temporary romantic suspense with an extra dollop of dripping Spanish moss" and went on to write eight before turning to the more lucrative field of historical romance.[8]

Next, publishers mined mystery and suspense fiction of the 1930s and 1940s for *Rebecca* clones, perhaps feeling (or hoping) some of the same elements would appeal to modern female audiences. A number of romantic suspense stories, set in big English houses that resembled Manderley but without much else to recommend them as gothic, were recycled as gothics during the early '60s, when publishers were seemingly desperate for material. Packaged with the requisite cover and given enticing blurbs that might or might not accurately represent the contents, these stories were as coy and chaste as their youthful heroines, remaining proudly (though inadvertently) out of touch with the more permissive 1960s. The old-fashioned aura of their Victorian or wartime settings would eventually become a staple of mass market gothic romances (and, in the 1970s, a threat to their continued existence).

One such "recycled" author was Mabel Seeley, who had started writing mystery fiction in 1938 and retired in 1954. Twelve years later, her mysteries were rereleased with the banner "A Gothic Suspense Novel" above the title. Both 1939's *The Crying Sisters* and 1940's *The Whispering Cup* feature small-town intrigues and adultery with nary a manor house in sight, though the 1966 reprints show a castle in one instance and a grand Victorian manor in the other. Helen MacInnes' 1940s World War II espionage novels received the same treatment, though at least their European setting justifies the addition of a medieval-style keep on her 1943 work, *Horizon* (among others). Another wartime drama is Sheila Bishop's *The House with Two Faces* (1960, reprinted in 1964 and 1971), which promises a woman's struggle against "the quicksand of an evil past." In fact, the story is dominated by a flashback involving a failing marriage and a 1940s love triangle (most assuredly not involving "evil"), some of it likely based on Bishop's own nursing experiences in a converted English manor house. Its main point of interest is its use of a mostly unrepentant adulteress heroine who seems only slightly interested in saving her marriage. However, this same trope makes it entirely unsuitable as a gothic.

Also retrofitted as gothics were a number of cozy mysteries, including Margaret Erskine's Inspector Finch novels, which publishers probably seized upon as a ready-made gothic series. Finch first appeared in 1938 and proved reasonably popular with, if not beloved by, U.K. mystery fans. Since many of his cases revolved around big houses with wealthy suspects and dysfunctional

4. Gothic Flower Power

families, the books were reissued in the United States with the proverbial fleeing woman, and not Finch himself, gracing the cover. The series continued until 1977, seven years before Erskine's death; only the last volume was not packaged as a traditional gothic. The title of *The Devil's Church* by F. Draco (1951) would seem to mark it as a prime candidate for the gothic treatment, with the back cover singling out its titular "edifice ... built for worship, consecrated by rites which are best forgotten, given over to arts too black for recounting, dedicated to the worship of the Devil." Alas, though there is some talk of witchcraft and curses among the attached manor's residents, the story is yet another cozy murder mystery without many thrills. As in *The House with Two Faces*, World War II casts a long shadow over its European characters. If anything, this touch of depressing realism detracts from its gothic atmosphere.

In some (or perhaps many) cases, the quality (or even the coherence) of the story wasn't all that important as long as a manuscript had at least a few of the requisite elements to be released as a gothic. In her bibliography of 20th-century gothic, Elsa J. Radcliffe identifies several books that tried her patience. "Not gothic," she writes beside several entries, most of them run-of-the-mill romantic suspense or manor-house cozies. A 1946 mystery, Alice Campbell's *With Bated Breath*, earns particular scorn: "This appears to be something the author dug out of a back cupboard and got published due to the new fad for supposed Gothic stories," she notes. "An incredibly jumbled writing style made very tough reading; half-way through the book I gave up in dizzy despair. I didn't even care enough to read the last chapter. Avis joins a bunch of crazy folk bombing around in an old English manor house and it's all really too too confusing."[9]

Yet there were some bright spots in the growing pantheon of gothic authors. In 1963, sisters Joan Aiken and Jane Aiken Hodge, both daughters of American author Conrad Aiken, burst onto the scene with two original novels. Joan's *The Silence of Herondale* told the suspenseful tale of a woman protecting a child prodigy from a malevolent stalker, while Jane's *Maulever Hall*, a historical romance in the style of Jane Austen and Georgette Heyer, pitted an amnesia victim against the brooding master of the eponymous manor. Eventually, Jane would transition to writing a series of well-received Regency romances and Joan would drift toward the children's books for which she became best known. In the beginning, however, Joan preferred to write contemporary tales featuring modern, liberated heroines. She was surprised to find that the covers misrepresented her short-haired, jean-clad protagonists by giving them flowing manes and fluffy nightdresses, but she was amused all the same.[10] She followed up with *The Fortune Hunters*, another novel of suspense revolving around a bohemian artistic circle and an independent woman guarding her newly inherited wealth from silver-tongued grifters.

Another consciously literary effort, Charlotte Armstrong's 1965 thriller *The Turret Room* was reprinted as a paperback in 1967. Billed as "an unforgettable thriller," the Fawcett-Crest mass market edition employs a modified version of the familiar gothic scenario. The woman is clad in a nightgown, but is not running. Instead, she faces forward, hands clasped in front of her, and the effect is one of her rising from wispily drawn water. A hip '60s-style young man stands between her and a tilted close-up of a moonlit tower. A jaunty scarf flaps at his neck and half-obscures his face. His look is inviting and flirtatious but not menacing.

The plot involves a young man (presumably the one on the cover), Harold Page, who sneaks out of a mental hospital and walks 75 miles to the house of his former in-laws. The house is a modified gothic setting, modern but with a turret room and a brewing mystery. Edith Thompson, a poor relation dependent on the charity of the family who owns the house, hides Harold when he is wrongly accused of assault. By modern standards, the book is slow-paced, with endless stammering and rounds of questioning between the in-laws and Edie. After much paranoia and manipulation, the tale concludes with some hearty bludgeoning and falls down the cellar stairs. Except for the turret room, there is nothing especially gothic about it except the poisoned relationships among the family members. It is a domestic melodrama with lots of claustrophobia as people move from one room to the other, the house closing in on them and their schemes. Harold's escape leads not to freedom, but to horror and death.

The Turret Room is a hybrid typical of many mid–1960s gothics: romance is implied rather than explored, the technique remains psychological rather than potboiler, with hints of melodrama poking through on occasion. The primary obstacle to the characters' happiness in almost every early gothic is lust and family corruption (usually of a fairly dreary sort) rather than outside evil. Ghosts, if any are even mentioned, remain projections of the characters' guilt and not visitors from beyond the veil of death. A woman's perspective is always primary, even when the author is a man (generally using a female pseudonym).

Other gothic paperbacks were more successful at integrating the features of the cozy mystery with the new gothic elements. The popularity of these

4. Gothic Flower Power

stories would eventually solidify into what would become known (and in many cases ridiculed) as the mass market gothic romance formula. A 1963 release, *That Night* by Jane Blackmore, echoed *Rebecca* as its heroine tried to solve the murder of her employer's first wife, at one point reminding herself, "This was no *Jane Eyre*. There was no locked room in the attics with its secret of wild and horrifying madness."[11] She does confront plenty of domestic drama, unruly teens with cars, and a terrible secret keeping her from the man she loves. The following year, Anne Maybury's *Brides of Bellenmore*—identified on the cover not as a gothic but as "an unforgettable mystery-romance in the tradition of Victoria Holt and Mary Stewart"—used a Victorian setting to excellent effect, as an orphaned heroine is courted by two brothers—James, who happens to be already married, at least for two-thirds of the book, and Mark, whose wife died under mysterious circumstances. An interesting subplot involves the possibly sinister Mark's forays into the new and distrusted science of chiropractic. The back of the book advertised "three more memorable romantic-suspense stories."

Maybury (whose real name was Anne Arundel) had been writing thrillers geared toward female audiences since the 1940s, and by the mid–1960s she had become a fixture in the gothic landscape (also writing under the name Katherine Troy), turning out at least 25 titles by 1981. Prolific as this rate seems, it appears virtually slothful beside authors like Michael Avallone, who wrote as Edwina Noone and Dorothea Nile, among many other names, or W.E.D. Ross, better known as "Marilyn," "Clarissa," or, in person, "Dan." The early gothics supplied by these two men, though never critically acclaimed, would prove influential based on the sheer number of titles they produced. Both got in on the game in its early rounds. In 1965, "Edwina Noone" released *Dark Cypress, Corridor of Whispers*, and *Heirloom of Tragedy*, which was touted as both "An Original Lancer Gothic Never Before Published" and "A Best-Seller Gothic Novel." With so much buildup, one expects an exciting and perhaps lurid tale, but *Heirloom* turns out to be a fairly routine costume drama involving light mystery and a blizzard that traps all the suspects inside the manor house until the somewhat clumsy denouement. Unlike the resurrected 1940s-style whodunits, though, the focus here is not on the murder and theft, or even on the supposed evidence against the heroine, but on the effect it has on the characters' relationships, extending even to the servants. Solving the mystery and restoring the castle or manor goes hand in hand with reuniting the family as, presumably, only a woman's love can. In dramatically forgiving the future mother-in-law who framed her, and repairing the shredded fabric of the squabbling family, Sue prefigures many gothic heroines to come.

Ross's contribution to the mass market gothic romance was even more pervasive. Like Payes and many other authors, he had come to the gothics via the nurse romances, and in fact many of his first gothics (such as *Durrell Towers*) are really just "nursies" with a gloomy house as the setting instead of a hospital.[12] A nurse is also a secondary character in *Beware My Love* (1965), a typical early gothic that could almost serve as the blueprint for many more to come (including many more by Ross himself). Set in contemporary Maine, *Beware* features a newly-married woman who grows increasingly frustrated as her once-doting bridegroom turns surly and leaves their manor home for days at a time. Eventually, he accuses her of being childish when she (rightly) complains that someone from his household (possibly the sexy young nurse) is trying to kill her. When he suggests that she is hallucinating and might want to see a psychiatrist, she (and the reader) wonders if he is gaslighting her to cover his crimes, including some attempted rapes on the lonely road that runs past the estate. The frightened bride (which would actually become the title for one of Ross's *Dark Shadows* novels), the troubled husband, and the hostile extended family would all become and remain staple ingredients for Ross's stories, published under several different names, and mass market gothic romances in general.

One surprising aspect of early gothic paperbacks (or at least those marketed as gothics) is the unexpected variety in the contents. As much as these books are (and were, even in their own time) characterized as endless variations on *Jane Eyre* or *Rebecca*, they actually contain stories featuring many different settings, themes, and tropes. A 1960s reader might have purchased a gothic and find most anything inside the standard cover—an imitation Golden Age murder mystery (or an actual reprint of a 1940s whodunit), a Peyton Place-style saga dramatizing small town sins, or an espionage caper set in a foreign country. Some of the tales even dispensed with the expected castle or manor house (though these would still show up on the cover): for example, Ross's *Desperate Heiress* (1966) features a "haunted showboat" where a grisly magic act gone wrong may have spawned a ghost; Daoma Winston's *Shadow on Mercer Mountain* (1967) is set at a redwood lodge in the early 1970s. Either publishers were trying to provide readers with variations that would expand their interests and enhance reading pleasure, or, more likely, they were rolling out so many manuscripts they didn't pay much attention to the contents.

4. Gothic Flower Power

The later 1960s saw much less variation. No doubt this was partly due to readers buying the kind of novels that pleased them most, and there can be no doubt that whatever their literary flaws, Ross, Avallone, and Maybury knew how to deliver a fast-paced, entertaining page-turner that kept their fans coming back for more. Another factor may have been the steady production of similarly packaged novels over the course of the decade. As supply caught up with demand, and more paperback originals reached the shelves, reliance on 1940s reprints faded and gothic tropes began to solidify. The popularity of Virginia Coffman, Dorothy Daniels, and Ross, among others, inspired budding authors or served as models for existing ones, thus shaping future entries in the genre. The easily recognized gothic cover format may have played a role as well. In the beginning, the covers of the gothics had only slightly reflected actual story events. Now the covers of previously successful novels were on display in countless stores and libraries. In a sort of reversal of the usual mode of cover production, authors could and probably did tailor their plots and settings to the familiar artwork in hopes of making a sale. It is therefore understandable that newer manuscripts increasingly began to resemble one another. The framework became sturdy, dependable, and instantly recognizable: a gloomy house or castle filled with sinister family members and frightening servants, a heroine the reader can identify with, a thread of romance that usually that usually goes no further than a few stolen kisses, and an abrupt declaration of love or a marriage proposal near the last page. With the machinery in place and by now well-oiled, mass market gothic romances began to appear at a brisk and, to some, alarming rate.

In 1967, Simon and Schuster's Parallax division released an entirely different kind of gothic novel. Subtitled "A Gothic Spoof," humorist and editor Hester Jane Mundis' *Mercy at the Manor Manor* poked fun at the well-known gothic cover, with a circular framing design reminiscent of the Dan Ross novels. In this case, the woman running from the house is a pop art caricature, decked out in white go-go boots, tight striped shirt, and a miniskirt, her cartoonish features a bland mask as she flees an equally impressionist manor situated "on the seacoast of Brooklyn." The front cover blurb proudly proclaims that *Mercy* is "as unlike the novels of Mary Stewart and Daphne du Maurier as you can get!"

A no-holds-barred gothic parody was probably overdue by 1967; with the market saturated and the storylines beginning to repeat themselves, it must have seemed to publishers and readers alike that the genre would soon go into decline. Spoofs, then, would be a logical development. Tongue-in-cheek gothics had been attempted before, though their authors were usually subtle enough to escape detection. Elsa Radcliffe's bibliography identifies at least one such effort by the probably pseudonymous Wilma Winthrop, whom she called an "anonymous hack" who attempted to write with "a humor not intelligent enough to qualify as cynical."[13] Looking at Winthrop's murder mystery, *Hostage of Evil* (1966), it is difficult to disagree. Rife with dreadful phonetically rendered Southern dialects, ludicrous plot twists, and wooden characters, *Hostage* lacks the respectful earnestness that makes even the less technically proficient gothics entertaining. Readers hoping for an atmospheric southern gothic must have been seriously disappointed by the unpleasantly arch style and silly plot, and it is doubtful they found much to admire in the dully self-referential humor.

Mercy at the Manor Manor made no attempt to disguise itself or its purpose. The story begins as the heroine, Mercy Klog Manor, travels to the ancestral home of her new husband, Arthur Manor. The two meet when he drops a hot dog in Woolworth's (typical of the novel's playful Freudianism—the narrative also notes that Arthur and his previous fiancée had spent long hours in the study not of fine literature or old maps, but sex manuals) and are married nine months later. Arthur is the typical gothic hero, though this time with an underwhelming twist. "All she could feel were Arthur's fingers gripping her arm. The long tapering fingers that she had come to know so well over the past months, watching them as they nimbly flew up and down the long columns of figures on hundreds of balance sheets throughout the endless nights of the tax season."[14]

The book cheerfully includes (and explodes) all the usual gothic tropes, the humor arising from their literal application. For example, like many a gothic heroine, Mercy starts to fear that the man beside her is no longer the husband she married:

> Mercy shuddered and turned, seeking the protective comfort of her bridegroom, but the face that she saw before her was not that of the man she had married. It was that of a complete stranger.
> An icy chill gripped Mercy. What had happened? This was not the man from whom she had vowed only death could part her. This was not the intense, volatile young accountant who could open champagne bottles with his teeth and balance her check book with flawless ease. No, this man was not her husband…"Over here, Merc," a voice called.[15]

Cheerfully overwrought descriptions crowd the book's pages, the tortured prose exaggerating Mercy's "Pickfordian curls" until they obscure her

4. Gothic Flower Power

vision and detailing interior monologues that reveal not just harmless naiveté but a dull ignorance that soon annoys not only her husband but presumably the reader. Like all gothic heroes, Arthur has a dark secret that left his first fiancée dead and himself with a mysterious limp. At the Manor family manor, things deteriorate quickly. After a fall down the stairs, Arthur takes to his bed and leaves Mercy to deal with a cursed stuffed fish, sinister paint-by-numbers artwork, and the scheming housekeeper's Hawaiian Baked Alaska dessert. Meanwhile, Arthur's eccentric relatives show little appreciation for either Mercy or her African paisley and white vinyl outfits. The traditional gothic settings are also lampooned. The dining room features a folding aluminum table, while the library holds no antique books, or books of any sort, but only a stack of outdated *Life* magazines. The manor also boasts a tiki bar and a television that takes up one entire wall, ironically anticipating a reality of 50 years later (and, given that it is 1967, one wonders if the Manors ever watched *Dark Shadows* on it).

To solve a convoluted murder mystery and end the Manor curse, Mercy summons memories from her old Nancy Drew books and peeks into her husband's grade-school diary, autographed by a variety of other young women who met with tragic fates. In the end, the mystery is solved in the same way as most other gothic domestic dramas—with the heroine confronting the second male lead, who longs to break up her relationship with the man who truly loves her.

The humor in *Mercy* tends to fall flat, despite its slightly manic pace and reliance on puns (as well as a few unsavory jokes that would not pass muster in a more politically sensitive era). Perhaps one reason gothic parodies tend to fail on the whole is that the mass market gothic romance is already a kind of burlesque—or what critics now tend to characterize as camp, with purposely exaggerated emotion and a sort of deliberate naiveté. Melodrama, after all, can only be stretched so far before interest diminishes, and most mass market gothic romances succeeded by at least pretending to take themselves seriously. Lacking this disingenuous approach, parodies like *Mercy* come off as little more than curiosities, about as amusing as outdated political humor from *Mad Magazine*.

What the publication of *Mercy* does suggest is that by 1967, publishers assumed that audiences were growing weary of the gothic formula, or at least beginning to recognize its sameness. Their concerns, luckily, were premature. The gothic was about to change again. Gloomy domestic dramas focusing on marriages gone sour were soon to merge with more outlandish tropes. The

The Gothic Romance Wave

changes would re-energize the genre and bring in millions more fans—and sales.

In 1966, the ongoing popularity of gothic paperbacks inspired a venture into a new medium: a daily soap opera based on the familiar storylines readers couldn't seem to get enough of. If even a percentage of these same women could be persuaded to tune in for half an hour every day, network executives reasoned, the show could not fail to be a hit. The new series, like so many gothics, began as a literal dream in the mind of its creator. Producer Dan Curtis often recounted how he dreamed of a young woman on a train, traveling to a spooky and mysterious gothic house on the coast. On June 27 of that year, *Dark Shadows* premiered. The first episode depicted the arrival of Victoria Winters, an orphaned and naïve young governess, at the seaside estate of Collinwood in Maine. The idea was to dramatize the popular gothic novels, taking plot threads from the supermarket bestsellers by Holt, Whitney, and others. Various threatening plot devices were introduced—a murderous caretaker, sinister family members, secrets and blackmail and thinly veiled seduction attempts that adhered to the G-rated afternoon code at the time. The pace was slow and deliberate, the mood carefully orchestrated, the sets atmospheric and claustrophobic. The early episodes, aired in black and white, evoke the Joan Fontaine versions of both *Jane Eyre* and *Rebecca* as Victoria explores the manor and tries to solve various mysteries that plague the apparently cursed Collins family.

At the same time, ABC contracted Dan Ross, the prolific author of mass market gothic romances, to write a series of tie-in novels under his familiar pen name "Marilyn Ross." Presumably readers of gothics would be expected to sample the novels and then turn on the show out of curiosity, while viewers of the show would buy the novels to enjoy the continuing adventures of their favorite characters. There was one problem: Ross, a Canadian, did not watch the show. Perhaps for this reason, the novels did not follow the storylines being broadcast on TV, but they were carefully packaged with similar gold-bordered covers and series-style titles.[16] Though the early editions were adorned with the typical "woman running from the house" artwork, the woman in this case representing Victoria Winters and the house Collinwood, reprints featured a photograph from the series inside an oval.

Unfortunately, coaxing the large gothic readership to switch on their televisions each day proved more difficult than expected, and early ratings for *Dark Shadows* were not promising. Faced with imminent cancellation, producer Dan Curtis decided to spice up the storylines with supernatural

4. Gothic Flower Power

characters and events. On April 18, 1967, the show introduced a new character—debonair vampire Barnabas Collins, half villain and half heartthrob, who would quickly elevate the show to ratings prominence and a cult status it still enjoys to this day. Jonathan Frid, a Canadian Shakespearian actor, had been cast as the vampire, and he brought to the show a classic approach that instantly elevated the material. Barnabas soon displaced Victoria Winters as *Dark Shadows'* central character in both the TV and paperback versions, with his photograph (and later, the show's sexy werewolf, Quentin) featured on the covers. After only five novels, Dan Ross adjusted the original formula for the tie-ins so they became a series of vampire romances, kept suitably chaste for the TV show's legion of teenaged fans.

The sudden and pervasive popularity of *Dark Shadows* and its literary progeny pushed sales of mass market gothic romances even higher. The addition of vampires, werewolves, and witches, often presented in a sympathetic light on the show, offered new avenues for paperback gothics to explore. A few mass market gothics even refer explicitly to *Dark Shadows*, such as 1971's *Castle Mirage*: "Abel was bubbling over with laughter now, bending with it. 'You should be a TV actress,' he told her, 'in one of those soap operas on TV where there are monsters and vampires pursuing the heroine through the entire show.' His hand on her elbow urged her along the path that led back to the house."[17]

As Barnabas began marauding around the cobweb-strewn set, ratings began to soar. Fan mail poured in by the truckload. No one was more surprised by elevation of Barnabas from villain to romantic hero than the actor who portrayed him. "I thought the role on *Dark Shadows* would go on for about three or four weeks," Frid later recalled. "And then, the phenomenon began, the role caught on, the mail started to flood in."[18] Teen magazines of the time show a somewhat embarrassed middle-aged Frid posing among younger men like David Cassidy, the Monkees, and various teen idols. Plans to kill off the vampire were quickly scrapped and Barnabas became first the anti-hero and then the hero of the show. Other characters were pushed aside and their relationships rearranged so that Barnabas, the undead idol of millions, could become the center of the ongoing drama.

Despite the focus on the vampire, neither the series nor the novels retained much that might be considered horror. The TV version of Barnabas was a bit more violent than his paperback counterpart, occasionally killing or threatening to kill various characters who got in his way or found out his secret (he even walled up one of the villains à la "The Cask of Amontillado").

The Gothic Romance Wave

Though his first appearance in the novel *Barnabas Collins* presents him as somewhat sinister and hairy-palmed, literary Barnabas is nowhere near as frightening. He is a gentleman on every page, a tragic soul yearning for a lasting love his curse prevents him from attaining. He is described (repeatedly, in fact) as a handsome and articulate man, a welcome guest at any party, a patron of the arts fond of attending and financing the London theater of the 1800s (taking some of the actresses as willing mistresses/blood donors) and even performing in the Collinsport community theater himself. His tastes are impeccable—he "dresses in the mod style," his enamored cousin Carolyn remarks in more than one of the novels. Villagers are suspicious of him, but not just because of the rumors that he is descended from a vampire (himself, of course, which no one figures out). They also dislike his English frippery, his aloof manners (honed in the 19th century) and his aristocratic bearing.

These refined qualities only make the heroines (and, presumably, the readers) even more attracted to him. Though Barnabas does bite a few women, it happens off-stage (or, more accurately, off-page). It is stressed that he takes only a small amount of blood so that the women are just a little hung over the next morning, remembering nothing and physically unharmed except for two mysterious "insect bites" on the neck. When deaths do occur, it is invariably another character framing Barnabas in order to separate him from the heroine. In turn, Barnabas functions as a kind of vigilante, removing the evil-doers once they have been identified, though usually without undue violence.

In almost every novel, Barnabas eventually summons the courage to reveal his true nature to the heroine. Her reaction is generally closer to sympathetic awe than terror.

> As Diana stood there gazing at the coffin with startled eyes Barnabas shut the door after them so they could not be heard outside the room. He moved closer to her. There was a strange expression on his gaunt face that made her feel he was about to reveal something of overwhelming importance.
> "Does this coffin upset you?" he asked quietly. "Have you a fear of the dead?"
> She studied him and tried to fathom what he was attempting to tell her. "It is a strange thing to find in your room," she said. "What does it mean?"
> "In telling you, I will risk your turning from me," he warned her.
> "That is not likely to happen."
> There was a moment of silence in the eerie atmosphere of the shadowed room. The candle by the head of the coffin offered a feeble, flickering glow. The empty coffin was like a grim question mark. Why was it there? What was it for?
> Barnabas' face was solemn. "The coffin is mine."
> "Yours?"

4. Gothic Flower Power

> He nodded gravely. "Yes. It is where I spend the days from dawn to dusk."
> "But why?"
> "It's a long story," he said.

After confessing that he sometimes "must forage for innocent blood to keep myself alive," he tells her that he is currently seeking a medical cure for his condition. This cheers the heroine up considerably, to Barnabas's immense relief.

> He stared at her in surprise. "You're not afraid of me? You don't hate me? The chill of my hands and lips doesn't cause revulsion in you?"
> "Not when I understand," she said with admiration. "I never hoped to win a love like yours. And I promise you I'll try to be worthy of it."[19]

By 1969, the series had undergone some changes. Another male character, the werewolf Quentin Collins, played by David Selby, was beginning to gain on Frid's popularity. Accordingly, Ross was instructed to work this new character into his stories. As a result, another potential suitor was brought into the mix for the heroine. Prefiguring the *Twilight* series, she now had a vampire, a werewolf, and usually another, safer (and human) man to choose from. Ross also added a twist to Quentin by calling him a master of disguise, though in practice this disguise seldom amounted to much beyond shaving his head, growing a beard, or donning an eye patch (nonetheless making it surprisingly difficult for his cousin Barnabas to recognize him). His name was incorporated into the brand of the series: every title now began with *Barnabas, Quentin, and the...*, even those in which Quentin played a small role.

Dan Ross admitted in interviews with *Dark Shadows* fans, conducted long after the series ended, that he had little interest in following the scripts from the show. He decided to strike out on his own, creating new characters and situations. He was interested in exploring avenues the show could not due to time, cast, and budget constraints (for example, forays into baroque Italian villas and Barnabas's adventures in Victorian London). Jarringly, continuity in the books is virtually nonexistent. Though the novels set in the present day use most of the familiar television characters, others set in, say, 1870 and 1880 feature a cast of Collins relatives that do not overlap. The servant, Hare, dies in some books and is alive and well in others; he also moves effortlessly and inexplicably from the Victorian era to the 1960s. Only Barnabas appears, more or less unchanged, in the stories not set in the present. The thought seems to have been that as long as Barnabas appeared and behaved heroically, winning and gently breaking female hearts, readers would be unconcerned with the rest of the details. This seems to have been the case, as sales were strong. The books were released at the staggering rate of one a month until the show inevitably waned in popularity and was cancelled. The last episode aired in 1971, but the books continued until March 1972—managing to sell over 17 million copies, according to author Ross.[20]

The *Dark Shadows* novels had no literary aspirations. They do function as a kind of compendium of gothic elements, as Ross used every known gothic plot device and setting (sometimes more than once) to keep the series going. The usual locked rooms, mysterious coffins, and crazed relatives stashed in the basement or tower all appear, along with ghosts both real and hoaxed. Mummies, aliens from outer space, Dr. Jekyll's son (which Ross recalled as one of his favorite books) and Quetzalcoatl all make appearances. Occasionally serious issues were touched upon, such as the struggles of shell-shocked World War I veterans and mental illness. A few genuinely frightening scenes emerge; the ballet dancer sees her murdered rival dancing alongside her during the recital, and the Satanic-style rituals conducted by Quentin in his rented Italian villa suggest the Manson family, a provocative topic at the time. Other novels are thinner in content and do not seem adequately resolved or explained, particularly those involving time travel (a staple on the series after 1968). Whatever the problems with continuity, the stories are engaging and entertaining. Prose is sparse, lean, and fast-moving. There is no attempt at poetic description and even the melodrama is kept to a minimum in the service of pace. None of the books would exceed 150 printed pages, with a formulaic plot hastily wrapped up in the last few pages as Barnabas leaves his lady love yet again to wander the world alone.

ABC cancelled *Dark Shadows* in 1971, though the novels continued for another year or so. Its popularity on both screen and paper infused new life and new themes into mass market gothic paperbacks. Dabblings in the occult would continue to spice up the expected romantic melodramas. Many stories would now populate their manor houses with werewolves and vampires, not to mention witchcraft and sorcery. Just a few examples of mass market gothic romances with Barnabas-type characters were Michael Avallone's *The Vampire Cameo* (writing as Dorothea Nile) in 1968, Ross's own *Secret of the Pale Lover* in 1969, Coffman's *The Vampyre of Moura* in 1970, and both Daoma Winston's *The Vampire Curse* and Elna Stone's *Secret of the Willows* in 1971. Werewolves began popping up too, probably thanks to the popularity of Quentin, Collinwood's resident lycan, from 1969 on. Two such examples from 1970 are Sharon Wagner's *Country of the Wolf* and Florence Stevenson's *The*

4. Gothic Flower Power

Curse of the Concullens. Even when a character wasn't an actual vampire or werewolf, authors were all too happy to use imagery that suggested otherworldly connections. In *Carlotta's Castle*, the heroine is startled when she sees an unexpected side of a new acquaintance claiming to be her cousin: "He cupped his hand around the flame of his lighter to ignite a cigarette. In the brief flare his face looked like that of a satyr, slightly evil."[21]

Around the same time, *Rosemary's Baby* was released as both a bestselling book (1967) and popular film (1968). Mass market gothics sought to capitalize on the story's titillating depiction of Satanic cult activity, giving rise to the subgenre eventually known as the "Satanic gothic." These novels would be suspenseful and even frightening, but without gore. The feminine take on the horror genre pioneered by *Dark Shadows* would add a new dimension to the gothic, making it a story of supernatural beings who deserved to be understood and loved just as much as (or perhaps more than) the human characters. It is not a stretch to say that the modern publishing phenomena of *Twilight* (and thus *Fifty Shades of Grey*) could not exist without *Dark Shadows*. Barnabas's many stepchildren live on today, in the romantic gentlemen vampires that haunt the shelves of the romance novel section in any chain bookstore.

As the new decade dawned, the mass market gothic had touched and even merged with every other genre of popular fiction: romance, mystery and suspense, and horror. Readers could find a gothic to satisfy virtually any taste, guided by the still-ubiquitous covers depicting a woman in a flowing gown running from a gloomy house or tower. Lists of similar books filled the back pages of every mass market gothic romance, with mail order forms included to expedite the purchase process. Far from waning, the mass market gothic romance was about to reach its creative and economic peak.

5

Gilded Peak and Gloomy Valley
1970s Gothic

> I stared up at the dark stairs. Out of the corner of my eye I could see Mrs. Raven toss her head back in a motion of dismissal. Then the shadowy forms of the Reynolds moved back from the dining room door.
> I climbed the stairs thoughtfully. Something was coming to a head at Raven's Cliff. I could feel it. And I was part of that something. I shuddered. The thought of spending another night in the red room seemed suddenly horrifying.
> The gloom of the upstairs settled on me heavily. Then, as I twisted the knob of the red room's door, a hand reached out of the gloom and grasped my arm. I started to scream, but another hand covered my lips and a frantic voice whispered in my ear.
> "Don't scream. It's me, Melody. I want to talk to you."
> —*The Demon of Raven's Cliff*
> by Patience Zawadsky, 1971

The 1960s had been a decade of turbulence, change, and modernization, as youth culture, women's liberation, and civil rights challenged social norms and transformed the look and mood of cities and small towns alike. As the new decade began, the U.S. population had reached 205 million, with an average household income of $9400. The average cost of a new house was $23,450, and a gallon of gas cost 36 cents, meaning that the price of a typical mass market gothic romance equaled about three gallons. A larger segment of that growing population was about to gain a political voice, as President Nixon, with the specter of Watergate still years away, signed a bill lowering the voting age to 18 from 21 in June 1970. The previous month, the National Guard had killed four student protestors at Kent State University, and that

5. Gilded Peak and Gloomy Valley

fall would see the deaths of Janis Joplin and Jimi Hendrix. On TV, the highest rated nighttime show was *Marcus Welby, M.D.*, with 13 million weekly viewers. The gothic soap opera, *Dark Shadows*, had just completed its highest ratings period ever, with 20 million daily viewers,[1] but was beginning the steady decline that would result in its cancellation in April 1971. The release of the final Beatles album, *Let It Be*, in May 1970 serenaded the end of an era.

Many signs pointed toward the 1970s as the decade when women would finally come into their own. Already things were changing. California became the first state to adopt "No Fault" divorce laws, forever altering the structure and even the concept of the American family, while San Diego State University opened the first Women's Studies department. Two groundbreaking books, Kate Millett's *Sexual Politics* and *Sisterhood is Powerful: An Anthology of Writings from the Women's Liberation Movement*, took the feminists' message mainstream. Elsewhere in bookstores, the melodrama-rich *Love Story* by Erich Segal became the bestselling book of the year (Tim Burton's *Dark Shadows* 2012 revival would contain an in-joke about the vampire Barnabas studying the book as a guide to his new century).[2]

Meanwhile, the tidal wave of gothics continued to swell. Janice Radway calculates that "[a]t the peak of their popularity, from about 1969 to 1972, gothics were issued at the rate of thirty-five titles a month, over four hundred per year. In the peak year of 1971, gothics constituted 24 percent of Dell's paperback sales. At that time, Dell was publishing four to five titles every month."[3] Other imprints proliferated and began crowding the shelves, including Candlelight Gothics, Belmont Tower Big Print Gothics, Bantam Gothics, Manor books, Unibooks, Pocket Books' Ravenswood Gothics, and Fawcett Crest, which published larger and longer novels with crossover appeal by Barbara Michaels, Andre Norton, and Nora Lofts along with others now forgotten.

Paperback Library decided to go a step further, redesigning the format and scope of the books (though keeping the traditional cover style and plot tropes) and pitching them at class-conscious female readers. "Queen-Size Gothics are a new idea," the back covers proclaimed. "They offer the very best in novels of romantic suspense, by the top writers, greater in length and drama, richer in reading pleasure. Each book is guaranteed to be: 'READING FIT FOR A QUEEN' [sic]." Queen-Size employed many familiar gothic authors, such as Dan "Marilyn" Ross and Michael Avallone, who wrote several books for the line under the name Jean-Anne De Pres (perhaps consciously echoing the name of a pivotal *Dark Shadows* character, Josette DuPres). Not

The Gothic Romance Wave

to be outdone, Curtis Books came out with a competing imprint called, naturally, Empress Gothics.

Later in the decade, the actual reigning monarch of romance, Harlequin, launched Harlequin Mystique, the first books appearing in 1977. Oddly, this time Harlequin seems to have missed the trend; the line lasted only until 1982 with 162 books, which is far from impressive by Harlequin standards. At that point, the line morphed into one called Harlequin Gothic (perhaps the name Mystique being too vague and foreign to attract buyers—indeed, most of the manuscripts were reprints translated from French) and lasted for another six years and 18 more titles, including two by the reliable Marilyn Ross and one by Avon Gothic veteran Jane Toombs.

Another innovation of the early 1970s was the Gothic magazine, some containing digest-style stories and some featuring comic book-style panels and tales that continued over several issues. These included *Dell's Gothic Romances*, which ran from November 1970 to September 1971, Stanley Publishing's *Gothic Secrets*, which ran for only two issues in August and September 1971, *Gothic Tales of Love*, and two from DC Comics, *The Dark Mansion of Forbidden Love* (later changed to *Forbidden Tales of Dark Mansion*) and *Sinister House of Secret Love* (later changed to *Secrets of Sinister House*).[4] None of these ventures proved successful, most folding after only a few issues. Possibly gothic readers preferred novels to stories, and most likely the comic-book format, traditionally a male-oriented medium, did not appeal to female romance fans. The only gothic comic to endure turned out to be yet another *Dark Shadows* tie-in series, which continued for five years after the show was canceled in 1971.

Mass market gothic romances were now an entrenched feature of the pop culture landscape, and had been around long enough to have their own, self-referential history. Rather than advertising new entries as "in the tradition of *Rebecca* and *Jane Eyre*," gothics could now pitch new entries as ideal "for those who love Victoria Holt and Mary Stewart" or "In the Tradition of Virginia Coffman and Dorothy Daniels."[5] But with the exponential growth in gothic lines and eager readers came the same problem the early gothic imprints had faced. This was the issue of quantity—there seemed to be more demand than publishable manuscripts. "The rise of the Gothic over the past decade is one of the more astounding phenomena of book-publishing," Isabelle Holland, herself a successful author of gothics, wrote in 1974. "What the classic detective story and the novel of suspense were to the publishing world in the '40s, '50s, and early '60s, the Gothic now is in the '70s. An

5. Gilded Peak and Gloomy Valley

extremely profitable genre sought by editors and publishers as gold was hunted by the Conquistadores."[6] Even the steady supply of manuscripts from hard-working authors like Dan Ross, writing at breakneck speed, proved insufficient to meet the demand of early 1970s fans.

A decade earlier, publishers had mined older, out-of-print hardbacks from the du Maurier era for material, but this supply had either dried up or seemed hopelessly out of date as the age of polyester and disco dawned. One solution was to recycle earlier gothics, sometimes with cover art reused from other books or with updated covers. Running women were now decked out in '70s-style clothing and hairstyles or posed more sensually. Another was to accept manuscripts with content that did not quite fit the usual gothic mold (though they would all be given the uniform cover with the woman running from the house). This resulted in some creative developments that expanded the gothic's story possibilities. Many authors experimented with setting, bypassing the usual Victorian and modern time periods for other eras, including Edwardian and World War II. The well-crafted *De Witt Manor* by Elizabeth St. Clair (1977) used 1940s small-town America as a backdrop as her wartime widow heroine tries to unravel the secrets of her late husband's family. This novel was also innovative in the sense that the heroine has no intention of moving into the titular manor house and spends most of the story trying to avoid visiting her in-laws there. Many American authors dabbled in Southern Gothic and tales set on haunted plantations during the Civil War era, such as Janet Louise Roberts' *Dark Rose* and Jan Alexander's *Darkwater* (1975).

Another unique American twist was using Hollywood settings and characters, which could be exploited for their own titillating brand of corruption, born of the mythology of show business. Television personalities, it turned out, could easily substitute for the traditional feudal lord. Patty Brisco's *Mist of Evil* (1976) used the clever device of having washed-up horror-film actors in costume stand in for actual otherworldly monsters. A few stories even used political themes. Kate Ostrander's *The Sea Tower* (1974) dabbles in Irish terrorist politics, and in AnneJeanette Scott's *The Count of Van Rheeden Castle* (1976), the lingering specter of Nazism has terrible implications for a family of modern Dutch aristocrats.

The gothic's geography was no longer confined to medieval British castles, Victorian estates or the cliffs of Maine. To be sure, Cornwall and New England remained popular choices, with plucky American ingénues poking their way through frightening Old World architecture, but heroines (and

The Gothic Romance Wave

readers) could also visit more exotic locales such as India (Mary Margaret Lawrence's *Seven Thunders*, 1974), Mexico (June Wetherell's *Legacy of the Lost*, 1970), Iceland (Sharon Wagner's *Dark Sun at Midnight*, 1976), and Greece (Ellen Morley's *Sinister Isle of Love*, 1977). Madeira was a popular choice for several novels, as were other assorted and sometimes fictional tropical islands on which ancient spirits might be expected to run deliciously amok. One title by Claudette Nicole [Jon Messmann] aimed to have it both ways: "her" Queen-Size Gothic, *The Chinese Letter* (1973), was set in California at the "sinister Institute for Asian Studies."

Beyond the heroine's fashion choices, gothic covers yielded little ground no matter what the intended setting might be. Though some of the designs tried to incorporate tropical or exotic motifs, many times the illustration gave no hint as to which side of the Atlantic, or even which century, the author had chosen. This could get downright silly, as with Manor Books' oddly titled *Moon of the Lost Frenchman* by Kitty Mendenhall (1977). Though the tale is set in "northern Wisconsin," the cover shows a woman apparently having crossed a roaring sea channel on foot as a medieval castle looms behind her. Most gothic publishers thought nothing of showing a woman in Victorian garb in front of an antebellum plantation-style manor, even if the back cover copy described the heroine's tragic car accident on the New England seaside (as was the case with the Dan Ross "Dark Harbor" series). It seems likely that the flowing white nightgowns remained popular attire for heroines because of their timeless quality as well as their adaptability.

Storylines were evolving too. In the 1960s, many, if not most, of the gothics concentrated on domestic dramas, with marriages upended by paranoid spouses and conniving in-laws rather than restless spirits or marauding supernatural beings. As in the 1960s, a number of what could more accurately be called murder mysteries were packaged as gothics (the novels of Rae Foley and Elizabeth [also known as E.X.] Ferrars providing two obvious examples), but the public's increasing fascination with the occult inspired a new subgenre of mass market gothic romance. Increasingly, books used peripheral characters who dabbled in séances or occult practices until these storylines became the central theme of the books.[7] Like *Dark Shadows*, many of the new gothics sought to combine and expand the familiar tropes. If 1960s heroines worried that their new husbands were plotting to kill them for financial gain, their 1970s counterparts feared even more gruesome fates. These ranged from slaking a vampire's thirst to bearing a demon child conceived during a Satanic ritual or even serving as a human sacrifice herself.

5. Gilded Peak and Gloomy Valley

Publishers were quick to exploit these new supernatural themes, the covers promising exciting and even lurid mystical content. Charlotte Hunt's 1970 *The Lotus Vellum* featured two male characters vying for the titular artifact, with nary a governess or frightened bride in sight, but the cover still featured the usual woman running from a house (this time clutching a vellum folio). Ace labeled the book Occult Fiction rather than Gothic, seamlessly combining the two genres through a trick of marketing. Ballantine went further with its Zodiac Gothic series in the mid–1970s, blending newfound public interest in astrology with gothic plotlines and even including a horoscope for each heroine by noted astrologer Sydney Omarr. A competing "Birthstone Gothics" line came from Beagle Books.[8] An astrologer heroine served as the sleuth in *Orion Was Rising* by Rose Palmer (1970—billed as "an occult mystery") and *The Black Dog* by Georgena Goff (Unibooks, 1971) is billed as "a Gothic novel of the psychic occult." A reprint of 1964's *Secret Melody* by Paula Minton was updated to include a male ghost superimposed over a stone archway as the heroine cringes in fear. Also in 1973 came a unique gothic "of color." *Tule Witch* by Jane Toombs (Avon) featured an African American couple, the nurse-heroine and the doctor hero, combining gothic, nursie, and modern horror tropes. This time, the woman running from the house sports an attractive Afro and a colorful 1970s mini-dress.[9] There is even a *Rosemary's Baby*-style subplot about a child fathered in a cult who has the appearance of a gargoyle (a creature popularized by a successful horror movie, *Gargoyles*, 1972).

As Toombs' title might suggest, witchcraft proved a particularly popular direction for 1970s gothics. *Dark Shadows*, of course, featured several storylines revolving around spells and sorcery, and the vampire Barnabas's ex-wife, the witch Angelique, had become one of the show's most popular villains. Mass market gothic romances did not hesitate to capitalize on the public's fascination with the dark arts, with many titles promising coven-based excitement. These include Florence Stevenson's *Witches' Crossing* (1975), Marilyn Ross' *Witches' Cove* (1974), and Miriam Lynch's 1976 *Witches' Holiday* ("Hell-spawned death traps Amy Vaughn in a house built of family hatred"). For a slight change of pace, Jean-Anne de Pre (Michael Avallone) contributed *Warlock's Woman* in 1973, a book which outraged bibliographer Elsa Radcliffe with its "slip-shod plotting, absurd and unbelievable characters and a stifling verbosity."[10] Another intriguing twist came with Alice Brennan's *To Kill a Witch* (1972), which was clearly indebted to Daphne du Maurier's "The Birds" ("A Satanic inheritance traps Laurie Brooks in a world without love—a place

The Gothic Romance Wave

ruled by Death!"). This time, the cover shows not a woman running but daydreaming while sinister gulls, who play a delightfully gruesome role in the story, gather ominously around her head.

Along with witches, demons and devils of various sorts made numerous appearances in 1970s gothics, some of the metaphorical type and others literally trailing brimstone. Presumably, both the 1971 book and 1973 movie adaptation of *The Exorcist* helped stimulate public interest in possession. Examples include Patience Zawadsky's *The Demon of Raven's Cliff* (1971), Cathy Cunningham's *The Demons of Highpoint House* (1973), Virginia Coffman's *The Devil's Virgin* (1970), Dorothy Daniels' *Diablo Manor* (1971), and the oddly titled *Lucifer Was Tall* by Elizabeth Gresham (1976). Demonically possessed children sometimes appeared to torment the governess heroine, recalling Henry James' seminal Victorian gothic *Turn of the Screw* (which had been adapted for and thus popularized by two different *Dark Shadows* storylines). Willo Davis Roberts' 1973 Easy-Eye gothic left nothing to the imagination, being called, simply, *The Evil Children*, while Audrey Leech's *Pawn of Fear* (1971) deliberately confuses the issue of exactly who is the pawn—the naïve governess or the manipulative little boy whose eerie likeness shares the cover with her.

None of these publishers, however, was prepared to go as far as Avon, which had recently risen to prominence with women readers. Flush with the success of the first erotic historical romance in 1972, Avon decided to pull out all the stops and present a line that many readers must have considered both shocking and irresistible. To some extent, the new offerings resembled the typical "Avon Gothics" they had offered for years. One title, *When the Century Blooms* by June Wetherell (1973), suggests a genteel Edwardian drama, perhaps complete with a governess and a taciturn but passionate master. In fact, it is anything but, instead involving a bloodthirsty Satanic cult on a remote island. Like the others in the series, the book featured a horned goat-head silhouette in the corner and the chilling logo "A Satanic Gothic" inside its borders. Other, more provocative titles included *Vengeance of the Cat Goddess* by Jennifer Stephens, *The Devil's Dance* by Jan Alexander, and *The Sorcerers* by Dorian Winslow, in which the heroine works as a companion to "handsome Mason Walker's invalid wife," who "amused herself with talk of black magic and playing with dolls." These creepy toys have been symbolically "mutilated in various forms of violent death." Soon real bodies begin piling up, their mortal wounds resembling those found on the dolls.

In a gloomy attic (of course) the heroine discovers a diary in which her

5. Gilded Peak and Gloomy Valley

predecessor laid out her fears: "They are devils, devils disguised. They are witches. With power. I have seen them perform. Doors don't close to them. The nights are unsafe. The mirrors ... dear God save me, preserve me from the mirrors." The heroine is compelled to glance up at just such a mirror hanging in her room, and a nasty shock awaits. "I looked up at the reflection in the wardrobe mirror. I made my mouth turn up in a smile. The smile became a grimace of horror." She makes a terrifying discovery: "The figure I had seen had been that of the doll in the dress Caretha had made for it. The doll ... in my mirror.... The doll was me."[11] It was a plot twist that might easily have graced a script for the horror series *Night Gallery*, then in its final season on NBC.

Best remembered today are two series entries, *Lord Satan* (1972) and *Her Demon Lover* (1973), written under the intriguing pen name Louisa Bronte (reprints in the late 1970s restored the author's real name to the cover). Only the missing umlaut separates Louisa from Haworth's most famous family, and one senses that Charlotte and Emily's influence is not far off in any case. Louisa was, in fact, Janet Louise Roberts, a veteran of more traditional gothics, daughter of a conservative missionary family, and an Ohio reference librarian in her daily life.[12] *Lord Satan*, which the online readers' group Goodreads identifies as her most popular title out of over two dozen, was part Regency romance, part *Jane Eyre*, and part *Rosemary's Baby*. This novel, along with its follow-up, pushed the gothic limits, and fans apparently loved it. Today, both books command high prices on used book sites.

The front cover of *Lord Satan* is unremarkable (a woman in a bridal dress, carrying a black-ribboned bouquet and surrounded by candles), but *Her Demon Lover* (1973) offers an interesting variation on the usual woman running from the house. As lightning strikes and thick mist rises, the heroine stands in front of a primitive-looking castle. Her dress whips in the wind, her arms raised in triumph and her face tilted toward the sky as she seems to command the elements around her. The blurb promises a sensational tale: "On her honeymoon in a Balkan castle, Sophia made a pact of passion with the devil!" The back cover explains further: bored with her new but "timid husband," the heroine meets Count Vlahos in the Balkan mountains. Before long, she has gladly "accepted the potion the count gave her and ... found herself stripped of all inhibitions, alone in the tower with a strong-willed, fiercely passionate man." Appropriately enough, right below the back cover copy is an ad for a "#1 Bestseller" called *Open Marriage, A New Life Style for Couples* by Nena and George O'Neill.

The Gothic Romance Wave

Set in 1892, *Her Demon Lover* gleefully subverted the usual "frightened bride" gothic trope. At the beginning of the story, Sophia is already feeling stifled in her new and respectable marriage. Once the couple accepts the count's invitation to visit his castle, her extramarital attraction to him grows. His personal magnetism has an immediate effect on her: "She gazed, enraptured, in spite of her doubts and fears which had kept her awake much of the night. She was submitting herself, and Greg also, to the hands and uncertain quality of a man she did not know. He was a strong man, a charming man, but she sensed that he was also ruthless, carrying all in his path, like a sudden torrential mountain stream which carries rocks and pebbles alike along in its plunge from the mountains. A cold, icy mountain stream—refreshing but deadly."[13]

Later, in the castle, Sophia experiences the raw power of her own natural instincts. A shadowy figure whom she assumes to be her husband joins her in the privacy of her chamber and introduces her to pleasures hitherto unknown.

> Lightning flashed from the windows. She could just make out the lean head bending over her body, the darkness of his body over hers.
> The storm outside and one inside, with her, in bed!
> She could not control herself. She felt a flood of desire, a weakness, an intense emotional heat, and her hips heaved up. Something flashed through her, like an involuntary sneeze of her whole body, a contracting and expanding again and again, of her female parts. She cried out softly at the strange experience, and clutched at his shoulders.[14]

Now sexually awakened, she gives into temptation with Vlahos, throwing off the guise of a staid and loyal Victorian wife and betraying her husband with a smoldering kiss.

> Her voice was smothered, as he took a quick step forward, and his arm drew her in to him just as though he would dance with her. Only he held her still, and his full sensuous lips came down roughly on hers.
> And some insanity possessed her. Instead of wrenching herself free—if she could have accomplished that against his hard arms—she pushed herself hungrily to him, and one arm went up around his neck. She was bent back across his arm, and his lips claimed hers even more wildly.
> She had never in her life known such kisses.... Nothing had ever prepared her for the madness of that embrace. His lips pressed hers again and again, his mouth opened against hers, and his tongue licked against her lips as though he would taste of her sweetness. His arms were so tight that she was crushed against his hard-muscled strength, her breasts flattened against his chest, her limbs knowing the hardness of his thighs through their clothing.[15]

No complex literary analysis is needed to decipher passages like this one. With its repetitive refrains of "hardness" and "insanity," it seems obvious that

5. Gilded Peak and Gloomy Valley

this particular brand of fictional occultism is a metaphor for the heroine's newly unfettered sexuality. Anything more blatant had, until the early 1970s, been forbidden to most romance novel heroines and, presumably, respectable middle-class female readers. Disguised as light horror, with the heroine mesmerized and not fully in command of her own body, the Satanic gothics could venture into hidden places their predecessors had not dared to go.

It might seem that, with these final barriers smashed, the mass market gothic would forge even further ahead, redefining popular romance novels and joining the newly vocal "women's libbers" in trumpeting female sexual liberation (who were presumably the intended readers for the *Open Marriage* book). Curiously, this was not to be. The authors of the Satanic Gothic line were destined to remain outliers, with the bulk of mid-1970s gothics sticking to the tried and true. The usual tropes prevailed in abundance, with stories revolving around a reasonably chaste and modest heroine as she navigated her unwelcome arrival at a large, mysterious house, a pair of competing suitors (the innocuous one usually turning out to be the secret villain), mysterious parentage, multiple attempts on her life, a child to protect, amnesia, secret wills, the rediscovery of long-forgotten murder victims, and assorted family scandals, often involving congenital madness and illegitimate births.

At their best, some gothics became less about the melodramatic trappings of the gloomy old house and more about the truths of human nature metaphorically expressed by the tortured souls who inhabit its labyrinthine chambers. On occasion, as in *Secret of the Willows*, they might slip in a reference to the social issues of the day, in this case racism in the post–Martin Luther King South. The cook has asked her employers about a summer job for her college-student daughter:

"I don't suppose you could hire Carlotta to help in the house as you did last summer?" Hattie asked without much hope in her voice.

"I'll try to work it into the budget, Hattie, but right now it doesn't look promising. Meanwhile, I'll ask around town and see if I can find something for her."

"I'd appreciate it. She is coming in later this morning to help me make jelly."

"One of these days, Hattie, I'm going to have the help you deserve in this house. But right now—" he sighed.

"Don't worry about that, Mr. Bart. I like to be busy. You pay me a good salary, and you know I feed my own family out of your kitchen. If I could just find a summer job for Carlotta—"

"What can she do?" I asked.

"Oh, she can do any kind of cooking and housekeeping," Hattie said. "I trained both the girls myself—brought them to work with me all their lives."

> "But isn't there anything else? I mean, can't she type or something? It seems to me with two years of college—"
>
> Hattie and Bart looked at each other with an understanding that made me feel suddenly like a gauche outsider. "There aren't many typing jobs in Malone," Hattie said.
>
> In her voice was an intimation of something left unspoken, Bart said it: "For Negroes." Again that look of understanding passed between them.[16]

At their worst, though, the mass market gothics had begun to resemble the nurseries of the previous decade: little more than paint-by-numbers collages of various genre trappings with no real truth behind them, the characters empty-headed and soulless puppets being danced in front of an elaborate set. Readers were expected to (and apparently did) buy, consume, and forget each slim volume just in time to purchase replacements during their next trip to the supermarket, where gothics were sold alongside other household commodities (presumably including the cigarettes whose ads were often bound into the center of the novels).

Some of the similarity and lack of originality might have resulted from the incredible output of some of the more prolific authors like Dan Ross, Michael Avallone, and Dorothy Daniels (who may or may not have co-written her books with longtime pulp author Norman Daniels). The rush to pump out gothics at all the major paperback houses had certainly led to relaxed standards and questionable quality. Elsa J. Radcliffe pulled no punches when expressing her distaste for some of the hack jobs she categorized in her comprehensive bibliography of gothic fiction in 1979. To Daniels' *Poison Flower*, she assigns a "D" with the comment "It takes a third of the book and pages of trivial dialogue to get the story off the ground. And what follows is so grossly melodramatic and senseless that I truly regretted my patient waiting for action. Daniels consistently provides a dependable standard of mediocrity." Radcliffe also singles out Dan Ross, author of what she calls the "eminently dispensable" *Dark Shadows* books, for censure for the same reason: "[Ross] turns out a mind-boggling number of books per year and writes under more than ten pseudonyms.... The reader of any discrimination whatsoever would very soon recognize and avoid his name." Yet she concedes that "[o]ne gets the feeling that Ross could write a 'good Gothic' if he ever bothered to take the time."[17]

Radcliffe's suspicion that a good many mass market gothics were hastily cobbled together in order to turn a quick dollar cannot be disputed. Not only is it obvious from the proliferation of hackneyed plots and scenes, awkward writing, and rushed endings common to many 1970s paperback gothics, it is

5. Gilded Peak and Gloomy Valley

confirmed by several books and articles that provide tips to aspiring writers. Following in the footsteps of Louisa May Alcott, who like her character Jo used a pseudonym to earn money with lurid gothic tales in the mid–19th century, many gothic paperback writers were or soon would be well known in different genres. These include Dean Koontz, John Dickson Carr, Richard Matheson, Elisabeth Ogilvie, and four female authors who may have found their gender a barrier to publishing serious science fiction: Angela Carter, Marion Zimmer Bradley, Anne McCaffrey, and Andre Norton. Likely there are many others whose pseudonyms have not yet been identified. In his 1972 book *Writing Popular Fiction*, Koontz describes his entry into the gothic field with undisguised cynicism:

> For a year, an editor friend had been urging me to try a Gothic novel since the form is perennially one of the most popular in the paperback field. I declined, principally because I didn't think I could write believably from a woman's viewpoint, but also because I simply did not like Gothic novels. I felt they were so formulized as to be mirror images of one another, and I didn't see how I could write in a field for which I had no respect. When the science fiction market remained tight, however, I finally tried my hand at a Gothic. I finished the book in two weeks.... The editor read it, made a few suggestions, and bought it for $1,500....Within a single year, taking only five weeks away from my serious work, I made $5,000 from my Gothics, enough to relieve immediate financial problems and let me get on with my more important work.[18]

George R.R. Martin, author of the hugely successful *Game of Thrones* series, recalls that his editor also once suggested he try his hand at gothics. Martin refused, but wonders, "Who knows, had I done otherwise today I might be Georgette Martin, beloved of Harlequin readers from coast to coast."[19] Joseph Hansen, known for his groundbreaking hard-boiled detective series featuring an openly gay sleuth, took the name Rose Brock to deliver some less controversial fare while he hammered out his first Dave Brandstetter book. "'Back in '67,' he said, 'when I was writing the first Brandstetter, *Fadeout*, I became uncertain. I faltered and thought I couldn't go on. This was the time when Gothics were covering every rack, and I felt maybe I should find out what they're all about and do one of them instead. I bought a half-dozen, read them and made a bet with myself I could do better.... The book was called *Tarn House*, and readers who come to it knowing my Dave stuff will find the style somewhat different. Plummier.'"[20]

In retrospect, it is easy to speculate that repetitive storylines, a flooded market, and formulaic writing by bored (not to mention condescending male) authors began to erode the playing field from the roots up. Yet readers remained

The Gothic Romance Wave

loyal, even if they might have been secretly dissatisfied with some of the books. After all, the traditional gothic romance was inexpensive light entertainment and had little real competition. Its contents, even if some entries contained hints of demon worship and allusions to sexual perversions, remained chaste enough to tantalize without crossing the line into embarrassing or even offensive. All that was about to change.

Soon after Koontz had transformed himself into gothic novelist Deanna Dwyer and started cashing her checks, a new author exploded onto the scene in a shower of sparks. *The Flame and the Flower*, a sexually explicit historical romance, was the work of Kathleen Woodiwiss, a first-time author who had experienced countless rejections before she sent her book to Avon in 1972. There, an editor plucked the 600-page manuscript out of the slush pile and decided to take a chance on it. What happened next must have stunned even Woodiwiss's publisher. *Flame* became a bestseller and ushered in a new era of blockbuster historical romances that eventually pushed gothics to one side of and then finally off the bookstore shelves altogether. By the time Woodiwiss died of cancer at the age of 68 in 2007, she had written 11 more books, which collectively went on to sell more than 36 million copies.[21]

As late as 1975, journalist Pam Proctor was asserting that "romance, and not raw sex, is still what most women like to read about. That's the message that comes through loud and clear from the perennial success of the Gothic novels—romantic suspense stories where the bedroom scenes take place after the book closes."[22] *The Flame and the Flower*, along with its many successors, was prepared to take that claim to the mat(tress). Their books were red, scorching hot. The sex was graphic, sensual, and, at least for the time, shocking. Descriptions and plot devices pushed the edge of propriety. *Beyond Heaving Bosoms* coins the word "rapetastic"[23] to describe *Flame*'s explicit scenes of scandalous sexual coercion. This novel, along with Rosemary Rogers' *Sweet Savage Love* (1974) are generally the ones the public thinks of when people joke (or complain) about the purple prose and excessive, overly detailed sex scenes in romances. Yet female readers who had grown used to (and perhaps grown up on) coy, slow-paced gothics that emphasized suspense over sexuality suddenly couldn't get enough of either.

Woodiwiss had submitted her work at an especially opportune time. In 1972, the women's movement was growing and the sexual revolution was in what might facetiously be called full swing. Premarital sex was on the rise as new social attitudes and standards followed the turmoil and liberation of the 1960s.[24] *Flame* adapted some of the gothic tropes readers enjoyed and

5. Gilded Peak and Gloomy Valley

expected, like the brooding aristocratic hero who is in this case almost twice the heroine's age, the historical setting, the arranged marriage between virtual strangers, the journey to the hero's home, and the solution to a murder. It also added exotic locations, swashbuckling-type adventure, and of course, frank and detailed sex scenes. The emphasis was no longer on the mysteries or the moody intricacies of the setting, but on the scorching physical relationship between the hero and heroine, which in this case started almost at the very beginning of the story.

Meanwhile, gothics remained stubbornly resistant to the lure of the erotic romance. In the same year *Flame* hit the shelves, Dean Koontz cautioned would-be gothic authors, "Stories containing explicit or even implied sexual content are especially taboo.... A Gothic must contain no bedroom scenes. As one Gothic editor once told me, 'the villain can want to beat her, torture her, and even kill her. But he mustn't contemplate rape!'"[25] Many readers, however, were ready to embrace the taboos. Feminist critics like Joanna Russ might complain about the distant and supercilious "Super-Male" found in the gothics, but even the surliest master of the manor looked like a retiring milquetoast next to Woodiwiss's hero, Brandon, who mistakes the heroine for a prostitute and forcibly deflowers her upon their first meeting. To an early 1970s reader, *The Flame and the Flower* must have seemed much like *Fifty Shades of Grey* did in 2012. If the explicit sex scenes in *The Flame and the Flower* fail to shock today, it is because such terminology and descriptions have become so thoroughly integrated into the romance novel vocabulary.

Other genres besides romance were changing and expanding as the 1970s moved on. Horror, for example, came into its own as Stephen King released *Carrie* (1974) and *Salem's Lot* (1975), a fast-paced and bloody vampire thriller that made small-scale, deliberately paced gothics like Ross's *Dark Shadows* novels or Virginia Coffman's *The Vampyre of Moura* seem quaintly old-fashioned and naïve. King's success inspired a host of imitators, who preferred the raw approach of straightforward horror and gore without the veneer of mystery and romance. Radcliffe complained of one such novel, Michael Hinkenmeyer's *Summer Solstice* (1976), "I found this an exceedingly unattractive horror Gothic.... The author also saw fit to lace his tale with a good bit of what amounts to 'little-boy-back-of-the-barn' sex which seems to me an insult to adult readers."[26] In one sense, fictional characters had come a long way since the naïve Sophia shuddered her way into full womanhood in the shadows of Count Vlahos's castle. In another, they had apparently regressed.

The Gothic Romance Wave

What happened to the mass market gothic romance in the late 1970s and early 1980s is still mostly a matter of conjecture. One commonly accepted narrative supposes that as time went on, only a few purists and women who objected to sexually explicit passages in their romantic novels continued to prefer the gothic, with its lack of sensual detail and light, nonviolent mystery. Many more were curious about sexy romance and graphic horror, so they tended to abandon the genteel but decaying manor and strike out for the uncharted but alluring land of the bodice ripper. With *Dark Shadows* gone from the airwaves, and romance turning in a new and sexier direction, the ancient castle was left to crumble around its cast of eccentric characters as all but the most ardent fans abandoned the gothic. The genre limped along for a few more years, but by the late 1970s the thick, racy historical and light, contemporary Harlequin-style romance[27] dominated the bookstore shelves. By 1980 there was nary a woman running from a house to be seen.

In this version, the *Flame and the Flower* acted almost as a stealth assassin for the gothic novel. It offered readers something different and gave the romance genre a new direction at a time when gothic ingenuity was fading. After Satanic weddings and ritualized couplings, the thinking goes, what was left? Prim governesses quietly longing for the master of the house had nothing on lusty, half-naked pirate heroes who traveled the globe and heroines whose bedroom techniques would shame professional courtesans.

Another theory is that unrelenting feminist critiques of the mass market gothic romance eventually turned readers away from its supposedly dimwitted heroines, overbearing master-heroes, and old-fashioned domestic-drama plots. Women now had a much wider variety of novels to pick from, including horror fiction with female characters (like *Carrie*) and sexually aware (and titillating) mainstream fiction like Judith Rossner's *Looking for Mr. Goodbar* (1975). Beside such fare, the plucky heroine traipsing through a gloomy European castle in search of a hidden diary or perhaps a ghost seemed downright laughable. As for the readers, they were growing out of stories that revolved around a young ingénue setting up a household with a wealthy, domineering man. The 1970s had given them new opportunities to forge meaningful careers and set up households of their own, with or without husbands to share them.

No doubt both of these theories have a grain of truth (and they are not, after all, mutually exclusive—it is reasonable to suppose that a career-oriented woman with feminist sympathies might enjoy a historical bodice-ripper as a fantasy escape on her days off). Yet neither pat summary seems to tell the

5. Gilded Peak and Gloomy Valley

whole story. *The Flame and the Flower* did not represent the end of the gothic, for the genre continued for many years after its 1972 release, and it seems likely that Avon's relatively explicit Satanic series of 1973 represented an effort to heat up the traditional gothic structure. As for the heroines, as time went on they did become more resourceful and determined rather than simply plucky. Despite the stereotype, it is not all that easy to find governess tales in the later gothic era. More typical are heroines like the one who appears in Elaine Booth Selig's *Mariner's End* (1977): "From the corner of his eye, he saw the new proprietor, a man up from New York, holding open the door to the kitchen as a young and pretty waitress made her way toward it with a trayload of dirty dishes. As she paused, a hand flicked out toward her posterior, the girl gave a start, and the tray came crashing to the floor. Almost simultaneously, the girl's arm reached out and gave the startled proprietor a resounding slap across the face. En route to the exit, she balled up her apron and tossed it angrily over her shoulder as Hayes looked on dumbfoundedly."

Hayes offers the newly unemployed waitress a chair in his nearby office, and she tells him that she is no ordinary hash-slinger. She is in the area for a specific and professional purpose: "Introducing herself as Claudia Adams, a graduate student in anthropology at Boston University, she explained that she had come to the Cape to work and to study the Wampanoag Indian culture in her spare time.... This year she had chosen Coombe's Corners because of its proximity to Mashpee, where the majority of the remaining Wampanoags had settled."[28]

Like Claudia, plenty of gothic heroines were changing with the times, demanding respect and equality in their careers as well as their marriages to supportive heroes. As for those heroes, the gentler, modernized male was making a comeback, with feudally-minded despots like Rochester largely confined to the historical novels of Victoria Holt (and Louisa Bronte).

At the same time, there can be no doubt that, as the 1970s moved toward the 1980s, there were rumblings that traditional gothics might be going out of style. Radway identifies a downturn in sales as early as 1972–1974 (coinciding with *The Flame and the Flower*'s popularity), and afterward, "[r]eturns increased to such an extent that many houses cut back their gothic output."[29] Publishers were also beginning to rethink the traditional gothic packaging and even the name "gothic." In the late 1970s, Candlelight Gothics become Candlelight Intrigues, with new cover designs attached to fairly typical gothic storylines. A 1974 entry from Signet, *The Shrouded Way* by Janet Caird, called itself "A Novel of Romantic Suspense," returning to the roots of *Rebecca*,

The Gothic Romance Wave

which had not been known as a gothic until the 1960s. The woman, dressed in chic 1970s street clothing, is skipping, rather than running, from a much-modified house, which this time is little more than a cottage in a charming green landscape. In 1975, *The Moonlit Way* by Alice Dwyer-Joyce, though designated by Bantam Books as a "Gothic Novel" with cover copy promising hijinks in "a castle on the jagged cliffs," showed two people embracing by a twisted tree. No house was in sight, and no one was running. By 1977, Alicen White's *The Watching Eye* showed a woman who is neither barefoot nor in a nightgown, but instead is dressed in ordinary 1970s garb. With a thoughtful look on her face, she heads toward a cliff edge at a casual stroll, fully in control of the situation and seemingly well aware of the direction she is taking. Like her, the gothic trend was slowing down, but wearing a determined look as it headed toward an inevitable precipice.

6

Destined for Darkness
The Gothic Heroine

> Could a young bride, brought to the seacoast of Brooklyn, be completely unaware of—everything? You bet!
> —*Mercy at the Manor Manor*
> by Hester Jane Mundis, 1967

There can be no doubt that popular fiction is gender-oriented both in content and marketing technique. In the early 21st century, a trip to any chain bookstore will reveal rows and rows of genre novels, their target audience clearly defined by their covers. Upbeat contemporary romances and cozy mysteries feature pastel color schemes, curly fonts, cute pets, and a variety of baked goods (some mysteries even promise a recipe section). Steamy historicals offer muscular young dukes in open shirts and tight trousers. Still others, darker in both design and theme, display weaponry, military paraphernalia, or scantily clad women in an attempt to interest male readers. If gothic romances were displayed today, it would be obvious whose interest they are angling to catch. Their modest heroines, clad in long Victorian gowns or ankle-length nightdresses, offer no encouragement to the male gaze. If a man is shown on a gothic cover at all, the heroine is attempting to put as much distance between them as quickly as her possibly bare feet will allow.

Just as she is central to the mass market gothic cover, the heroine is central to the story underneath. She is the catalyst for the events that make up the novel; it is through her eyes (either via a first-person or a limited third-person viewpoint) that the audience experiences each event, filtering every other character and every plot development through the heroine's consciousness. The reader inhabits her body for the duration of the book, seeing what she sees and feeling what she feels.[1] The story is hers to tell. Her ultimate triumph is also that of the reader, who cheers her on for defeating the villain and claiming the love she deserves.

The Gothic Romance Wave

The mass market gothic romance is the product of a unique time and place, a crossroads where several paths converged. An explosion of creativity in popular culture, the rise of the mass market paperback, women's rights, and sexual liberation all came together in a frothy concoction. It stands to reason that the heroine of gothics, mostly written by women and always aimed primarily at women, would reflect the concerns of their creators and, in turn, should fuel awareness of these concerns (perhaps rising to the level of demands) in their readers. Therefore, one might sensibly ask what this character's relationship to the female reader might be, and how this has changed (if in fact it has) from the days of Ann Radcliffe to the era of Phyllis Whitney.

In *Female Gothic Histories*, Diana Wallace points out that the popularity of the gothic romance tends to peak during times when real-life feminists are on the move.[2] In other words, Radcliffe's novels roughly correspond to the release of Mary Wollstonecraft's *Vindication of the Rights of Woman* (1792), the era of the Brontës foreshadowed later 19th-century feminist activism, and modern "women's lib" took flight right around the time the mass market gothic was registering its highest sales. For Wallace, the safety of the historical (or at least the fantastical) mode may allow covert protest, and the heroine's progress from danger to safety may be a metaphor for feminist social gains. Likewise, Kate Ellis sees the work of Radcliffe, Charlotte Smith, and Jane Austen as rife with political commentary and insight.[3] These writers, she suggests, broke new ground by challenging the limits of domesticity (and the male-authored literature of domesticity like *Pamela*) and male authority by employing the castle, the ultimate symbol of patriarchy, as an object of revulsion and an impetus to rebellion. Likewise, the Brontës subvert the sentimental novel of the Victorian era, with the madwoman in the attic (or the ghostly waif on the moors) replacing the angel in the house. Women's private turmoil in an age of blunted opportunity gives rise to metaphorical (and sometimes literal) howls of rage that shake Thornfield and Wuthering Heights to their foundations.

The 18th-century gothic heroine was, unsurprisingly, shaped by and for the interests of a new class of readers—women with leisure time. As England settled into an industrial economy, rather than an agricultural one, more women began to stay inside the home and enjoy a life of limited physical labor as well as domestic comforts. This redefined their place in the family and in the society at large. It enabled women not only to become avid readers, but authors. Mussell has suggested that the act of writing for public consumption, even more than the content of the novels, makes the woman-penned gothic political. In 1799, 331 of 1171 titles published in America were by women, she notes, each publication representing an act of independence and vocational commitment.[4] Women continued to write, and earn a living from their novels, throughout the 19th century. Most of these novels, whether gothic or not, were so sentimental as to be generally unreadable today. Yet they formed the basis for what was to come in the age of mass market publishing and represent the first modern industry in which women were able to assert economic power.

Ann Radcliffe's Georgian heroines were clearly meant to appeal to these members of a non-laboring class, who had the time to read novels. Ideally, they would also serve as role models to help women adjust to new social mores in a time of rapidly changing (some might say evolving) standards. Sexual temptation and economic freedom were two possibilities for women that had never really been considered as pressing threats by the literate class. This new anxiety led to the publication (and popularity) of books like *Pamela*, which Regis describes as if not the first romance novel, the first "courtship novel" and possibly the first commercial best-seller.[5] The heroine in this story is physically but never morally overpowered as she struggles through a series of temptations, kidnappings, and threats. Throughout it all, she sticks to her virtues (in other words, successfully defends her virginity) and is rewarded with marriage and prosperity, and even a kind of economic independence bequeathed to her by her husband. As jarring as this might seem to modern readers, at the time it was viewed as a progressive step away from women being viewed as chattel.

The early gothic novels of Radcliffe recast Pamela (or Clarissa) with heroines like Emily St. Aubert in *The Mysteries of Udolpho*. Like her predecessors, Emily is also kidnapped by a villain who expresses great passion not for her, but for her inheritance. It would be tempting to view Emily as a victim or at best a passive sort who is pulled in two directions by the villainous Montoni and the virtuous Valancourt. Yet the story suggests that she is more than this. The newly orphaned Emily learns to navigate her way around Europe without either of them at her side (something Pamela and Clarissa never quite managed), solves the mystery of the waxen figure along with several other plot points, and emerges from Montoni's castle victorious and economically independent. At this point, she chooses a husband—the good-natured Valancourt—out of love rather than necessity.

Jane Austen was to repeat this trajectory for Catherine Morland, though perhaps her brilliantly subtle humor prevents some readers from fully appreciating the metaphorical value of Catherine's journey across England. At first, as a sheltered ingénue, she travels with her guardians, and then, in a large step toward independence, with her new friends, and finally back to her parents' home on her own. This time, "the journey in itself had no terrors for her; and she began it without either dreading its length or feeling its solitariness." Her mother praises the accomplishment of traveling alone, which was not often undertaken by ladies of Catherine's age and social class in the Regency period. "'Well,' continued her philosophic mother, 'I am glad I did not know of your journey at the time; but now it is all over, perhaps there is no great harm done. It is always good for young people to be put upon exerting themselves; and you know, my dear Catherine, you always were a sad little scatter-brained creature; but now you must have been forced to have your wits about you, with so much changing of chaises and so forth; and I hope it will appear that you have not left anything behind you in any of the pockets.'"[6]

Over the course of her gothic journey, Catherine has found maturity and courage. She unmasks liars, forces Henry to confront the sad truth about his parents' marriage (perhaps avoiding a similar fate for his own), and ultimately attracts and wins the heart and husband of her choice.

In this respect, Catherine prefigures Jane Eyre, perhaps the quintessential gothic heroine. Beloved by readers (and by Mr. Rochester) for her feisty attitude, Jane is forced by circumstances to earn a living as a governess in a semi-servile position, but her will is strong enough to reject a comfortable life as Rochester's mistress as well as St. John's proposal—offers many women in her position would have found, respectively, tempting and spiritually advisable. Like Catherine, Jane journeys through harsh terrain both physically and mentally, only to emerge at the end of her gothic trials stronger and wiser. Returning to the blinded and maimed Rochester on her own terms, wealthy and with a refused proposal from the sanctimonious St. John behind her, Jane becomes his guide and, in a literal sense, his eyes, taking over for his makeshift service dog, tellingly named "Pilot." In the end, as Jane herself puts it, "Reader, I married him"—not "(thank goodness) he married me."

Ninety-two years later, the second Mrs. deWinter debuted, possessing few social accomplishments and not even a name of her own. A new bride at 21, with little experience of the outside world, Mrs. DeWinter is overwhelmed with the responsibility of running a great English house and worried that her husband married her only out of kindness or boredom. For the first

6. Destined for Darkness

half of the novel, the reader becomes increasingly impatient as the heroine allows the housekeeper to humiliate her and even try to strong-arm her into suicide with constant comparisons to Rebecca, the first and apparently perfect Mrs. DeWinter. As would be the case in almost all subsequent popular gothics, du Maurier is silent when it comes to details of the deWinters' intimate life, but it seems clear that they are initially mismatched both in terms of age and social class. After Max confesses that he murdered Rebecca and hid her body (a scenario softened to accidental death in the movie to avoid moral offense), however, the heroine's attitude begins to change. Not only does she not run screaming from a man who has apparently committed the ultimate crime, she actually begins to take charge of her life, her husband, and their marriage. In contrast to Mrs. Danvers' sexless sterility, the heroine reclaims her role as both a potentially fertile wife and as mistress of Manderley:

> It was going to be very different in the future. I was not going to be nervous and shy with the servants any more. With Mrs. Danvers gone I should learn bit by bit to control the house. I would go and interview the cook in the kitchen. They would like me, respect me. Soon it would be as though Mrs. Danvers had never had command. I would learn more about the estate, too.... I might take to gardening myself, and in time have one or two things altered.... That little square lawn outside the morning-room with the statue of the satyr. I did not like it. We would give the satyr away. There were heaps of things that I could do, little by little. People would come and stay and I should not mind. There would be the interest of seeing to their rooms, having flowers and books put, arranging the food. We would have children. Surely we would have children.[7]

The garden and the satyr are clear symbols of sexuality; the heroine's resolution to confront them and even alter them suggests that she is no longer frightened of these things, after which the possibility of children occurs to her. By the story's end, she has put away childish things once and for all and is literally in control. Like Rochester, Maxim pays for his misdeeds by losing his home (and social power) and spending his days in exile, a broken man. Despite his injuries in the Thornfield fire, Rochester had regained at least some of his sight and, with Jane's help, learned to live again; Maxim's psychological recovery is less certain, leaving his wife to nursemaid him and hover benignly while he reads the English newspapers and tries to forget all he has lost.

Many teenaged girls in the 1940s and 1950s probably started their journeys as readers with novels about plucky young heroines like Nancy Drew and Cherry Ames (in fact the final issue of *Gothic Journal* paid homage to the *Nancy Drew* series). By the 1960s and 1970s, this audience had grown

The Gothic Romance Wave

into other types of stories, especially those featuring young women who, like them, had reached marriageable age and were beginning to contemplate their futures as adults. In one sense, the sleuthing heroines of the paperback gothics had much in common with Nancy and Cherry (who probably prefigured the heroine of many a "nursie" romance as well). Borrowing the structure of *Jane Eyre* gave authors a fresh stage on which they could combine light mystery and romance, along with plenty of Victorian-style atmosphere and just enough pulp-style *noir* to keep things interesting, yet unobjectionable: while dodging attempts on her life, the heroine will be courted by two men and distrusted by various servants and family members. Eventually she will determine which man is innocent of wrongdoing and therefore worthy of her. They will then join forces and rehabilitate the house both physically and spiritually, assuming it hasn't burned down or exploded.

Most paperback gothic romances limited themselves to one of four basic types of heroine, with a few variations depending on the needs of the plot.

The first, who is closest to Jane Eyre, is the determined governess. Despite an exemplary background and character, she finds herself in an economic pinch with no responsible relatives or means of supporting herself. Forced to seek employment with a family in one of the few respectable positions open to women in earlier eras, she takes charge of protecting and rehabilitating a troubled child. On occasion, she may sign on as some other type of servant, such as a housekeeper or a paid companion to a recluse, or present herself as a long-lost relative, but her basic role in the household will be the same. Once she takes up residence, she must endure various frightening interludes and attempts on her life. During the course of her adventures, she develops feelings for the master of the house, who may or may not be her ward's biological father, but fears that he is too cold, too dangerous, or of too high a social station to return her feelings. Eventually, she will save her charge(s) from mortal danger before finding happiness in a committed relationship with the hero. The best-known example is Victoria Holt's *Mistress of Mellyn*, though many imitations followed.

The second, who is generally modeled on the second Mrs. DeWinter, is the frightened bride (perhaps the best-remembered style of gothic heroine thanks to Joanna Russ). Also alone in the world, either because she is orphaned or has indifferent or absent parents, this heroine has impulsively married a wealthy, worldly man and then finds out she doesn't know him as well as she thought. Once she accompanies him to his manor house or castle, she fears he is trying to kill her or drive her mad, as he may have done with

6. Destined for Darkness

his first wife or fiancée. She struggles to adjust to her new position in the manor while fending off the usual attempts on her life and trying to figure out her husband's motives. The marriages in these stories are seldom dealt with in any depth—they are plot devices to speed along the mystery and add a layer of danger by making the heroine more isolated (or to reward her for solving the mystery and saving a life). It might also be noted that although patriarchal structure demands that the man protect the woman, here he does not do so, for whatever reason, forcing her to protect herself. Sexuality is often dealt with summarily and even coyly—sometimes the couple does not consummate their marriage until after the book ends, but if they do, it is described only in the vaguest terms[8] and quickly glossed over.

A variation of this formula is the troubled bride-to-be, in which the marriage has not yet taken place. The bride to be is taken to the castle to get acquainted with the family, but both the heroine and the reader begin to wonder whether the marriage will ever take place. Meanwhile, another man presents himself as an alternate choice of groom. The heroine must decide which of them is genuinely in love with her and which of them is plotting against her. Depending on the outcome, she may or may not call off the marriage. Another is the sleuthing widow, whose wealthy husband has died or disappeared en route to the castle or shortly after the newlywed couple's arrival. While his widow tries to solve his murder, another man presents himself as a replacement husband and she must consider if he is sincere or more interested in taking over the husband's economic resources (and, in fact, helped usher her first husband off this mortal coil). An excellent example of this trope is Elsie Lee's *Mistress of Montfair* (1965).

Though a Victorian heroine might be expected to throw herself on the mercy of her financially solvent employers or relatives, in most of the novels with contemporary settings, the modern heroine must earn a living and balance her gothic adventures with the demands of the career that brought her to the mysterious old house in the first place. Thus, the third type of heroine is the modern employee. These stories, typically set in the late 1960s or early 1970s, depict a woman, often college-educated, who arrives at the house or castle in some professional capacity, such as a secretary, art restorer, library cataloguer, journalist, or in some other reasonably progressive but ultimately non-threatening and suitably feminine role. In some cases, her professional experience or knowledge will assist her in solving the mystery. Her vocation is presented as respectable and responsible, though she seldom encroaches on a field the 1960s would have considered traditionally masculine, such as

The Gothic Romance Wave

a lawyer, detective, or architect.[9] Generally she will keep working after her inevitable marriage at the end of the story, usually for the master of the house who is now her husband. Examples include *The House in the Woods* by Leslie Lance and *The Silent Place* by Rachel Cosgrove Payes (both from 1969). One popular approach to this type of story involved grafting the "nursie" formula onto a gothic framework (some covers substituted a uniformed nurse running from a castle for the usual barefoot woman in a nightdress).[10] A typical example is Dan (this time writing as Clarissa) Ross' *Durrell Tower* (1965): "Hired as a nurse for wealthy Jim Durrell's ailing uncle, Elaine Cary found herself strongly attracted to the handsome, brooding young master of Durrell Towers. Then suddenly Jim disappeared. In his place, terror stalked the corridors of the gloomy mansion. Slowly, Elaine found to her horror that she too began to question whether her beloved Jim was the sinister force behind the bizarre events that surrounded the old mansion and gave new life to its evil legacy."[11]

Perhaps the most progressive heroine occurs in the final category, in which the heroine herself becomes the female heir to or new owner of the house. In these stories, the heroine arrives at the manor or castle because a wealthy relative has left it to her (on rare occasions she has purchased it herself) or has been informed that she is the long-lost heir to some prominent family and must prove herself to claim the inheritance. The conditions of the inheritance may drive the plot too. In Alice Brennan's *To Kill a Witch* (1972), a reclusive author, somewhat like Victoria Holt herself, dies and leaves her haunted island to the heroine, who once interviewed her for a magazine, provided she can prove her psychological endurance. Another typical example is *Carlotta's Castle* by Jane McCarthy (1973), in which the newly enriched (and newly married) heroine quite sensibly wonders if she can afford to pay the taxes on her imposing but crumbling new acquisition.

As the 1960s faded into the 1970s, heroines were charging ahead along with their real-life counterparts. No longer are they limited to keeping house, accepting charity from the hero, or nursemaiding children or invalids. They also have little time or patience for outdated sexist assumptions. Cynthia, the heroine of *Terror at Tansey Hill* (Suzanne Roberts, 1975), finds herself in an embarrassing situation when she reports to an upscale restaurant for a job interview. She discovers that the hero, thinking he is meeting a male candidate, has invited her to an all-male enclave.

> The small room was pleasantly air-conditioned. She looked around nervously, and before she could decide which man might be Michael Coleman, a waiter came up to her, smiling.

6. Destined for Darkness

"Sorry, miss, ladies aren't allowed in here." He had a merry, round face and a twinkle in his eye. "At least—we didn't used to serve ladies, but lately we've had some—er—ladies from Women's Lib who've been rather unhappy with our policy. So if you care for a table, I'll seat you, even though—"

"There must be some mistake," Cynthia said, her heart beginning to pound in embarrassment.... She'd heard of places like this, traditional old places where masculine food was served, places men liked to feel were oases from females.

To her credit, Cynthia stands her ground, accompanies the hero to a more inclusive café across the street, and gets the job as caretaker to a remote house with a small staff and a child in residence. The hero, ultimately more amused than outraged by the mix-up, admits the need to "readjust my thinking,"[12] presumably in ways that will allow him greater comfort with the aforementioned "women's lib."[13]

The sexual revolution touched gothic heroines too. Though some "frightened brides" might have recoiled at ghostly figures and strange screams in the night, all of them actively sought and enjoyed the pleasures of the marital bed. "Never mind how we spent the hours between teatime and dinner," the 19th-century newlywed in Mona Farnsworth's *The Castle That Whispered* (1976) tells the reader with a figurative wink.[14] "They were spent as hours should be spent on a honeymoon." Contemporary gothics might even have a non-virginal, unmarried heroine. In 1965's *The Tuscany Madonna* by Miriam Canfield (a penname of Dorothy Fletcher), the French heroine agrees to a loveless marriage to an American to prevent her family's financial ruin. On the night before the wedding, she makes a bold choice and gives her virginity to Gil, a minor character who does not reappear in the story. She expresses no regret for her actions and suffers no external shame or punishment. Before long she is planning to seduce her new husband. In an entertaining reversal, he remains polite but distant toward her, inflaming her need even more. Of course, Denice de Bonneville is French and can perhaps be forgiven her Continental liberties, but her British and American sisters were not far behind her. "What's your sign?" became a clichéd pickup line in 1970s singles' bars, but the apparent interest in horoscopes reflected not just a longing for the numinous, as Victoria Nelson might put it, but an open-mindedness toward women's sexuality and the possibility of arranging sexual experiences outside marriage.

In 1975, Emma Mai Ewing observed in the *New York Times* that the current crop of novels featured a new type of protagonist:

The updating of the gothic heroine may seem slight—unless you knew her yesterday. Sometimes now she is a career girl, or divorced, intelligent, even believable. The gothic now can have an educational pitch. Catherine Gaskin's *Property of a Gentleman* (Doubleday, $7.95) describes antique collecting. Isabelle Holland's *Trelawny* (Weybright & Talley, $6.95; Bantam later in paperback) finds the heroine hoping to turn the family mansion in Maine into a discreet commune and art colony. *The Dark Below* (Fawcett, 95 cents) by Michael T. Hinkemeyer, a Queens College professor, even has a male lead. Maybe these don't seem too daring innovations for the seventies, but in the framework they're far out.[15]

Clearly, the popular image of the gothic ingénue as a stereotyped Pollyanna wailing for rescue in the villain's dungeon misrepresents both character and genre. The heroine of any romance, most certainly including the gothic, maintains a complex relationship to the (presumed female) reader as both Other and Self. Often, this blurring of identity is enhanced by the use of a first-person viewpoint. The experience is vicarious rather than voyeuristic, with the reader sharing, if only temporarily, the heroine's triumph as she resolves the story's conflicts, exorcises the evil plaguing the house, and claims her chosen mate in every sense of the word.

Not all interpretations of the gothic heroine's role have been as positive, however. Ellis, who concerned herself with 18th- and 19th-century examples, seems to have no difficulty describing the gothic heroine, and by extension her creator, as proactive and even progressive in her rejection of patriarchal oppression, but a number of other critics are less sanguine about the gothic's purpose and effect. Despite the almost miraculous social gains of women by the late 20th century, some critics of popular romance fiction find little beyond passive, disenfranchised heroines who embody modern women's fear of the opposite sex and even of their own sexuality. Either Georgian and Victorian heroines simply provided a starker contrast to their more conservative time period better or their Nixon-era counterparts have actually gone backward. The effect on readers is even more sinister, they insist. Reading women's popular fiction has been described as leading to emotional vapidity and political apathy, perhaps akin to popping the "Mother's Little Helper" pills the Rolling Stones sang about in 1966. It may even be a plot engineered by the smirking patriarchy, aided by a virtual army of Stepford-like female authors, determined to gull the readers they secretly (or perhaps merely unconsciously) despise.

Janice Radway, writing in the early 1980s, characterized the gothic as basically "reactionary" because it cultivates reader identification with a heroine who at first seems feisty and determined, but who ultimately capitulates to the patriarchy represented by the hero. "[T]he gothic successfully disarms the anger it induces," she argues, since "the feminist protest is not sustained....

6. Destined for Darkness

The gothic's fantasy resolution represents, finally, an imaginative compromise between slowly developing psychological needs generated by changing social possibilities for women and its readers' still more powerful desire to keep gender relations as they were."[16] Only when readers ceased to "fear" the reaction of men to their newfound individuality in the early 1970s, Radway believes, did they feel free to abandon the gothic formula and turn to sexually explicit fare like *The Flame and the Flower*. Kay Mussell, who generally defends the romance and its readers, concedes that "the relationship [between hero and heroine] is one of limits"[17] rather than liberation. The modern gothic romance is especially alluring because it "offers vicarious danger and romantic fantasy of a type that is particularly appealing to female readers. Women are cast as victims in a man's world, but through her demonstration of feminine virtues, the victim proves herself worthy of salvation through the love of the hero, who becomes her deliverer from the terrors that beset her."

She believes that "[w]omen in these books are doubly victimized: by their feminine powerlessness and by their location in a place ... where a gothic villain can threaten them."[18] Only marriage and an alliance with a powerful hero can save the heroine. The domestic, interior setting, typically the purview of the female characters instead becomes one in which she has relinquished that last bit of control, leaving herself in greater danger than she might be in a male-oriented space like a battlefield or the open wilderness. Modleski and Cohn go even further, Modleski stressing that an interest in gothics arises from women's own paranoia about enforced gender roles, while Cohn dismisses the entire romance genre as a hopeless tangle of conflicting and mutually exclusive values. Such fiction offers a degrading blueprint for the reader's own interactions with real-world men: "[Romance fiction] deconstructs itself through an unanswerable contradiction: to reestablish the power relations between men and woman through love and marriage is finally to accede to the conditions imposed by patriarchal society. Marriage remains woman's sole means of access to power, and romantic love—the supreme value in romance fiction—relentlessly defends women against economic self-interest in marriage. Thus, romance end where it began, its resolution endlessly reenacting the contradiction it exists to dispel."[19]

In other words, the popular romance novel is a quivering, bewildering mass of contradictions. It simultaneously gives lip service to and then undermines female self-sufficiency and independence through the actions of a simpering heroine who aspires only to become a subservient wife. It pushes the reader into bad relationships with domineering men and at the same time

The Gothic Romance Wave

keeps her isolated from real flesh-and-blood connections. It is both "deliberately apolitical,"[20] yet it is also heavy with social and cultural meaning (and proscription). Every time a woman picks up a romance novel from a mainstream, mass market publisher, she is tearing down the centuries of progress so hard-won by her sisters. To believe some critics, the tide that had turned for women by the late 1960s was either incomprehensible or entirely rejected by the readers of gothics. They enjoyed stories about brave women poking through a sinister house investigating murders or ghostly events, only to cheer inwardly when the heroine ultimately broke down and sobbed for a man to rescue her. Every fresh page turned made Helen Reddy weep. One wonders how the readers, stupefied and compliant in their own objectification, manage to make sense of such stories at all. One might also wonder how they manage to make their way to the bookstore on their own, make a selection, and approach the counter with enough money to buy even one, let alone form a steady romance novel habit.

Hyperbole aside, it is worth asking whether critics are justified in viewing the gothic heroine as little more than the embodiment of a system "in which social mobility occurs through family identity and marriage rather than through individual success ... thus elevating the place of family formation through love to supremacy."[21] It may seem a bit jarring to turn from this bleak critical landscape of oppression and feminine helplessness to a tip sheet for prospective gothic authors hoping to write for 1992's *Silhouette Shadows* line. The editors advise that the heroine should be "a strong, contemporary woman, capable of confronting and conquering the dangers that threaten her.... She is always a match for the hero as they play out a compelling romance in the midst of plot that may range from gothic in tone to a woman in jeopardy story [while] The hero may represent—even personify—the dangers she faces, or he may provide support and comfort in the midst of a dark and menacing world."[22]

Readers on the whole seem to be less patient with ineffectual heroines than critics suppose: gothic bibliographer Elsa Radcliffe gives Joan Ditzel Conway's *Island of Fear* a grade of "D" thanks to its clichéd "mish-mosh of disasters and melodrama.... This heroine gets top honors for all-time clod. Every ten pages the poor dear is tripping, falling, or getting injured, and generally through her own stupidity."[23] Conversely, a *Gothic Journal* reader review of the 1991 gothic *The Crimson Roses of Fountain Court* by Peggy Darty emphasizes that "Margaret's hobby of painting, her love of cats, and her self-supporting career as a working woman make her easy for a modern-day reader to identify with." She commands "reader respect."[24] When a loosely constructed plot demands that a heroine behave foolishly for the sake of the storyline, readers complain. "Too stupid to live"[25] has become a catchphrase among romance fans, meant to warn one another away from books lacking a credible female protagonist.

If the more pessimistic critics are correct, and the romance is used to disempower the readers by lulling them into a soporific acceptance of a subservient state, we might expect to see little change from the 18th century to the 1970s. The heroine would progress from an empty vessel with no political power (as dictated by 18th-century law and custom) to one who, perhaps, sees the possibility of power and either consciously rejects it or reconciles herself to permanent inequality. On the other hand, it seems plausible to construe reading a gothic (or other types of romance) as a liberating act. Women are choosing their own reading materials, spending their own money, supporting the economic prosperity of a female author, and boldly confronting forbidden topics and sexual taboos (often at least hinted at in gothics). The heroine becomes the reader's vessel, enabling her to experiment with identity and self-actualization. What critics like Cohn perhaps fail to see is that during the course of the story, the heroine transforms both the psychological space and the potential marital space she and the hero inhabit. The power balance is shifted, though perhaps not fully upended—after all, the couple does not have the power to institute an instant, society-wide matriarchy even if they wished to do so. Within the manor house, though, Victorian or 1960s conventions may be adjusted or ignored as the couple chooses.

Mistress of Mellyn's Martha suggests a test case. This heroine, modest in both temperament and circumstance, arrives at Mellyn much as Jane Eyre arrives at Thornfield: poor, plain, and homeless save for the shelter provided for her in her role as a governess. Yet to regard Martha as passive or powerless would be to misread Holt's conscious use of structure in the novel. As Mussell has demonstrated, Martha's journey through the plot is a variation on the time-honored quest tale, though with gender-appropriate challenges. Arthurian knights left the castle and proved their ability to kill and conquer; Martha, conversely, literally turns inward, enters Mellyn, and demonstrates her capacity for domestic skills along with kindness and nurturing. In fact, as quest narratives go, Sir Gawain shows himself to be far more passive than the typical gothic heroine when he feigns sleep to avoid the chatelaine's repeated attempts at seduction. In contrast, many a gothic heroine slips through locked doors forbidden to her, searches people's rooms, snoops through letters and diaries, and questions servants and guests in her quest for the truth. If it becomes necessary for her to confront her enemy with, literally, sword in hand, she can do that too. Though she might regret inflicting defensive wounds, in the heat of battle she can do what it takes.

After identifying the centrality of the domestic challenges to heroine's purpose, Mussell hedges when explicating the meaning of Martha's ultimate triumph. As she reads it, "The confirmation of Martha's success in the domestic test is certified not because she brings a murderer to justice but when Connan chooses her as his wife."[26] Separating the two goals (and rewards) is not exactly fair. Celestine, whose obsession with claiming both Mellyn and its master as her own (and in that order of importance), might almost be seen as a parody of the stereotypical gothic romance heroine. Her determination to marry the hero puts her in a murderous frenzy, and in her attempt to eliminate her rival, Martha, she betrays her guilt. Martha, who has passed the domestic test without losing her own personality and values, wins the house and the husband as a package deal, though she clearly regards Connan's love as the greater prize. Celestine, whose fixation on becoming Mellyn's mistress makes her perverted and cruel, is reviled and punished for her crimes.

Martha, like Jane Eyre and Mrs. DeWinter, is a heroine with whom most female readers can (and do) comfortably identify. Neither beautiful nor vain, all three use their intellect to overcome the obstacles that keep them in a subservient position. Connan, Rochester, and Maxim reject conventional and class-appropriate beauties like Celestine, Blanche Ingram, and Rebecca, women who are perfectly content to enter into outwardly traditional but loveless marriages for their own gain, in favor of an unassuming heroine who offers genuine love or, in Jane's case, witty sparring.[27] Having passed the domestic test, solved the mystery, and accepted the hero's flaws, these second wives are hardly passive ciphers, and there is no hint that they will capitulate to the heroes after the narrative has concluded. In fact, every gothic hero expresses excitement (perhaps even to his own surprise) at the prospect of an equal marriage. In stories set in the 19th century, such an arrangement would seem especially enlightened, which perhaps accounts for the popularity of a historical setting. Both the heroine's achievement and the hero's capacity to love seem that much greater when juxtaposed against the backdrop of a male-dominated world.

Much has also been made of the supposed psychological meaning behind the heroine's lack of close family members, which supposedly separates her from any meaningful matrilineal ties. However, the reality is simply that in

6. Destined for Darkness

a short book (most modern gothics are about 80,000 words or less), there is limited time for character development and thus the cast must be stripped down to those directly involved in the drama at hand. Also, the plot requires that the heroine depend on her own resources and not those of her family, a story arc that precludes the heroine remaining passive and helpless. One thing she does is learn to navigate the house or castle on her own and create family ties of her own (though marriage, stepchildren, siblings in law, or whatever). Occasionally, the heroine is on a quest for her biological family, from whom she was separated at a young age. For all these reasons, it is impractical for an author to include parents—though it can and has been done. Far from a deliberate attempt to exclude other women from the dramatic canvas, isolating the heroine is necessary so that her character may mature and develop.

It is true that most mass market gothic romances emphasize the hero's social position, which is always loftier than that of the heroine (one recalls that class differences caused much of the anxiety for *Rebecca*'s nameless heroine, who started off as a lowly paid companion and moved on to a brief and ultimately unsuccessful turn as mistress of Manderley). However, critics should not forget that literary comedy,[28] which like the romance novel ends with marriage, also involves the raising of one character's social status from low to high (the reverse of tragedy). Interestingly, even when she has the opportunity to assert her newfound economic dominance, the gothic heroine almost never decides to take the reins and become head of the family or matriarch of the castle. When faced with a choice between love and wealth, she always chooses love, which includes rejecting or repurposing that traditional (and often phallic) symbol of feudalism and patriarchy, the castle. The marriages they affirm at the end of the story break the chains that symbolize the old hierarchy. In *Carlotta's Castle*, the heroine even turns the structure over to a nunnery, reclaiming it as an all-female space free of the suffering engineered by its tyrannical male founder. Even when male characters like Rochester and Maxim deWinter try to maintain the structures of the past, or at least risk life and limb in trying, women step in to upend convention and redistribute the wealth fairly. They embrace modernity at the happy expense of the older and more rigid (or cruel) ways, dragging their (belatedly grateful) husbands along into the future.

To look at the heroine's effect on readers another way, virtually none of the critics who have studied the mass market romance (including the gothic) have given much attention to Herbert Gans' study of popular culture and its

The Gothic Romance Wave

consumers. Gans concludes that most readers likely consume such books as entertainment and do not draw political lessons or life guidance from them. Instead, critics place a staggering importance on the ingénue heroine of a 60,000-word melodrama, who assumes the influence of a world leader engineering the fates of an entire class of readers. Equally astonishing is the assumption that the authors of such paperbacks, most of them struggling freelancers desperately hammering out manuscripts to supplement their incomes, could have such a far-reaching effect on gender norms.

Perhaps some mass market romances do little to confront conventional gender relations (and the fact remains that many gothics were written by male authors taking a break from their usual science fiction or hardboiled detective stories). Still, the romance market was changing quickly in the gothics' heyday. Popular romances published since the late 1980s, after the mass market gothic romance's popularity had waned, increasingly offered valuable models for independent women: female sexuality was discussed frankly, male partners were expected to be both sensitive and responsible in the relationship, and in almost all cases the modern heroine continued her career after marriage. Gothic heroines of the late 1960s and early 1970s were already pioneering this more take-charge attitude. They thought nothing of ending curses, exorcising evil spirits, and exposing criminals while remodeling the castle (a symbolic feminist act if ever there was one) and engineering satisfying marriages.

Though she is generally running away on the cover, in every gothic novel the heroine chooses to stay and face her demons—whether they are psychological, supernatural, or merely plotting in-laws. True, her quest may lead to conventional marriage, an institution our culture still regards with a certain ambiguity. After all, does the traditional pre-wedding bridal shower celebrate a woman's passage to a new social and sexual maturity, or is it a consolation party for the freedom she is about to give up forever? No definitive answer can be true for all brides. However, one thing is true for almost every gothic: the heroine's days as a wife will not be spent in the dank, sunless recesses of the castle. Instead, she will stand in the center of its most fragrant and fertile garden to enjoy the light and warmth.

7

Melancholy Males and Demon Lovers
The Gothic Hero

> His hand took her by the shoulder, firm yet surprisingly gentle. "You've thinking to do, all right," he said. "Maybe more than you know. Enough in any case."
> His rugged face was just above hers, and Jean felt her lips part as she leaned forward, reaching up to his face. His kiss was soft but only for an instant, and then he gathered her into his arms and she felt the power of this man, and she liked the hardness of his kiss as he pressed her mouth open. When he drew back, his eyes were deep pools of black fire, but his face remained unsmiling and he said nothing.
> "Let's say that was a thank you for saving my life," she finally breathed.
>
> —*House at Hawk's End* by Claudette Nicole
> [Jon Messmann], 1971

In the early months of 2014, reports emerged that the erotic romance *Fifty Shades of Grey* had reached a publishing milestone by logging one hundred million sales across the globe.[1] The butt of endless jokes and the inspiration for the term "mommy porn," *Fifty Shades* had nonetheless captivated readers worldwide, almost all of them female. It would eventually spawn two sequels, a companion volume written from the hero's point of view, and a major motion picture, not to mention countless imitations by authors eager to share in author E.L. James' good fortune.

The *Fifty Shades* sensation may have been unexpected (and some might say undeserved, given the poor reviews), but it was not unprecedented. Six years earlier, Stephenie Meyer's vampire romance *Twilight* (also mercilessly savaged by critics) had broken records by racking up 22 million sales in a single year.[2] *Twilight* also became a series of books as well as films, with the

The Gothic Romance Wave

entire franchise bringing in some six billion dollars,[3] a figure that is still growing.

E.L. James, the author of *Fifty Shades*, must have hoped her novel would mirror *Twilight*'s success. After all, the book had started out as a fictional tribute to *Twilight*,[4] with erotic language and situations added for fans impatient with the original's emphasis on its youthful characters' chastity. This connection makes Christian Grey, the arrogant and sexually domineering hero of *Fifty Shades*, the stepchild of Edward Cullen, the surly but charismatic teenaged vampire. Both, in turn, are the direct descendants of the gothic hero.[5] They may live in modern West Coast homes instead of hereditary castles on the windswept coast of Cornwall or New England, but their stormy personalities, vast wealth, and instant power over the heroine connect their lineage to Rochester, the vampyre Ruthven, and finally to Lord Byron himself.[6] In fact, their origins reach back even further, to the days of supernatural-themed folk tales and ballads.

In her bibliographic guide to romance novels, Ramsdell contrasts the "[t]he sardonic, brooding hero of the classic gothic" to his literary cousin, the "engaging, competent hero of the romantic suspense" novel,[7] which suggests one way to tell the difference between the two subgenres. Yet romance readers (and writers) have never been shy about their preference for a "cynical man who makes life more difficult for the heroine"[8] over a more jocular and sensitive love interest (called a beta hero in romance novel parlance). Such a man is instantly recognizable, both to the reader and to the heroine, because of his air of privileged arrogance, volcanic passions, and stubborn melancholy. Billionaire Christian Grey, with his taste for sadomasochism, is only his most recent (though perhaps the most extreme) incarnation. It is no coincidence that such a man is called, in romance terms, an alpha hero (those who take their authoritarian role too far are affectionately known by romance readers as "alphaholes"). Evolutionary biology suggests that when it comes to choosing mates, human females are biologically impelled toward certain types of reproductively promising males. Generally, women prefer men who are tall, intelligent, able to protect a mate and children, and economically stable and prosperous enough to offer not only sustenance but creature comforts. One sees all of these traits reflected in the typical gothic romance hero. He is tall, dark, and handsome to a fault, with an impeccable pedigree (though perhaps compromised by a curse somewhere along the line), and a castle or manor house to demonstrate his wealth and social status.[9] His attitude brings instant conflict to the story; the heroine's efforts to solve the mystery inherent to the

7. Melancholy Males and Demon Lovers

gothic quest are confounded by his refusal to listen to or help her. Indeed, she may at times wonder if he might be actively working against her. Sorting out his feelings for her, as well as his possible involvement in whatever crime has been committed, heightens the narrative tension. In the case of a gothic, he need not even be a living man; a vampire, demon, or ghost, under certain circumstances, will do just as well.

Perhaps because of the alpha hero's exaggerated masculinity, critics, especially those with a feminist bent, tend to find the romance novel and the gothic novel in particular a bastion of male privilege and female passivity. To be sure, the gothic addresses male power in every chapter. The lord of the manor is the center of the action, even when he is offstage (or, more accurately, off-page). The heroine is constantly thinking about him, acting on his behalf, or perhaps trying to avoid him. Yet, even if the gothic is unarguably about patriarchy, it is not about subservience. Part of every gothic heroine's quest is to distinguish rigid and therefore malevolent examples of patriarchy from those open to being reshaped through feminine ideals and love (especially since it is usually revealed that an ostensibly helpful rival suitor has been the true villain all along). The readers of mass market gothic romances have long understood (even if they cannot always articulate the fact in critical terms) that the stories are about comfort and healing more than they are about evil and fear. It is the heroine who ultimately conquers and reforms (in both senses of the word) the hero who is willing to learn. He does not become her lord and master in anything but a playfully erotic sense; at the end of every gothic, her values triumph. She will either help destroy an institution that has become polluted (symbolized by a crumbling castle or burning manor house) or restore harmony to the hero's once broken, sterile home.

For example, Caroline Farr's *Witch's Hammer* depicts a heroine confronting a horror that can only be described as patriarchy gone wild. The lord of the manor, in this case a wealthy film star, has attempted to recreate pre–Revolutionary Russia in 1960s New England, right down to installing a community of serfs and employing a menacing enforcer figure who is reputed to be Rasputin's son. Worse, he maintains an uncomfortably incestuous hold over his daughter, who has subordinated her own personality to his. As in Russia, though, this strong-armed tyranny falls when the servants band together, organized by the heroine, and violently rebel, destroying the commune. The heroine, having recognized and defeated this malevolent arrangement, rejects this self-appointed tzar and chooses as a lover a gentler man with modern ideas and a healthy respect for both women and democracy.

The Gothic Romance Wave

Today we tend to think of mass market gothic romances, and romance novels in general, as the story of the heroine and her reaction to the male love interest. In early gothics, however, such as *The Castle of Otranto* (1764) and Clara Reeve's *The Old English Baron* (1778), the ingénue was simply one member of a larger cast, and hers was not the dominant point of view.[10] Not until *The Mysteries of Udolpho* did the heroine take control of the narrative. Interestingly, no male character in any of these works corresponds to the gothic hero as we think of him today. *Otranto*'s Theodore and *Udolpho*'s Valancourt are affable, loyal, and rather dull young men. Both are given to long sentimental speeches such as the one Valancourt bursts out with while he admires a dramatic landscape with Emily and her father: "'These scenes ... soften the heart like sweet music, and inspire that delicious melancholy which no person, who had felt it once, would resign for the gayest pleasures. They waken our best and purest feelings; disposing us to benevolence, pity, and friendship. Those whom I love, I always seem to love more in such an hour as this.' His voice trembled, and he paused."[11] It is not hard to imagine Edward Rochester turning away to sneer at this heartfelt declaration, or Heathcliff delivering the mawkish Valancourt an outraged cuff on the ear (if not a vicious punch to the throat). Emily, of course, is captivated by the young gentleman's sensitivity and kindness. Modern readers, most likely, react with an indulgent but bored smile.

Valancourt is a child of nature, drawn to its gentle music and in touch with the simple impulses of the romantic heart. The villain of *Udolpho*, Count Montoni, cuts a more dramatic figure. Montoni, like every gothic villain, is a remnant of the old feudal order. Enlightened 18th-century readers would recognize that his evil stems from the artifice and corruption of civilization, which has provided him with a castle that can double as a prison, not to mention an army of servants and sycophants willing to kill for him; Emily's plight and ability to evade these nefarious designs is at least partially a metaphorical escape. Similarly, *Otranto*'s Theodore and Isabella had defeated the lecherous Manfred and entered a passionless but apparently satisfactory marriage during which they spend most of their time mourning the death of the story's other heroine, Mathilda. In retrospect, it is not a broad jump from a woman trapped in a castle by an overbearing gothic villain to a modern woman yearning to escape the enforced domesticity imposed by family tradition. Senf points out that Victorian novelists recognized and exploited this metaphor by using gothic elements to express social critique. For Dickens, Eliot, and others, surly patriarchs and dank estates became symbols for outdated and oppressive British social institutions.

7. Melancholy Males and Demon Lovers

Few 18th-century readers secretly longed for Emily and Montoni, or Isabella and the aging, lecherous tyrant Manfred, to discover a forbidden passion; however, one can presume that all three Brontë sisters, and no doubt many other Byron enthusiasts of the early 19th century, found themselves more intrigued by the scheming Montoni than the stout-hearted but insipid Valancourt. By the time *Jane Eyre* appeared in 1847, life had imitated art in the brief but glorious career of Lord Byron, a kind of real-life gothic figure (and the model for the first literary vampire, Ruthven) whose magnetic personality and aura of wickedness sent young English ladies (and perhaps some not so young) swooning. This new generation of readers probably saw Radcliffe's characters quite differently than she had envisioned them. Even Emily St. Aubert had to admit there was something oddly alluring about her aristocratic nemesis. Her description of him prefigures Jane Eyre's later appraisals of her imposing employer, Edward Rochester:

> This Signor Montoni had an air of conscious superiority, animated by spirit and strengthened by talents, to which every person seemed involuntarily to yield. The quickness of his perceptions was strikingly expressed on his countenance; yet that countenance could submit implicitly to occasion; and more than once in this day the triumph of art over nature might have been discerned in it. His visage was long, and rather narrow; yet he was called handsome: and it was, perhaps, the spirit and vigour of his soul, sparkling through his features, that triumphed for him. Emily felt admiration, but not the admiration that leads to esteem; for it was mixed with a degree of fear she knew not exactly wherefore.[12]

Though Rochester is a less overtly savage love interest than Heathcliff, he still has far more of Montoni in him than he does of Valancourt—and, like Montoni, he even keeps a prisoner in the tower, though for arguably less nefarious reasons. The master of Thornfield is also a descendant of the wicked suitors in didactic books like *Pamela* and *Clarissa*, who kidnap and tempt the heroine until she either gives in and dies, like Clarissa, or holds onto her virtue and marries him, like Pamela.[13] Milton's Satan may also have lent a hand in his creation, as readers and critics alike have long noticed (and sometimes lamented) that Satan is by far the most interesting and appealing character in *Paradise Lost*, a favorite text of the young Brontës. Rochester never goes to the extremes of Lovelace or Montoni, though he does attempt to commit bigamy and later invites Jane to be his mistress, options sufficiently shocking to Victorian England. Yet, through it all, Jane continues to love him, to the extent that she decides to physically remove herself from temptation by leaving Thornfield. As Nelson suggests, Jane's yearning for Rochester, who would in an earlier era have been portrayed as the novel's villain, turned literary convention on its head. He is both hero and antagonist, both seducer and loyal husband. Their connection sparks, sizzles, and even frightens the heroine, who nonetheless cannot get enough of her enigmatic employer. Readers, in turn, cannot get enough of Jane and Rochester together, as the myriad of film adaptations and modern sequels attests.

Charlotte Brontë presents Jane's marriage to Rochester, and not the rigidly moral St. John, not as capitulation, but as a means to personal fulfillment and self-actualization. Her choice saves Rochester as well: the rejected St. John soon perishes, burning with a fever that may well be a metaphor for the fiery passions he denied himself in life, while Rochester, though maimed in the fire that purifies both Thornfield and his own body, fights his way back to health. Eventually, under Jane's guidance, he can see the world, including the son who will carry on his family name, with new eyes. Emily's heroine, Catherine, faces a similar choice when she is caught between the passionate savagery of Heathcliff and the cool stability of Edgar; in this case, she follows convention and as a result goes mad before dying in a paroxysm of sexual frustration. Only in Anne Brontë's *Tenant of Wildfell Hall* does the heroine reject the Byronic affectations of her husband, Arthur, boldly defying custom by packing up and leaving him to his alcoholism and his mistress. Upon his death, she accepts a less volatile suitor, the somewhat priggish Gilbert. The reversal of the suitors' personalities from those found in her sisters' works may have prevented Anne's novel from being held in the same esteem today as *Jane Eyre* and *Wuthering Heights*.

One of *Rebecca*'s many contributions to the gothic genre was to use a newly married but naïve woman as the protagonist (much as Anne Brontë had done, though less successfully) who is increasingly unsure about her husband's real feelings for her. The use of an unhappily married heroine allows an author to gloss over, or perhaps skip entirely, the details of courtship and consummation and move directly into scenes of detection. As the mass market gothic romance took on more of the characteristics of the mass market mystery novel, this becomes a fear that he is trying to gaslight or kill her. The untrustworthy husband would become a staple of the paperback gothic, though his role and his effect on the heroine is often mischaracterized or even misunderstood (most notably in feminist studies like those of Joanna Russ and Tania Modleski).

A typical example is found in Anne Maybury's *Shadow of a Stranger* (1960). After recovering from a serious accident and subsequent nervous

7. Melancholy Males and Demon Lovers

breakdown, Tess has impulsively married Johnnie and traveled to his family's Canadian estate, only to find his behavior drastically altered once they settle in. Johnnie takes perverse pleasure in reminding her that he holds the upper hand and in implying that she may be slipping into mental instability. It would be a mistake, however, to assume that Tess accepts his hovering control, much less enjoys it. From the beginning, she resents his tendency to treat her like a delicate invalid.

To Johnnie's chagrin, Tess is not as easily cowed as he assumed. She is not only willing to talk back to him; she even takes him on physically when she gets sufficiently fed up with his secretive behavior and domineering manner. The resulting confrontation echoes that between Emily St. Aubert and Montoni nearly two hundred years earlier:

> "You talk as though I needed a keeper!"
> "Well—when you behave as you are doing now—"
> "You can't make me stay here, Johnnie! I'm not a prisoner!"
> "You're dependent upon me. How do you think you will get back to England on your own, without me? Fly by jet? Book a luxury suite on a ship? Sorry, Tess, but I'm afraid your place is here. While Uncle Luke is alive, I shall never let you go! Did you hear that? I shall never let you go!"
> Tess put out her hands and pushed against him with all her force. Taken unaware, he staggered back a little and she tore past him to the front door, opened it and slammed it behind her.[14]

Tess, fortunately, has more options than did Emily. As tensions escalate, she is not shy about cutting her husband off sexually, moving into one of the guest bedrooms after one of his outbursts and retreating to it every time his smug derision crosses the line.

> "You talk as though I were on the razor's edge of insanity!"
> "Of course I don't! But isn't it natural that a man should want to take care of his wife, protect her from herself?"
> She felt weariness mingle with her anger. The urgency, the fluid speech, the seeming sincerity acted like hypnotism upon her. She saw danger staring at her in his troubled eyes, his soft deadly words and turning, she dashed into her bedroom and slammed the door.[15]

It is common for critics of modern gothics, or of romance novels in general, to disparage the blatant sexism in common scenes such as these. The males exist only to bully and harass the women, who nonetheless accept their subservient role in the relationship and in life. Yet it is important to note here that Johnnie is not, in fact, the hero of the novel. Soon enough, the reader, along with Tess, realizes that she has made a mistake to trust him even for a moment. A number of theatrical plot twists, including attempted murder, a priceless Ming Dynasty vase, and a stolen identity soon make Johnnie's real agenda clear. The alert reader will already have guessed at least part of the truth when a foil character, Angus, arrives in the middle of Johnnie's outburst to demonstrate how a real gothic hero should behave:

> She gave a little cry as his fingers lightened on her arms. "And please let go, you're hurting me!"
> "Perhaps that's the only way to bring you to your senses!"
> Her calmness seemed to increase his fury. He began to shake her so hard that she cried out.
> "I won't put up with an inquisitive, spying wife, do you hear? Do you hear?"
> "I beg your pardon!" said a quiet voice behind them. Johnnie dropped his hands and swung around. Angus stood still in the doorway.[16]

Unlike Johnnie, Angus—educated, respectable, and fully in control of himself—respects Tess and soon positions himself as the man she can and should align herself with. Whereas Johnnie's idea of manliness is to domineer and belittle, Angus exerts a strong, positive masculinity—firm, logical, protective and willing to listen.

Some gothic novels do show a heroine who attempts to rein in her own personality in order to appease a mate. However, in every case her efforts suggest a wish to compromise rather than capitulate. At first, the heroine of *Carlotta's Castle* is a bit too eager to throw herself into the role of accommodating new bride:

> All my thoughts were with Piers on the long drive back. I wondered ... about his keen desire to be the dominant one in this alliance, of the way he had warned me that he would tolerate no interference in his odd prejudices and strong opinions. Oh yes, he was masculine as well as manly, essentially male in every sense and I told myself happily that I'd have to move cautiously in many quarters, curb the independence that was so much a part of my character since I'd been on my own. I must learn to accede graciously to his wishes, to anticipate his desires. And I long to do just that and become totally absorbed by the man I adored.[17]

Predictably, though, she grows impatient with the "essentially male" self-centeredness she originally found so intriguing and begins to crave open spaces and independence. Frustrated with her husband's moods, she turns instead to building her own professional photographic portfolio: "Oh, when would this marriage really get off the ground?" she wonders halfway through the novel. "I had to try very hard to hang onto my patience."

Miriam Darce Frenier's *Goodbye, Heathcliff*, examines what she calls "nasty" heroes in "nursies" and mainstream romances of the late '60s and

7. Melancholy Males and Demon Lovers

early '70s. "Nasty" might almost be too soft a word for some of the characters she describes. They sneer, insult, and condescend to the heroine. Occasionally (like Johnnie) they even grab her arm or her wrist in a way that borders on assault. Though Frenier may overstate her case by cherry-picking examples and reproducing them out of context, gothic heroes seem like perfect gentlemen compared to their counterparts in "workplace" romances or early bodice rippers. For one thing, their threats (or romantic overtures) are never of an aggressively sexual nature—as Dean Koontz stressed in his 1972 "how-to" book, *Writing Popular Fiction*, the gothic hero "must never contemplate rape."[18] In addition, no matter what he might say, or even threaten, a true gothic hero never harms the heroine in any way. He may have political or social authority, and may even own a dungeon, but the feudalism of the gothic world remains benign. The worst he can really do is send her away—which he forces himself to do for her own good.

For the heroine of the modern gothic romance, the greatest satisfaction comes not only from winning the heart of, but taming such a man. An underlying theme of nearly every successful gothic is the progress of the hero from arrogant rake to dependable husband. In many cases, the heroine is willing to reject gossip about the hero's wickedness and thwart society's definition of a suitable match in order to hold out for one that promises both emotional challenge and sexual satisfaction.[19] In *Moura*, the heroine is even prepared to defend the hero after he is sentenced to the guillotine for a murder she half-believes he committed. In every case, though, her faith in him is justified. The gothic hero ultimately reveals himself to be anything but the stonehearted brute he first resembles. Instead, he is a sensitive soul who has simply learned to camouflage himself with the cultural expectations of his time and social class. Once the heroine sees through this, she can make what '70s psychological lingo might have called a therapeutic breakthrough. In return for her devotion and trust in his character, the hero does change. Though he may mistrust or even fear the heroine as much as she does him, he soon begins to accept her and ultimately depends on her. The dramatic (or some might say melodramatic) denouement is made all the sweeter when the previously stoic master of the manor throws off his mask and declares his passion for the heroine while saving her life at the last moment. At this point, he generally reveals that his previous apparent indifference or even hostility toward the heroine resulted either from a misunderstanding, a misguided desire to protect her, or an attempt to trap the real villain. At the same time, he is absolved of any crimes he has been accused of, the charges revealed as the

The Gothic Romance Wave

result of a grudge or misunderstanding; maybe even he believes himself guilty until the heroine clears his name and cleanses his soul as well (sometimes, as in *Rebecca*, his sins are so severe that the cleansing requires the burning of the house itself in a kind of sympathetic magic). He is now free to love her without fear of reprisal; the curse on him is broken, perhaps literally. The heroine's intervention may also help him reconcile with other family members, such as younger siblings or troubled offspring.

In *Carlotta's Castle*, the heroine eventually abandons her idea of capitulating to her arrogant husband and instead confronts him about his behavior and her expectations. They emerge with a new understanding and a new sense of equality. "There followed one of the most memorable hours of our marriage—an hour when all the misunderstandings and hurts were cleared away, one by one, and we sat with our hands clasped, knowing at last that our marriage had begun."[20] The heroine sees this as nothing less than a feminist triumph, even if she does not call it that, honoring the legacy of women who lived and died in less enlightened eras, sometimes at the hands of cruel husbands: "Sweet reconciliation strengthened by brave new resolutions! I had never been so happy nor so sad. Four women had died during the curse of Carlotta's Castle and I owed them this much: to be the best person I could and to treasure the legacy of love."[21] Her husband, Piers, agrees and admits that, thanks to the heroine's instruction and example, "all my values have shifted in these past weeks.... Out of the tragedy of the past, or of the 'curse' of Carlotta's Castle, your husband has gained some measure of wisdom, some semblance of peace."[22] By showing himself capable of understanding and rejecting the evil side of patriarchy, Piers becomes worthy of the heroine's love. Joined in purpose and spirit, the two donate the castle to an order of nuns, rendering it an all-female space devoted to charitable work.

Unlike their counterparts in steamy historical romances, gothic couples seldom indulge in explicitly described sexual romps. However, an erotic charge is present in all their relationships and burns even brighter after the requisite misunderstandings are resolved. The lovers in Janet Louise Roberts' *Ravenswood* (1971), whose marriage is off to a rocky start thanks to some Napoleonic intrigue, once reconciled, come together with all the breathless sincerity of Valancourt's declaration and the high-hearted fervor of the Victorian stage play.

> "I began to despair, and when I hurt you—I thought I had lost you forever."
>
> She drew his head down to hers, so breathlessly happy she thought she might die of it. They kissed, a long sensuous kiss of their lips and their hearts and their souls. He

7. Melancholy Males and Demon Lovers

held her closely, tightly, pressing his mouth to hers as though he could not stop.... And to know that this was truly the beginning for them, not the ending. The beginning of a long and happy marriage, with all they had wanted and waited for, and despaired of having. With all joy and happiness to come."[23]

Likewise, the hero and heroine of *The Devon Maze* (1971) suspect each other of terrible deeds—he thinks she has plotted to usurp his ancestral manor and she suspects him of pushing his wheelchair-bound father into the estate pond to drown. As a result, they have remained married in name only for almost a year. Now the true villain has been unmasked—to no one's surprise except theirs, he was posing all along as the gentle rival suitor. "It hadn't been easy for Ron or me to shed our protective layers of skins nor our former fears and doubts about each other, even though we knew they were false. After all, we'd nurtured them and worn our psychological armor too many months for a Cinderella consummation of our marriage. The love was there; the unreasoning, passionate physical love came first and paved the way for richer love sand understanding that now seemed forever growing."[24]

Surprisingly, this couple's approach is the reverse of what one might expect in a more traditional romance, which delays physical consummation until the characters form a solid emotional bond. If anything, it would appear that the fear and distrust the heroine initially experiences strengthens her erotic bond with the hero when at last the misunderstandings are cleared up. The familiar trope of the bad boy is given a twist—the bad boy turns out not to have been bad at all, which casts his dark charm and sardonic edge in a different and undeniably appealing light. The relief from the drawn-out tension preceding the reveal adds spice to the brewing sexual connection. If the characters' declarations seem overblown or trite, they nonetheless echo a fantasy common to many modern women, whatever path they have chosen in real life. Biological imperatives, after all, are not so easily suppressed.

Some critics have noted that the heroine's longing for an economically secure and somewhat older partner reflects the desire for a father figure—"this is the world of the paternal sublime," as Patricia Meyer Spacks puts it.[25] In many novels, the male love interest is not, at first, the husband but the heroine's employer. In these stories, his hold on her is primarily an economic one, echoing the dynamic of her preadolescence. Romance writer Kathleen Gilles Seidel agrees: "If you're a woman with a difficult life, if you're struggling to keep up in a competitive corporation, it might be pleasant to spend a few hours feeling as if you aren't always being judged and graded. If you're supporting your children by yourself, if you're having to make all those decisions about their curfews

The Gothic Romance Wave

and their schoolwork and their friends on your own, a father figure swooping in to take all that off your shoulders is a pretty thought."[26]

It is true that the hero is often approaching middle age while the heroine is an ingénue. He does offer wealth, protection, a magnificent house, and social position. There is another precedent for a man who bears these gifts, however. It seems equally likely that the gothic romance hero is the literary descendant of the demon lover (which is in fact the title of a 1982 gothic by Victoria Holt).

A staple figure in the folk ballad, the demon lover typically approaches a young married woman, often a former sweetheart, after a long absence. He suggests that they renew their relationship even though she has now married another man and in some versions has also become a mother. Soon the charismatic demon lover, sometimes called "Jamie Harris," seduces the young wife away from her dull but dependable tradesman husband (a "house carpenter" in the version popularized by Joan Baez in the 1960s). Along with the physical pleasures of this adulterous relationship, he offers her many gifts, often including a fine house on a remote island (a parcel of real estate familiar to many a gothic heroine). Swayed by his charms, she boards his ship, anticipating a life of romance and seafaring adventure. On the voyage, she discovers, too late, that he is in fact already dead and has tricked her into accompanying him into hell. Though the outcome is a dark one, the audience is invited to sympathize, at least temporarily, with the yearning of the young woman, trapped in a traditionally respectable but boring and empty existence. The ballad serves as a cautionary tale for young women, warning that the price of adultery and the disruption of the family unit, even (or especially) for personal fulfillment, is damnation.

Toni Reed associates the demon lover with Clarissa's Lovelace as a seminal figure in the development of the English novel and specifically the romance novel,[27] and it is easy to see the connection between Jamie Harris and the wealthy, reprehensible rake who lures Clarissa into ruin and, eventually, death. In contrast to ballads like "House Carpenter," however, is another known as "John Riley."[28] Here, a man approaches a young woman and proposes marriage. She declines, insisting she will remain faithful to her true love, John Riley, who has been away for seven years, even if he has died at sea or married another. The stranger then kisses her, reveals himself to be John (presumably in disguise), and the lovers are happily reunited as a reward for their (or at least her) faithfulness despite their physical separation.

By the mid–19th century, gothics (and two of the three Brontë sisters in

7. Melancholy Males and Demon Lovers

particular) were asking a daring question—what if the two could be combined? What if the demon lover, thrilling and dangerous, could be transformed into or merged with the steadfast John Riley, who offers the heroine a future of passion and excitement? Montoni, Lovelace, and Ruthven[29] are more Jamie than they are John, but Rochester and Heathcliff are men who could—and do—draw any woman with a beating heart from her stolid house carpenter (here in the figures of St. John and Edgar). Rochester's apparently psychic link with Jane, who hears his voice though she is many miles away, suggests the power of the demon lover, though it is a benevolent power in this case. Heathcliff's apparent communion with the ghostly Catherine is more ambiguous, but no less passionate. At last, the gothic had found its true voice and perhaps its true purpose: to express the deepest desires of women in a socially acceptable format. As Clair remarks in her discussion of the development of the mass market romance novel, "Emily and Charlotte Brontë gave a central place in their fervid, darkly romantic imaginings to what deep down all women knew, the thing that is buried in Ann Radcliffe's fiction. What women most loved, and most feared, was that dangerous, fascinating creature, Man."[30]

If Jamie Harris lives on in Rochester and all the mass market gothic romance heroes who came after him, the house carpenter endures as well, though his role in the female-centered narrative changes drastically. In most gothics, a demure, friendly young man will usually appear to compete for the heroine's love. He is everything the brooding master of the house or castle is not—he is younger, kinder, witty, and seems open to women's rights. He is in touch with modern trends, clothing, and manners, especially in the 1960s, whereas the hero is older and usually more old-fashioned. The heroine likes him, but does not feel heat toward him. Nonetheless, she considers taking him as a partner. He is also usually revealed as the true villain[31]—a sociopathic liar, perhaps using an assumed identity, possibly even plotting her death. Though she is seduced for a time by the secondary male's attentions, the heroine soon comes to learn that her erotic attraction is, after all, leading her in the right direction.[32] In the modern versions of the ballad's central premise, victory comes when she leaves the house carpenter, who did not have her best interests at heart anyway, and runs off with her demon lover. Best of all, she discovers that he is, in fact, her own devoted John Riley.

Demonic connections are made explicitly in one of Victoria Holt's later gothics, *The Time of the Hunter's Moon* (1983). The story involves a teacher at a girl's school housed in the ruins of an Abbey. Cordelia's first impression of the hero, Sir Jason, instantly recalls the demon lover in explicit terms:

"There was something satanic about him. He looked complacent too and I did not care for the boldness of his expression. It was as though he was making plans and was very confident of their success."[33] Later Jason confirms that her suspicions are justified—rumor has it that one of his ancestors was in fact Lucifer himself, whom Jason calls "my satanic ancestor," and whose influence he accepts almost cheerfully, joking about "the Devil in our blood."[34] According to some characters, Jason may be a little too invested in living up to his supposed supernatural heritage—he is suspecting of murdering his wife, impregnating his actress mistress, and making her disappear when his interests turn toward the heroine instead. Yet when Jason stops posturing, the heroine, Cordelia, finds something more. "I wanted to stay out in this magic night and learn more about this man, for he was revealing a great deal about himself. I had thought of him as brash and arrogant. He was; but there was something else about him—a sadness, even a vulnerability, something which touched me in a way."[35]

Eventually, the attraction progresses to a scene that apparently shocked many readers in 1983 and seems even more objectionable today. Jason locks Cordelia in a room and attempts to lure her into a sexual situation. "I was afraid," Cordelia confesses. "He was forcing me out of my coat." Still, Cordelia has no intention of yielding. She tries reasoning with him, to no avail. "Rape is not within the law, Jason Verringer, even for men like you.... He took me by the shoulders and laughed at me..." Jason, here at his most demonic, warns Cordelia that it would be his word against hers, and no one will believe her, or at least will pretend not to. His title and influence in the community suggest that he is correct. Even his housekeeper seems to be in on the plot—"she is obedient to my wishes as I expect all my servants to be."[36] Desperate, Cordelia escapes by breaking a window and cutting her hand in the process. Her blood flows, metaphorically substituting for the loss of her virginity and, apparently, shocking Jason back to his humanity. Stunned, he backs off and spends the rest of the book apologizing. Cordelia will have none of it until Jason proves himself by being "pretty well smashed up" in an attempt to rescue his niece from a dangerous Casanova. Like Rochester, the breaking of his bones and the battering of his body redeems Jason, forcing him to rebuild himself morally as well as physically. Cordelia will now marry him. Jason complains that she is accepting out of "pity for a man who will never again be what he was" and in fact he is exactly right. "You may be the wicked villain with a trace of the Devil in him," Cordelia teases, "but haven't I always known how to cope with him?"[37] Her friend, Lydia, was less fortunate, falling victim to

7. Melancholy Males and Demon Lovers

the murderous black-widower husband who had once courted Cordelia, killed Lydia, and then moved onto Jason's niece, Fiona.

The book ends with Cordelia and a redeemed Jason attending a real-life play, Ellen Wood's *East Lynne*, a popular didactic melodrama of the 1860s. The play chronicled the downfall of a woman who left her husband for the allure of an ultimately faithless lover and dealt somewhat frankly with sexual politics, women's repression, and the need for moral uprightness. The scene reveals that Jason and Cordelia have moved beyond the simple type of "stage" relationship they watch in the play, which happens to star Jason's former mistress. The birth of a son, Jason's longed-for heir, cements the legitimacy of their union. The novel's last line describes their marriage as an ongoing process of "education." Before her marriage to Jason, Cordelia manages to attract another suitor, a steadfast banker who offers her quiet stability and passionless love. Like any good gothic heroine, though, she chooses the challenge and excitement of the devil, secure in the knowledge that she alone can tame him.

Today, few readers remember or pine for the thousands of bland gothic heroes like Ron in *The Devon Maze*, whose attitude is mostly petulant rather than frightening. Instead, they recall—with various and no doubt conflicted emotions—the loud, passionate men of the Brontës and Victoria Holt, with their fiery sexual demands and sarcastic bombast. Their auras color the early 21st century's paranormal romances, with vampire and werewolf heroes who rely on the heroine's trust to keep them from losing control and unwillingly embarking on murderous rampages. They frighten the heroine even while she (along with the reader) falls in love with him and urges him to find the side of him that can love again. *Twilight*'s Bella even chooses to become a vampire after marrying Edward Cullen. Here, supernatural powers and the thirst for blood are presented as just another set of obstacles the couple has to work through in order to strengthen their commitment.

As Phyllis Whitney remarked while offering advice to aspiring gothic authors: "Even your dark-browed, sardonic hero might be able to learn a few things by the end of the story—it wouldn't hurt him at all!"[38] At the end of every gothic novel is a heroine who enjoys the satisfaction of watching her new mate cultivate the feminine side of his own psyche, embracing emotion and exchanging solitary power for a new kind of devoted John Riley-esque partnership. Yet, to her delight, he is still Jamie Harris in the bedroom—seductive, passionate, and maybe more than a little dangerous. The balance of the two personae, demon and consort, forms the basis of his redemption.

8

Numinous Melodrama
The Appeal of the Gothic

> In the morning sunlight the house still smoldered. The flames had roared through the shrubbery in the garden; the summer house was charred rubble. No bodies had been found although Abel had reported there were three people in it at the time of the fire; his father, his half-brother and a servant girl. The ashes were still being sifted for the bodies.
> Elizabeth, standing beside Abel, staring out over the scarred and blackened remains, shivered, and her hand clutched Abel's tightly. She said, "If they did not burn in the fire...?"
> Abel said, "They did. We must believe that they did! The good overcame. Elizabeth, we must believe that!"
> She nodded. "Yes," she said, "We must believe."
> —*Castle Mirage* by Alice Brennan, 1971

From its original 18th-century incarnation through its 1960s mass market form, the gothic novel has captivated audiences and inspired reader loyalty in a way few other literary genres can match. The more passionately critics (and later, feminists) railed against them, the more popular the books became. Only when a market glut led to a large number of substandard offerings did audiences tire of gothics and turn to something new—supposedly the historical novels of Sir Walter Scott in the 19th century or the erotic historicals of Kathleen Woodiwiss and Rosemary Rogers in the 20th.

Many critics have scoured the old Radcliffean gothics for clues about their appeal to late 18th-century readers. Fewer have attempted to discover what chord the Nixon-era mass market paperbacks struck in their original audience. Nevertheless, it struck hard and deep, its echoes still resounding through popular fiction of the 21st century. One might well wonder what, if any, overlap exists between the elements that drew readers in as the Age of Reason faded into Romanticism and again, a century and a half later, as Americans prepared to witness man's first walk on the moon.

8. Numinous Melodrama

In *Gothicka*, we will recall, Victoria Nelson suggested that public fascination with gothic fiction, then and now, soared as the Age of Reason ran roughshod over the outdated but comforting superstitions and simplistic religiosity of earlier eras. This triggered a search for the numinous and a longing for divine symbolism, largely absent from modern secular culture but alive and well, albeit in mutated form, in tales fraught with ghosts, vampires, psychics, and angels. These figures bridge some undefined "other side" that many readers find terrifying but psychologically indispensable. They are still drawn, therefore, not only to gothic novels but to movies, role-playing games, and other forms of entertainment with horror or supernatural themes.[1] Nelson believes this sideways approach to conventional religion accounts for the frequent use of nuns and monks as agents of darkness in Protestant countries' gothic fare. Matthew Lewis's *The Monk* provides the most obvious example, but one also finds frequent allusions to tormented clergymen and ghostly nuns[2] in modern fare. Virginia Coffman's *The Devil Vicar* comes to mind, as well as John Marsh's *Monk's Hollow* and Jennie Melville's *Nun's Castle*. Tellingly, Northanger was only the first of many novels to boast an "Abbey" in the title.

Some gothics, especially those that appeared after 1970, do contain a hint of the numinous and the occasional presence of full-blown supernatural entities. Many of what were eventually called "horror/occult gothics" or "Satanic gothics" attempted to capitalize on the popularity of *Dark Shadows*, with its vampire and werewolf heartthrobs, and *Rosemary's Baby*, which left its cloven footprint on at least a few gothic plots. Yet it is probably safe to say that the modern mass market Gothic of the 1960s and 1970s was only minimally concerned with religious ideas (heroines may sometimes give lip service to conventional religious beliefs, but the heroes are often openly agnostic). The deeply religious Middle Ages and Renaissance, favorite settings of both Ann Radcliffe and Matthew Lewis,[3] were abandoned in favor of contemporary or Victorian settings (though medieval-era castles continued to play a central role in many of the stories). Characters were nominally Christian, but only occasionally attended church, especially in books set after the 19th century. And the majority of mass market gothic heroines, after diligent investigation, fail to uncover any supernatural elements at all; the entire paranormal subplot is usually shown to be a machination of the villain, as in Radcliffe.

Nelson also suggested that, despite what critics would like to believe about themselves and their readers, humans are at their most basic level emotional creatures and therefore vulnerable to the allure of melodrama. "Addic-

The Gothic Romance Wave

tion"[4] is a word often associated with the compulsive buying and reading of romance novels among modern American women. It is a term that suggests immediate emotional gratification on the part of the addicted person (in this case, the reader). Titillated, excited, and aroused in ways they may not even have been willing to admit or able to articulate, readers of early gothics returned again and again to similar tales that promised to repeat the experience. Mass market gothics did not shy away from the concept or even the label "melodrama." In fact, they actively courted it, pushing plots and descriptions to increasingly lurid ends. Fans responded to this visceral stimulus by buying and devouring the inexpensive books in huge quantities.

Melodrama is often associated with childlike and primitive forms of discourse—"crude," as Eric Bentley puts it in reference to theater, though he explains that he does not mean this pejoratively, but rather as it "corresponds to that phase of a child's life when he creates magic worlds."[5] Romance author Susan Elizabeth Phillips (who has a degree in theater), would seem to concur when she likens the world building in romance reading to children "who deal with their fears of the real world by creating symbolic repositories of these fears" such as the proverbial "monsters who lurk in closets." The cynical hero who is both hero and villain, a staple in gothics, therefore becomes "a virile and powerful rogue male ... a potent symbol of all the obstacles life presents to women."[6]

Bentley stresses the melodrama's close connection with the dream self: in dreams, he suggests, one is heroic in the face of palpable (and exaggerated) threat as well as unfettered by the constraints of reality and even physics.[7] It cannot be a coincidence that so many classic gothics had their origins in dreams, from Walpole's *Castle of Otranto* through Dan Curtis's dream of the opening scene of *Dark Shadows* to Stephenie Meyer's dream of the sparkling vampire Edward and his human girlfriend sitting in a field. Heroines in gothics often have dreams too—vivid, terrifying ones as well as those that provide clues to the novel's central mystery from their own subconscious minds. Sometimes a dead character, perhaps a legendary woman with whom the heroine has come to identify, will contact her in a sequence that may or may not be the product of her imagination. Such scenes reinforce the bonds between fictional women, just as the novels themselves do when they inspire readers to join romance book clubs and online communities.

Unlike dreams, which tend to be formless, gothics have a structured plot—highly structured in some novels, and certainly stylized, resembling the deliberate artificiality of theater.[8] Perhaps in order to understand the mass

8. Numinous Melodrama

market gothic's popularity, we need to position it not among other, more "serious" or literary novels, but with the productions of the melodramatic stage. The connection is apparent not just in the types of stories and characters presented in each form, but through its ready availability to vast numbers of middle-class consumers. In the modern world, the supermarket rack of easily affordable paperbacks becomes roughly analogous to the cheap seats at a Regency or Victorian theater, the preferred source of melodrama in the days before widespread literacy and mass market fiction. Indeed, gothics were a staple there, and the gothic stage follows almost the same trajectory as the gothic novel, then and now. Stories were composed around recognized character types (ingénue, lover, villain, servant), employed rotating plots with predictable twists and endings, and pitched upper-class settings and situations to the middle class. Before long, or at least well before 1860, gothic parodies became popular on stage. By then the tropes had become so excessively melodramatic, Bloom states, that it was difficult to tell the difference.[9]

The suitability of the gothic novel for the melodramatic stage meant that, a century and a half later, it was also a good fit for television and film. Movies like *The Man in Grey* and *Rebecca* drew large audiences in the 1940s, as would the gothic Hammer Horror films in the 1960s and 1970s. *Dark Shadows*, the daily gothic soap opera, was heavy with melodramatic music featuring the theremin, an electronic instrument that produced a sound resembling a spirit wailing. The show released a soundtrack album and at least two 45 rpm singles, all of which sold well to the show's fans and are still available on CD today. One might even speculate that the highly recognizable covers of mass market gothics, showing the heroine in a desperate flight from danger, may have functioned like playbills in drawing audiences in with the promise of excitement and thrills.

The intersection of melodrama and gothic storytelling, especially with respect to a female audience, has been recognized as essential to understanding the appeal of 18th-century gothic to its middle class readership.[10] Gothic novels and melodrama, after all, are the cousins of literary romanticism. Since Romantic poetry could not easily be transferred to the stage for the entertainment of the masses, gothic novels were adapted instead. The works of Walpole, Radcliffe, Polidori and even, centuries later, du Maurier's *Rebecca* were all imported to the stage and were popular, along with many other Gothic tales of madmen, castles, and heroines in danger. These stage performances, popular in the last days of George III and into the Regency, often included music (the definition of "melodrama" in its most basic sense) and, of course, heightened emotion—what Jane Austen called "sensibility." Peter Brooks' characterization of melodrama might as well be a description of a gothic novel of the 18th century or one penned by Victoria Holt.

Brooks lists as crucial to melodrama the tendency toward depicting intense, excessive representations of life that tend to strip away the façade of manners to reveal the essential conflicts at work, leading to moments of intense, and highly stylized confrontations. These symbolic dramatizations rely on what Brooks lists as the standard features of melodrama: hyperbolic figures, lurid and grandiose events, masked relationships and disguised identities, abductions, slow-acting poisons, secret societies, and mysterious parentage.[11] It is through this stimulating world the gothic heroine moves, and the reader along with her, vicariously sharing the challenge of being alone in the world, traveling to a new and perhaps exotic place, making a fresh start, building a new identity. Critics who, like Joanna Russ, deride the gothic heroine as passive are missing (or dismissing) the actions she does take in the course of every gothic story. Eventually, she will solve a mystery (possibly a murder), prevent her own injury or death as well as that of the hero, and claim the lord of the manor as a husband.[12] Her eventual triumph is made all the sweeter because she is generally a young woman with little or no domestic, political, or economic clout, even if the story is set in the 20th century. Often orphaned and without protection, she hovers one step above the servant class, entering a strange household as a poor relation, a housekeeper (in the case of the *Moura* series' heroine, Anne Wicklow) or a nanny or governess (the Jane Eyre prototype). The gothic heroine has only determined pluck and a sharp wit to secure and keep her place in society—and if she has none when the story begins, it is assured that she will rise to prominence before the story ends. It should be obvious that watching Blanche Ingram, a woman of wealth, beauty, and position (cemented by wealthy male relatives) verbally thrash Mr. Rochester would never prove as satisfying as seeing Jane Eyre, with nothing but her intellect and quick tongue, not only best him in debate but win his love and a life of economic security.

The connections to stagecraft extend to the importance of setting as well. The central position of the castle or manor house, not just on the covers of the novels but in the story itself, cannot be overlooked. From the early days, starting with Prince Manfred's Otranto, the castle has been fundamental to the gothic experience. Radcliffe trapped Emily in a castle to heighten her audience's fear for her well-being. Her aunt was imprisoned in Montini's ancestral keep as a reflection of the poor and debasing marriage she entered into. Finally Emily finds herself inheriting land and estates of her own. This makes sense, given the term's original connection to architecture, especially that of a crude, barbaric design (later, the cloyingly ostentatious Victorian-era manor offered an easy substitution). The modern gothic's requisite use of the castle (or its stand-in) represents more than just homage to Walpole and Radcliffe, however. Historical castles represent patriarchal feudalism in all its savage splendor, but literary castles suggest the possibility of a feminine (perhaps even feminist) reclaiming. Though the castle's walls and towers remain masculine constructs, originally designed for military purposes, its inner spaces tend to be feminized, decorated and tended to by the wife and an army of maidservants.

In Europe, the presence of such monuments commemorates a harsh feudal past, a source of both pride and indignation, depending on one's political standing. For Americans, they represent a connection to ancestral roots or perhaps an exotic vacation destination (which may also explain their common position at the edge of the sea and the heroine's frequent excursions around the grounds on horseback). As in fairy tales, the basis for gothic romance and romance in general, castles represent the primitive pageantry of the Middle Ages, but also its inhuman brutality. For every tapestry-lined solar there is a lightless dungeon or horrifying oubliette (always the most popular stops on the modern castle tour). Mass market gothic romances, like their 18th-century predecessors, make full use of all these features, as well as hidden rooms, secret dungeons, and booby-trapped doors that lead to a deadly plunge down the castle wall.[13] Yet, as Felski points out, their rounded design and labyrinthine catacombs may also suggest a metaphorical womb: "While Gothic novels are full of dead or absent mothers, Kahane suggests that we can see the castle itself [as] an anxiety-laden symbol of the maternal body, imagined as both womb and tomb."[14] When the heroine enters the castle, she may in fact be re-entering the womb in order to rewrite her beginnings—especially since the search for family, biological or adoptive, is a theme that runs through every mass market gothic romance. In some cases, she may discover her literal mother, either dead or alive, stashed behind the layers of stone. The castle or manor, therefore, may represent for the female reader a chance to remake herself vicariously, trading her dull suburban middle-class home for an exciting space laden with romantic tension and the chance to start over (not to mention a small army of servants to attend to the housekeeping).

Herbert Gans' *Popular Culture and High Culture* was published in 1974, just after the peak of the mass market gothic romance's popularity, and many of his conclusions help explain readers' (and critics') ongoing engagement with the genre. Gans found that, contrary to what many literary and cultural critics assumed, enjoying a popular culture product (in this case, reading a mass market paperback) has no lasting effect on the consumer at all, though it will of course bring economic growth to both publisher and author (and, by extension, the retail establishments that offer the goods, such as chain bookstores or supermarkets). The reader consumes the product, experiences a few hours of enjoyment, the nature of which may be debated, and afterward discards the material (either shelving it or passing it along to other readers as a used copy) while remaining essentially unchanged. Soon enough, the details of the experience are forgotten and the reader seeks out a new book, looking to repeat the pleasurable experience. This does in fact describe the repetitive nature of romance reading. The materials are basically similar, especially within each type of romance; yet readers never seem to grow weary of reading, say, one hundred gothics or two hundred Regencies, and it is not uncommon to encounter readers with vast collections. Today, Harlequin's subscription service sends readers four to six books of the same series each month, and readers sign up in droves. Some speculate this is Harlequin's main source of income.

An invaluable source for studying the tastes and expectations of mainstream gothic readers is *Gothic Journal*, a desktop print publication edited and distributed by Kristi Lyn Glass from 1991 to 1998.[15] The black-and-white newsletter/magazine hybrid focused on classic gothics, articles about the genre and its prominent authors both living and dead, along with reader reviews of 1990s releases that could be considered retro-gothic or romantic suspense. Many of the genre's longtime readers wrote letters and articles recalling their favorite novels and authors, and a number of the original 1960s and 1970s authors contributed columns, articles, and opinions, including Rachel Cosgrove Payes, Virginia Coffman, and the legendary Phyllis Whitney. Authors of the then-new Zebra Gothic line, such as Lee Karr, were frequent letter writers. Profiles of classic gothic authors like Dan Ross, Barbara Michaels, and Victoria Holt provided background information about both the writers and their careers (including identifying their various pseudonyms). Occasionally, other industry professionals, such as editors and publishers, joined the discussion. Later issues contained sections specially directed at professional writers of gothics and romances as well as advice for aspiring writers of gothics or romantic suspense novels.

In the letters column, fans debated such topics as sexuality in the gothic,

8. Numinous Melodrama

the art of gothic covers, marketing strategies, and the types of heroes and heroines they preferred. These readers provide a strong corrective to critical studies that portray them as simple-minded, subservient women trying to compensate for sterile love lives by reading romance novels (in fact, many interviews with authors note the support of their husbands, or report that they remained happily single by choice, as did Virginia Coffman). The readers and writers who contributed were sharp, witty, literate, and highly specific about what they found appealing in gothics and why. Most were not scholars, though some academics did contribute sophisticated articles.

As fans, the women (and a few men) who contributed were able and willing, even eager, to articulate their preferences, sometimes at length. No one in the journal's entire run ever longed for books featuring more passive or dim-witted heroines or begged authors to make their heroes more brutish. Not a single contributor expressed relief or gratitude at being put in her place by the machinations of patriarchal publishers and conspiring authors. If anything, they complained about exactly those things scholars insisted they loved to read and were probably addicted to: "dumb" heroines who found fulfillment only in the arms of domineering men and repetitive, predictable storylines. Some even complained about the ubiquitous "woman running from the house" covers and cloyingly alliterative titles like Sharon Wagner's *The Lost Lilacs of Latimer House* (which apparently contained no lilacs, lost or otherwise).

The illustrations in *Gothic Journal*, no less than the articles, provides insight into what drew readers to these books (and to the journal in hopes of hearing about new titles or a full-scale gothic revival). The February/March issue of 1995, for example, features a cover drawing of a reader in a rocking chair with a book upside down on her lap with her eyes closed. Her velcro-strap sneakers lie, discarded, beside her feet. Behind her sprawls a Victorian manor, where a woman in a hoop skirt is walking toward a horse-drawn carriage and a waiting man in a top hat. Another cover, fronting the December/January 1998 issue, depicts a romance writer at her computer, wistfully gazing out a window at a 19th-century heroine wandering alongside a medieval castle.

Among gothic fans, the shared daydream need not be explained or excused. It is taken for granted among like-minded aficionados, who require no assistance in interpreting the illustrations. No one (except possibly a non-reader of gothics who picked up the *Journal* by mistake) would stop to wonder how or why a modern woman has attained such close physical proximity to the past, as though she is gazing through a time portal. The imaginative landscape is the same for both writer and audience (and as the letters column

The Gothic Romance Wave

shows, many ardent readers have tried their hand at writing, to varying degrees of success)—an elegant historical fantasy, complete with a well-dressed suitor and a dash of haunted house drama to ratchet up the excitement. This is, surely, the world not just of costume drama but of melodrama, to use that word in its most neutral and judgment-free sense.

Pamela Regis, like Nelson, points out that female writers have always approached the love story with a perspective unique to their gender. Love at first sight, for example, is much more the product of male fantasy than female[16] and thus seldom appears in mass market gothic romances (even those written by men under a female pseudonym). Instead, the love relationship develops slowly (some would say with agonizing slowness) as the heroine questions the hero's attitude toward her, hers toward him, how much credence to give external judgments of his character, and how to eliminate the barriers and obstacles to learning the truth about him. In the gothic, she also wonders if he might be the story's villain. Often this is not resolved until the very last page. In some cases the two do not even declare their love for one another until the very end of the story, sometimes in an epilogue. In more than one, the bulk of the courtship is left to the reader's imagination.

Susan Elizabeth Phillips, who started off as an ardent reader of romances and eventually became a successful author herself, believes that romance readers achieve catharsis by projecting contemporary fears and the problems of women's lives, both real (bills, children, health) and metaphorical (feminine disenfranchisement, powerlessness in the home) and then vanquishing them along with the heroine. Her triumph over the hero's resistance to her charms, which usually include a fiercely independent streak, symbolizes her mastery over personal and professional anxieties. Phillips goes so far as to call the romance novel's effect on the reader a "fantasy of empowerment."[17] In every romance novel, from the most chaste and old-fashioned gothic to today's red-hot erotic romps, no matter what the obstacles, "what happens? She always wins! Guts and brains beat brawn every time. What a comforting fantasy this is for a frazzled, overburdened, anxiety-ridden reader."[18] One might go so far as to suggest that modern women seek their "buried life," as Matthew Arnold once called it, in literature that reaffirms their self-worth simultaneously as wives and mothers. Beneath the bustle of modern economic life, perhaps, lies a longing for the simplicity of the feudal world of fairy tales, where love was forever, good was lavishly rewarded, and evil punished. Gothics describe not a monster under the bed (even if there may be a vampire at the door), but the very real fears that come with women's puberty and reproductive responsibilities.

8. Numinous Melodrama

This aspect of the romance fantasy may also account for a staple ingredient of gothics, often vilified by critics but embraced by readers: the feisty younger heroine clashing shields with an older, wealthy and insufferably arrogant hero. Modern authors aren't simply cribbing from *Jane Eyre* when they compose such scenes. They are explicitly rejecting the "sensitive, caring" male Phillips claims to avoid in her own reading material because the contrast between the two potential lovers is not great enough, and their verbal sparring would generate little heat. The heroine (like the contemporary female reader) must work her way to a position of equality or the catharsis remains ineffectual and incomplete. As Phillips puts it, satisfaction results when the hero realizes that "[a]ll this muscle, wealth, and authority are useless against her courage, intelligence, generosity, loyalty, and kindness."[19] In the world of romance novels, feminine qualities (especially those of empathy and compassion) overpower masculine tyranny simply by existing in their purest and most natural form. Readers know what they want: very few romances, and none achieving any lasting success, depict a younger, inexperienced man falling in love with, say, the powerful widowed matron of an estate.[20] The seductive Mrs. Robinson and her ilk remain a male-centered fantasy.

Still, the gothic heroine must work for her empowerment. She must avoid falling statues, spooked horses, and severed brake lines. She must outwit serial killers, fight off shadowy attackers, and wend her way through labyrinthine secret passages and down crumbling staircases. She must also win the hero's love without yielding to his seductive offers of premarital (or at least pre-commitment) sex, and at the same time she must weight a competing offer of marriage from the villain, whose charm usually masks a dangerous psychopathy. If she is already married or engaged, she must struggle against the temptation to betray her husband or fiancé until she has proven his unworthiness or actual crimes. Her sexual chastity (or reserve, if she is married) throughout the gothic is not a matter of prudishness, but of self-preservation. As in real life, she must use every skill at her disposal to determine what kind of mate the hero will be, and ensure that he will value her love and her body alike. Anxiety, fear, and despair eventually give way to hurricane-force passion and the exultation of vanquishing adversity and evil.

Clever but not arrogant, feisty but not combative, she maintains a strong sense of self despite her physical and economic powerlessness, which assuredly do not equal helplessness in her case. She knows how far she will go and knows what she will not do. She holds fast to her morals. Critics who call her weak have somehow managed to miss plenty of scenes in which she stands up to those who insult and push her around, protects the children, elderly people, and animals in her care, and brings wrongdoers to justice.[21] In some cases, her opponents may include powerful warlocks, demons, or vampires. In nearly every case, these supernatural beings also wither under her perseverance. Could the puzzles solved by the heroine represent, metaphorically, the complexity of daily living in the modern world—perhaps specifically in the world of hippies, women's liberation, and the sexual revolution, when gender roles and standards of living were changing rapidly?

On this subject, Gans again provides insight, for he discusses the way in which audiences may use popular culture's (and in this case fiction's) brand of melodrama as a personal resource, though they do not do so in the way scholars might expect. In other words, this is not accomplished through targeted, issue-specific lessons, since melodramas do not attempt to present things as they happen in real life. Instead, melodrama leads by metaphoric example, showing individuals taking charge of their lives and mastering (or least learning to accommodate) obstacles.[22] Romances, both gothic and otherwise, appear to offer the same sort of encouragement to their readers, who translate the heroine's problems with pirate attacks, surly feudal lords, and deadly traps hidden in castle stones as metaphors for their own modern struggles with family, career, and identity. The gothic heroine often faces these very problems, but with heightened stakes. For example, she must secure her place in the manor despite hostile relatives (stand-ins for the modern woman's in-laws?), work at a vocation, perhaps as a governess or an amateur sleuth, and she has a family to take of—comprised of the hero and sometimes a child for whom she serves as tutor, stepmother, or informal protector. Her triumphs, then, are the reader's—at least until the book is finished. Soon enough, though, the sense of power fades as the daily routine grinds on. Another, similar book is opened and the journey begins anew.

Much has been made of the supposed "formula" that dictates the progression of every romance novel, including the mass market gothic. As many romance writers have pointed out, "formula" is a misnomer, implying a rigidity of form that does not exist. What actually drives a romance novel might more accurately be called a set of elements that must be rearranged into something fresh, but not too different, from constructions that have preceded it. Readers are particular and demand recognizable obstacles and resolutions for the characters, above all the "happy ending," or commitment between the lovers at the end. The challenge for the writer is to select and organize the ingredients in an appetizing way that is unique to her own vision and yet will

8. Numinous Melodrama

satisfy the readers. In *Beyond Heaving Bosoms,* Sarah Wendell and Candy Tan compare the process to two chefs riffing on the same recipe and coming out with two different but delicious end products. The difference may be subtle, but experienced diners can taste it.[23] (One supposes it would be possible for one of the chefs to diverge from the recipe too much, perhaps adding too much sugar or pepper, and come up with something inedible.)

There can be no doubt, however, that as the number of titles grows exponentially, much repetition occurs. Readers, especially those who are voracious in their habits, will begin to notice a certain sameness and perhaps even predictability. This does not seem to be a problem for most of them, who are less concerned with plot structure than they are with appealing characterization and satisfying chemistry between the central couple, along with, in the case of a gothic, some suitably hair-raising suspense along the way. For a romance, the happy ending is the only necessary element and is always the expected result. How the authors get there is for the most part up to them.

The combination of predictability and melodrama, not to mention the prevalence of castles and surly aristocrats, suggests the mass market gothic's affinity to another related genre, the fairy tale. Like the gothic, the fairy tale flirts with supernatural elements,[24] repeatedly places the central character (usually female) in mortal danger, and results in a happy ending that restores order. The denouement also celebrates the heroine's coming of age by reaffirming traditional marriage and hinting at the newly joined couple's fertility.[25] Often, the central male character is a prince or other highly placed nobleman who raises his bride up from a lower social class or position. Melodrama and the numinous, therefore, may find their intersection in the fairy tale. This juxtaposition in turn provides the basic pattern for the gothic romance in particular, with its suggestions of otherworldly influence lurking just beneath the surface and its simultaneous placement in the modern, secular world. As Jack Zipes notes,

> Fairy tales are informed by a human disposition to action—to transform the world and make it more adaptable to human needs, while we also try to change and make ourselves fit for the world. Therefore, the focus of fairy tales, whether oral, written, or cinematic, has always been on finding magical instruments, extraordinary technologies, or powerful people and animals that will enable protagonists to transform themselves along with their environment, making it more suitable for living in peace and contentment. Fairy tales begin with conflict because we all begin our lives with conflict. We are all misfit for the world, and somehow we must fit in, fit in with other people, and thus we must invent or find the means through communication to satisfy as well as resolve conflicting desires and instincts.[26]

The Gothic Romance Wave

In her bibliography of modern gothic novels, Elsa Radcliffe called gothic writers, both past and present, "storytellers, in the most ancient and venerable of traditions. They have written about and elaborated on the everyday fairy tales, myths, fantasies and dreams that were once told around campfires and hearths and are basically as old as humankind on earth."[27] Current writers of romance, gothic or not, would seem to agree. Kathleen Gilles Seidel might as well be describing any number of traditional fairy tales (or their Prince Charmings) when she says of the romance heroes, "They surprise you, they unsettle you, they bring drama and excitement, but in the end they make you feel safe." She goes on to speculate that the romance's relative simplicity of form and comforting outcome may represent a temporary "return to childhood," when life seemed no more complex than the average fairy tale and the reader, like the innocent, youthful heroine of either type of story, deserves and receives love just by virtue of her existence—in most gothic romances, she is dispossessed of wealth or social position, even parents, before the story begins. By the end, she has regained all she has lost and more.

Gothic heroines, like the protagonists of fairy tales or perhaps like modern women, are not always sure which tools (or weapons) will best suit them in their quest for a personally fulfilling role, or at least a stable place, in society. The influence of money, or the intervention of ghosts or witchcraft might work equally well as far as she knows. The hero's love, along with his social and economic power (symbolized in a gothic by the house or castle he rules) surely provides one such "means" of reconciling individual consciousness with social acceptance and respectability. Yet obstacles intrude: the gothic hero is tainted, perhaps accused of murder or afflicted with a curse of some sort. In most cases he blames and hates himself for an injustice he believes he caused or was at least powerless to stop (in many cases, the death of his first wife). Before a marriage can take place, the heroine must first satisfy herself of his worthiness and, second, convince him that he is worthy to claim her and persuade him to offer his love and resources to her. The plot of the gothic, like that of a fairy tale, details her efforts to accomplish that goal.

One contributor to *Gothic Journal* took this connection further. Waverly Fitzgerald's "The Heroine's Quest in the Gothic Novel" claims that the roots of the gothic romance go even deeper, to the earliest sacred myths of civilized people. Its traditional plot points match that of the purification myth, in which the female protagonist journeys to an enchanted castle for the express purpose of lifting the curse on hero king and restoring his family and lands.[28]

8. Numinous Melodrama

Far from being a "passive" participant in the drama, as so many critics charge, the heroine begins her own journey with a "willful act of disobedience" that matures her[29] and later shows courage and resourcefulness in cleansing the sickened land and society infected by the king's cursed state. The hero-king then proves his worth by saving her and affirming their mutual fertility through marriage. Both the myth and the romance place emphasis on the domestic, the traditional sphere of women, where the female protagonist exerts her magical powers as the biological life-giver. This is, Fitzgerald stresses, an "archetypal experience shared by many women." Gothic romance fans therefore participate in an eons-old life-affirming ritual every time they re-read the familiar story in a fresh guise.

It might seem paradoxical that a literary form grounded in fertility ritual and myth is as staunchly chaste as the traditional gothic novel. Even into the 1970s, with the sexual revolution in full swing and historical romances turning up the heat to scorching levels, most mass market gothics resisted anything beyond innuendo, even between husband and wife. Yet sexuality is assuredly present in gothics, just as it is in fairy tales, Regencies, and other forms of "sweet" romance that still exist today. Though there is little or no overt description of bare flesh or body parts heaving and thrusting, the symbolism of the castle or manor, with its peaked towers and dark, forbidden tunnels, as well as the heightened emotions and conflicting feelings that crackle between hero and heroine, convey the promise of passion perfectly well. The gothic couple is rather like the couple of Keats' Grecian Urn—once he catches her, consummation must eventually, and inevitably, yield to disappointment. Instead, gothics capitalize on the stress of thwarted longing and unacknowledged desire, shrouded in an atmosphere of fear and the threat of violence.

Readers seemed well attuned to the inherent tension in the gothic's mixture of fairy tale escapism with the slightly darker veil of implied sexuality and a dangerous hero. Taking things to the next level, as the "bodice ripper" authors were wont to do, would presumably spoil (or threaten) the dreamlike, fairy-tale (some might say childlike) atmosphere of the traditional gothic. There, readers (and writers) can foray safely into the hidden world of evil people and happenings. There is no gore, no strong sexuality, no real or lasting pain, and above all no sexual violence. Occasionally a bloodless murder, of the sort found in a cozy mystery, takes place (falling off cliffs or being swept out to sea are useful for this purpose). Even a vampire's interest is not terrifying—the mass market gothic vampire is a much tamer species than that found in a horror novel or film. Since the story is generally told in the

The Gothic Romance Wave

first person, or at most the third person limited, the reader knows the heroine will find her way out of whatever trap holds her and will soon be reunited with the hero so that the narrative can continue. Gothics accept the reality of violence, both against women and children and against people in general.[30] Yet it remains at one remove, leaving the reader safe in her middle-class surroundings. The castle dungeon is less threatening when the reader can look up and see her familiar kitchen or living room around her; the villain's threats can be interrupted at any time by setting down the novel; the heroine's fears of starvation as she lies locked in the tower can be banished when the reader strolls to the refrigerator for a snack. Later, she can head back to the supermarket, browse the paperback rack, and choose another novel in the same genre. Inside its pages, the heroine, her hero, and the familiar castle will all be waiting to welcome her again.

9

Critics on the Gothic
The Flame and the Pitchfork

> We should have known better.
> We should have known that romance authors aren't bored housewives who sit around eating bonbons while they write formulaic tropes to fulfill their unachievable fantasies.
> Yet before we began our participant-observation research with romance writers four years ago, we bought into the same stereotypes so many outside the genre do. And we didn't realize we held these views until we found ourselves surprised.
> Surprised to find authors were professional and really, really smart.
> Surprised by the seriousness with which authors approach their craft and their profession.
> Surprised by how well written and entertaining romance fiction can be.
> These surprises tell us we expected less, a realization that simultaneously humbles and embarrasses us.
> —Professors Jen Lois and Joanna Gregson, "Stigma and Surprise," http://popularromanceproject.org, 2014

In October of 2015, *The Washington Post* reported on a romance publishing scandal when a promising new author was caught plagiarizing another's work. Outraged, the writer whose novel had been stolen did some research and was shocked to find that most of the offender's literary output could be traced back to previously published works by other writers. Her "books" were little more than cut and paste jobs with only the names, locations, and the genders of certain characters altered.

The plagiarism itself, though an affront to the victimized authors, was sadly nothing new. Big-name romance authors Janet Dailey and Cassie Edwards had been publicly accused of similar deeds in years past. What made the 2015 brouhaha notable was that the *Post* seemed oddly sympathetic to her actions. After all, the paper noted, "the fill-in-the-blanks quality of some romance novels" seemed almost to be asking for duplication. The article expressed something close to surprise that anyone had even noticed: "Though some bodice-rippers are dirtier than others, there is a formula—at some point, the wealthy heiress or the lady-in-waiting hooks up with the horse wrangler or the errant knight, and jeans come off or, well, bodices get ripped."[1]

Responses to the *Post*'s condescension came fast and furious. The cheekily-named website "Smart Bitches, Trashy Books," known for its outspoken defense of romance novels and writers, blasted the article in typically brash language:

> But hey, romance novels. We can't take those seriously. Much like classical music, they're all the same. Same notes, same letters, same formula, bunch of chapters or movements and really, they're all fill-in-the-blanks, right? ... fodder for tired jokes and the dismissal of an entire literary genre, the people who write it, and the people who read it.
> Gosh, golly, gee penis, I can't imagine why that is.[2]

The author of the web page, "SB Sarah" [Sarah Wendell], went on to express her disgust that such "flaccid sexism and tired clichés" could still exist at all, much less make it into the pages of a respected newspaper in the 21st century. "I'd like to think that the language and attitude surrounding the genre has begun to change," she wrote, "to become less misogynist and dismissive in the past few years." To her dismay, and to the dismay of many romance fans who wrote comments both to support her point and shame the plagiarist in question, her optimism had proved premature or perhaps even unfounded.

Still, Wendell and the readers of her website were probably not caught wholly off guard. Ridiculing romance novels and their readers has been something of a spectator sport among journalists, feminists, and academics for at least half a century—more if one counts the invectives against the original gothic novels of the 1790s and Nathaniel Hawthorne's infamous 1850s rant against "scribbling women" and their quaint domestic dramas.[3] When sociologists Jen Lois and Joanna Gregson set out to study the genre from an ethnographic perspective in 2013, they soon found themselves thoroughly taken aback—though not in the way they expected. After examining a few representative novels and interviewing a few authors, they concluded that "the stigma against the romance genre is so strong that even our background as scholars in the sociology of gender wasn't enough to inoculate us" from "[t]he sexism, the hostility, and the condescension" they had unwittingly absorbed.[4] Their experience echoes that of countless other researchers.

9. Critics on the Gothic

Romance novels have been around in their recognizable mass market form since the early 1950s; yet, as late as 2012, Mary Bly could still say "[a]cademic study of popular romance fiction is clearly in its infancy" in Franz and Selinger's aptly titled collection *New Approaches to Popular Romance Fiction*.[5]

Since the mass market gothic romance generally avoided "bodice ripper" scenes and emphasized mystery and horror rather than courtship and sexuality, it escaped some of the critical drubbing administered to its literary cousin, the historical romance. It is probably safe to say that few, if any, readers picked up a 1960s or 1970s gothic in search of sexual titillation. However, it has certainly been dismissed as poorly written, repetitive, and simplistic. Even admitted fans of the genre are more likely to regard the gothic as a guilty pleasure than a legitimate choice in reading material. For example, blogger "Spectergirl" prefaces her web page on gothic mass market romances with an apologetic disclaimer: "Several years ago I had the good fortune of stumbling across a collection of '60s and '70s Gothic romance novels at a garage sale. The use of the term 'good fortune' has nothing whatsoever to do with the quality of the novels themselves. In fact, they were all equally terrible."[6]

Avid readers of the genre, as well as its authors, might well find themselves puzzled by such negative attitudes (as well as the juxtaposition of experiencing "good fortune" in finding something "terrible"). Whatever the romance novel's literary merits, its cultural importance cannot be denied. In a capitalist society such as ours, one might expect that legally sanctioned earning power should bring with it at least some measure of admiration. And gothic writers earned plenty of capitalist tender in their heyday, sometimes blatantly using the form as a financial stopgap. Dean Koontz, beset with financial worries when the market for his more "serious" work, science fiction and horror, temporarily dried up, turned to the gothic in 1972. He wrote one book in two weeks and another in one week, earning $1500 for the first and $1750 for the second. In one year, he recalls, he made $5000 (the figure is in 1972 dollars; it would be worth about $29,300 in 2017).[7] Koontz's success was modest by gothic standards. Dorothy Daniels, a staple on gothic shelves, contracted for 12 novels a year with an advance of $3500 each (about $20,500 in modern dollars; still high for a category romance novel, which generally advance $8000 to $10,000 today). Phyllis Whitney, perhaps the most successful American Gothic writer, started publishing at age 48, and eventually *Spindrift*, her 19th Gothic, sold 57,000 hardcovers upon release. After that, she typically started with a print run of 80,000 copies and by 1975, she had 55 books published in 17 languages. Whitney earned approximately $1 per hardback sold in royalties and, according to Doubleday, "$125,000 for paperback rights, in addition to revenues from book clubs, foreign rights, and sales of her juvenile books."[8] In 2017 currency, these paperback rights alone would be worth over half a million dollars.

Whitney was born in 1903, some 26 years before Virginia Woolf championed a woman's right to claim "room of one's own" in which to write, never mind cultivate substantial wealth and international fame. Yet financial success may actually have worked against the most popular gothic writers, both in Ann Radcliffe's day as well as our own. In 1974, Gans noted the "anticommercial bias with which many scholars look at culture; they often deem it worthy of attention only if it is created by unpaid folk and by 'serious' artists who do not appear to think about earning a living."[9] It is not difficult to see how purveyors of highbrow literary fiction, the majority of them male, would chafe at the high sales made by female romance novelists in comparison to their own less accessible and less profitable works. Even Hawthorne's complaint about "scribbling women" was explicitly triggered by his perception that their novels were siphoning sales from *The Scarlet Letter*. Academics, struggling to publish for comparatively few readers and little or no money, would also have reason to resent the romance novel's fiscal and popular success.

Class bias, too, has doubtless played a role. Regis states, "unapologetically," that the "values" of the romance novel "are profoundly bourgeois,"[10] and no one has so far proved otherwise (or even attempted to do so). It makes sense that in his study of popular culture and its critics, Herbert Gans suggests that "the most popular creators come from much the same socioeconomic and educational background as their audience and therefore share its taste, much like the real or idealized folk-artist who shared the culture of his audience."[11] The gap between this perceived group of non-academic readers, here one made up of middle-class women, often leads to caste-based hostility: "high culture needs to think of popular culture as of low quality, of its creators as hacks, and its audience as culturally oppressed people without academic standards."[12] When it comes to romance novels, it appears, "high culture" can even be replaced with "other mass-market literary genres." As noted, Dean Koontz, who self-identifies as a science fiction and horror writer in his *Writing Popular Fiction* guide, sees nothing amiss in denigrating his fellow gothic authors while describing the novels of which he was especially proud. One such work is *This Haunted Earth*, which describes life on a planet inhabited

9. Critics on the Gothic

by characters from popular horror films, like Dracula and the werewolf. One cannot help but suspect that the assumption of a masculine audience for this book, as well as its cast of predominantly male characters, accounts for its perceived literary value.

If male critics are sometimes scathing toward romance novels and gothics, their remarks seem like bemused indifference compared to the vehemence (and sometimes venom) directed at the field by feminist critics, who have shown no reluctance to attack works predominantly written by and for women. The first widely-known serious study of the romance, *Reading the Romance*, appeared in 1980, followed by Tania Modleski's *Loving with a Vengeance* in 1982 and Miriam Darce Frenier's *Goodbye, Heathcliff* in 1988. None of these studies examines the mass market gothic romance as distinct from the more general field that includes short category romances, Regencies, and long "bodice-ripper"-type historicals. However, Radway's study contained a brief history of the mass market gothic romance, Modleski addressed the theme of paranoia in the typical gothic, and Frenier examined the decline of brutish, sarcastic Brontë-esque heroes in Harlequin-style contemporaries. For the most part, these early studies expressed, at best, ambivalence and, at worst, disdain for the popular romance and its supposedly disempowering patriarchal message.[13]

During the same decade, two studies by Kay Mussell, *Women's Gothic and Romantic Fiction: A Reference Guide* (1981) and *Fantasy and Reconciliation: Contemporary Formulas of Women's Romance Fiction* (1984), discussed a number of gothic tropes and their significance within the genre. Mussell does not challenge some of the earlier assumptions about gothics, such as describing their basic premise as that of a passive heroine reacting to a repressive, sexist environment. However, her *Reference Guide* raises some interesting questions and, by summarizing many studies with differing attitudes and conclusions, dismantles many stereotypes about romance and gothic romance novels, authors, and readers. *Fantasy and Reconciliation* explores the "quest" motif common to many mass market gothic romances, examining the various tests the heroine (in particular the protagonist of Holt's *Mistress of Mellyn*) faces in her journey toward the requisite happy ending.

While Mussell views the dramas of the gothic as a kind of testing ground on which the heroine proves her worth to the master who will eventually marry her (or choose to transform a marriage of convenience into a love match), Frenier comments on the ways in which women's liberation has modified, though not neutralized, the basic premise that women find their greatest pleasure and fulfillment in marriage and family. Either way, both say, the romance reinforces the traditional role of women in society, even if more modern heroines pursue careers after marriage to the hero. Readers therefore come to these novels to affirm, and perhaps rehearse the stages of, a standard heterosexual courtship. Any other choice for the young, fertile heroine (or, by extension, the reader) is discouraged—perhaps unthinkable.

As far as the mass market gothic romance is concerned, more influential than all of these books combined, however, was a caustic article that appeared in *The Journal of Popular Culture* in spring 1973 (and later reprinted in the 1995 collection *To Write Like a Woman*). "Someone's Trying to Kill Me and I Think It's My Husband," by feminist science fiction author Joanna Russ, is still widely consulted (and usually taken at face value) by both readers and scholars seeking information about the popular gothic. Russ begins by considering the types of fiction favored by American women in the early 1970s (though it should be noted that all the gothics she analyzes, save one, are from the mid-1960s). The answer, to her chagrin, is "confession magazines, nurse novels—and the Modern Gothic."[14] No doubt Gans would be intrigued by the class distinctions she makes between the readers of the three: "Modern Gothics, unlike nurse novels and the confession magazines, are read by middle-class women or women with middle-class aspirations, and for some reason the books written by Englishwomen have remained the most popular, at least at Ace [one of the leading publishers of mass market gothics at the time]." Russ does not ask an obvious question: did American women favor the works of "Englishwomen" because they entertained fantasies of British gentrification and imagined the characters speaking in posh accents they heard on *Masterpiece Theater*? Or might it simply have been that these stories resembled the familiar and beloved British tales of du Maurier, Henry James, and the Brontës?

Curious about the gothics' appeal, Russ exchanged some correspondence with Terry Carr, a male editor at Ace books, known for its successful gothic line. Carr explained that one draw of many gothic stories was the conflict between the heroine and a new husband, "who may or may not be a lunatic and/or murderer." Russ therefore concludes that matrimonial terror was what resonated most with female readers: "it remained for U.S. women to discover they were frightened of their husbands," she remarks.[15] Carr's letter to Russ is reproduced with a few points of ellipses that may obscure his original intent, but his point seems to be that women sought the gothics out because the books mirrored real-life anxieties. Russ, despite (or because of) her fem-

9. Critics on the Gothic

inist sensibilities, does not challenge this assertion. Instead, she is almost too eager to concede that the typical gothic heroine is little more than a shrinking violet who spends most of the novel kowtowing to what Russ terms "a *Super-Male*, who treats her brusquely, derogates her, scolds her, and otherwise shows anger or contempt for her. The Heroine is vehemently attracted to him and usually just as vehemently repelled or frightened."[16] Complicating the heroine's problem is the Other Woman, a worldly type who competes for the Super-Male's attention even if she is dead, and a Shadow-Male who offers an alternative to committing to the Super-Male.

Such plot devices (at least in this boiled-down form) seem to offend Russ, since to her they reinforce what she perceives as the heroine's feminine powerlessness and reactive nature. Gothics are, for Russ, "*adventure stories with passive protagonists*"[17]—or, in her words, heroines who spend most of their time trying to "'read' other people's faces and feelings. This is what most real women spend their time doing." To Russ, this type of internalized detection is "boring," and the character's effort to unravel the domestic mystery at hand little more than a "sacred version of everyday gossip."[18] Worst of all, "Gothics obviously envision the relation between Super-Male and Heroine as neither abnormal nor unusual, but as the standard, even ideal, relation between men and women."[19] Presumably to prove that such novels are ill-written and superficial, she presents a disjointed list, running several pages, of phrases from one novel, strung together with ellipses, tedious to read and incoherent without context or any connecting storyline.[20]

Clearly, Russ's critique of the mass market gothic romance is based on generalizations labeled by invented jargon (her "Super-Male" is roughly analogous to "alpha male" in more modern romance parlance, though with a more facetious and perhaps sinister aura) and what she considers overly emotional prose (which she calls "bathetic" but does not quite go so far as to label "purple"). She takes special aim at gothic novels' reliance on descriptions of food, clothing, and domestic props, which she recites in some detail. By isolating these elements, and using her own barbed wit and a supercilious writing style, Russ succeeds in making the novels in her sampling look foolish and shallow. Yet it seems a bit disingenuous of her to separate, say, a description of a meal from its context and complain about domestic details when gothics have traditionally taken place within a household setting beset by mysterious and even otherworldly events. Any writer of fiction that includes a dose of fantasy knows that such mundane details add verisimilitude to a plot that might otherwise seem too outlandish. They can also be used to heighten suspense, lulling the reader, along with the characters, into a familiar atmosphere before shocking them out of their complacency with a startling plot twist.

Descriptions of clothing, as well, can serve as a kind of shorthand to themes of social class in a novel. This is especially true for stories set in the Victorian era, as many gothics are. Heroines with only a few shabby gowns will feel their outcast status, a central gothic trope, more keenly if the castle is filled with finely dressed ladies and sophisticated gentlemen she cannot befriend. This obvious characterization device seems to escape Russ, along with the fact that readers might enjoy such details in order to visualize, movie-style, a country or century other than their own and identify more closely with the heroine (which is also the goal of the often-employed first person viewpoint).[21] Finally, in gothics that center on a heroine's place in and duties toward a functioning upper-class household (not to mention her need to wear costumes, assume other identities, or avoid pastries poisoned by the villain), detail may be useful as well. Again, without context, there is no way of knowing. It would be hard to imagine a mystery novelist being chided for including a number of fine details, since these are recognized (and welcomed) by mystery aficionados as possible clues. Science fiction novels, likewise, often itemize alien or futuristic homes, foods, weapons, and vehicles. Though sometimes too much description can become overwhelming and dull in any novel, to say it is a feature (never mind the distinguishing feature, as Russ implies) only of mass market gothic romances is an exaggeration. One suspects that Russ would also be only too happy to deride a paucity of description.

Russ's article probably had no effect on mainstream readers who did not subscribe to *The Journal of Popular Culture*, and one of the authors she targets, Susan Howatch, went on to enjoy bestselling status and critical acclaim (for her part, Howatch notes elsewhere that she did not set out to make the novel in question, *The Dark Shore*, a gothic; that label was supplied by the publisher[22]). Gothic fans continued to buy and enjoy gothics well beyond 1973, apparently unfazed by the books' endless patter about emotions, gowns, and Super-Males who lived in mysterious houses with names like Hawkshurst, Ravensridge, and Shadowwood. The article did, however, taint the critical well for years to come. It clearly made a strong impression on Tania Modleski, whose 1982 book *Loving with a Vengeance* tackles both the gothic and other types of mass market romance, such as the short Harlequin-type novel that had steadily been gaining popularity since the late 1970s. Modleski contrasts (not entirely accurately) the two in terms clearly inspired by Russ's focus on the heroine's wariness of the "Super-Male" and his intentions toward her:

9. Critics on the Gothic

"Another way of expressing the difference between the two types of narrative is to say that the Harlequin heroine's feelings undergo a transformation from fear into love, whereas for the Gothic heroine, the transformation is from love into fear."[23] Like Russ, Modleski connects the heroine's fear in the castle, among hostile strangers, to the process by which women struggle to find identities in male-dominated Victorian or modern society (the two most common settings for gothics). Both Harlequins and gothics, Modleski believes, "deal with women's fears and confusion about masculine behavior in a world in which men learn to devalue women." These observations lead her to conclude that the mass market gothic romance is actually about female paranoia, especially after a relationship with a man has been formed: "In Harlequins ... the preoccupation is with getting a man; in Gothics the concern is with understanding the relationship and the feelings involved once the union has been formed."[24]

At first glance, a view of the gothic as anti-feminist appears plausible. Since most mass market gothic romances revisit, in one way or another, the love story of Jane Eyre and Edward Rochester, one might theorize that the heroine's (Jane's or her stand-in's) quest to turn the hero from a taciturn and sarcastic bully into a devoted mate is an attempt by the reader to rewrite the struggles of her own life, casting herself simultaneously as victim and heroine, in order to psychologically assuage the disappointments she experienced with her own father[25] and then with a spouse. Besides, Mr. Rochester, to say nothing of his many doppelgangers in gothic romances, may not have been such a catch after all. Jean Rhys's *Wide Sargasso Sea* repositions Mr. Rochester as a villain who made his wealth through the typical Victorian means of economic exploitation, drove his first wife mad, and even forced her to take an ugly name of his own invention, "Bertha." Not surprisingly, once she is forcibly transported from the freedom of the Caribbean to the structured society of England, Bertha gives up on life and draws in on herself in madness, living only to exact revenge on Rochester while assimilated females like Jane Eyre do their best to contain her. The fact that generations of readers appear to prefer the original novel to Rhys's reimagined version speaks to the degree to which women readers have been conditioned to accept the ends of the patriarchy, just as Bertha was forced to accept her new name and identity as Rochester's chattel.

Modleski also suggests that "a core of truth" in the "paranoia of married women"[26] as exhibited in these books strikes a chord with women readers, themselves oppressed and devalued if not in literal jeopardy like the heroine.[27]

The Gothic Romance Wave

Could a possibly-villainous husband poisoning her soup in the novel echo a real-life husband's complaints about one's cooking? By reading gothics, the modern woman may be trying to make sense of her own depression and anxiety and even, Modleski suggests, reconcile herself to being "devalued" or actually despised and victimized.

Certainly devaluation on a scale leading to abuse and attempted murder would be justifiable cause for paranoia in the gothic heroine, and, if demonstrated by real-life angry, vicious men, in the reader. However, Modleski glosses over an important distinction between the gothic heroine and the modern middle-class reader. In a gothic, the heroine is constantly beset by falling statues, locked rooms, failing brakes, sabotaged stair treads, hungry vampires, and angry spirits, to name just a few possible dangers. Though she is usually mistaken about the identity of the perpetrator, as in any mystery novel, she is not mistaken that someone is trying to kill her. To recast the thrills and chills inherent in a gothic plot to metaphors for domestic discontent seems unnecessarily and misleadingly reductive, not to mention the assumption of bristling masculine hostility in the reader's (and possibly the author's) own home. After all, similar dangers routinely befall the male protagonists of mystery and horror novels written by male authors and aimed at male readers, but their use of tropes (sometimes the very same ones used in the gothic) is seldom subject to the derision romance novels receive.

Whatever their missteps, critics are correct that the relationship between the romance fan and her preferred reading material (gothic or otherwise) is worth examining. Ironically, this may be where their efforts have gone most awry. The impressive sales of mass market gothics and other types of romances prove that readers welcome and enjoy the familiar motifs, even if they are not familiar with the exact critical terminology to describe their use. Why they enjoy them, and how they put that enjoyment to use, is far less clear-cut than some of the more cynical critics would have us believe.

As Pamela Regis points out in *A Natural History of the Romance Novel* (2007), Janice Radway originally criticized the romance novel for, among other things, failing to offer its disenfranchised reader "a comprehensive program for reorganizing her life." Regis finds such an expectation unrealistic, at best, since in her view not even an established classic like *Pride and Prejudice* makes any such attempt[28] (not to mention the fact that not all readers may want or need their lives reorganized). Glen Thomas has likewise rejected the "behaviorist model" of consumer and mass market. Both Radway's pitying descriptions of romance readers growing addicted to books that subtly alienate and

9. Critics on the Gothic

undermine them, and Modleski's alarming image of women using romance novels to drug themselves into accepting their oppression[29] are fundamentally flawed, Thomas suggests. Instead, the relationship between the producers, consumers, and conveyers of any mass-media product should be viewed as a complex interplay of economic, psychological, and cultural factors, with the consumer (in this case the middle-class woman) actually holding the most power. She is not a dupe of a patriarchal system using romance novels to lull her into a passive or even subservient state, but rather a discerning purchaser who can use her discretionary income to influence the market to meet her own needs. "My point here is that criticism and discussion of the readership of romance fiction needs to move beyond the circularity of the debate over a fantasy reader who is oppressed and relieved by turns, be that oppression by the heavy hand of patriarchy, or the relief that stems from feeling happier or enjoying enhanced sexual relations with a significant other. Rather than focus on the unitary fantasy reader of romance fiction, it's time to talk of readers in the plural, and how these readers' choices are one element in constructing and shaping a complex reading position and identity."[30] Herbert Gans would also reject the idea that genre novels are (or should be) used primarily to resolve specific short-term personal anxieties. The disconnect between consumers and critics of popular culture arises because of the different focus each group brings to the product; Gans suggests that "[p]eople pay much less attention to the media and are much less swayed by its content than the critics, who are highly sensitive to verbal and other symbolic materials, I believe. They use the media for diversion and would not think of applying its content to their own lives." It has escaped the notice of many romance-novel commentators that, as Gans puts it, "few people seem to use the media for problem solving, or media fiction for descriptions or explanations of reality."[31] Academics, whose chosen media tend to be scholarly texts they must master, might be said to operate in the reverse of mainstream culture. They must therefore discard (or at least suppress) learned attitudes towards written artefacts in order to understand the layperson's casual reading experience.

Several papers and studies support the conclusions of both Gans and Thomas. One survey, reported by Mussell, reports that heavy readers of romances (both gothics and other types) had pleasing social lives, happy marriages, took pleasure in family, and found their reading a source of pleasure, not anxiety. Romance readers are not solitary and lonely at all, according to this study, but are instead active and engaged in many areas of modern life. Depressed, solitary people were actually found to read less.[32] It seems

The Gothic Romance Wave

hard to believe that researchers have assumed so much about readers without talking to any, but in many instances this seems to be the case. Even Radway, who monitored a group of romance readers and collected their impressions of various books, filtered their responses through her own academic bias. This disconnect becomes even more apparent once one leaves the pages of academic discourse and walks among the readers themselves. Romance-novel collecting is an active pursuit for many women, especially those who are older and have more leisure time—as any visit to a used-book sale or the romance section of a chain bookstore will attest. The women shopping there (many armed with computerized lists of books they own and books they are looking for) welcome the chance to discuss favorites, suggest titles and authors, and trade information on upcoming sales and releases with one another. Romance conventions draw large numbers of excited readers who interact with authors, editors, and one another; book clubs and web pages devoted to romances of all sort flourish. Far from cowing, silencing, or shaming the women who read them, romance novels of all sorts deliver excitement, intellectual stimulation, and a genuine community of women (exemplified by the lively discussions in the pages of *Gothic Journal*) the most ardent feminist would have to admire.

Even a rudimentary understanding of human nature suggests that if the ultimate outcome of gothic (and other romance) novels were to make women more aware of their own "devalued" status, they would either stop reading or, brimming with newly awakened anger, move on to more enlightened, feminist-authored literature that was readily available even in the 1960s.[33] The critics admit (or complain) that this doesn't happen—instead, readers have continued to consume romance after romance in what cynics describe as a kind of compulsive, chain-reading pattern. Yet, for all this pathology and addiction, there are no stop-romance-reading support groups, therapists, or hypnotists as far as is known. Is it possible that readers are simply missing or misinterpreting what is on the page in front of them—that women, especially, are so subconsciously invested in patriarchal models that they willingly internalize its disempowering messages over and over again? Is this how gothic novels, even (or especially) those penned by women, foist the inevitability of patriarchal oppression on the reader? Do the actions of the heroine, while seeming proactive and independent on the surface, actually demonstrate capitulation?

A careful examination of the feminist arguments and the texts themselves, not to mention history itself, shows that these dire interpretations are,

9. Critics on the Gothic

at best, misguided. Far from training women to accept that men "devalue" them and are only too eager to brutalize and subvert them, the romance novel can empower and inspire its readers. Daphne Clair, writing in Jayne Ann Krentz's *Dangerous Men and Adventurous Women* (1992), suggests that this was no less true of the 1790s gothic than it is today:

> Mrs. Radcliffe put into print women's deepest fears: the fear of being trapped and imprisoned in the house to which all women were supposed to confine their lives; the fear of male sexuality, male power, and male duplicity; and, not least, the fear of losing their own identity ... [these themes] still echo strongly in category romance. Heroines commonly are orphaned, come into a small inheritance, travel to foreign parts, and are employed—sometimes even kidnapped—by the dark, ruthless owners of large, isolated mansions. They often spend a chapter or two "finding themselves" or establishing their sense of identity, frequently assert their independence in the face of masculine assump-tions of authority, and nearly always feel under threat emotionally if not physically from the dominant male in the story. But in one way or another, the heroine emerges victorious, enriched and with enhanced social status.[34]

The "danger" and "fear" described by Russ and Modleski are indeed present in romances, as every contributor to *Dangerous Men and Adventurous Women* readily admits. However, both serve a specific purpose—to educate and strengthen the heroine as she faces and overcomes various obstacles. By the time she is ready to solve the mystery and claim her mate, she can meet him on even ground and use her heightened feminine power to revitalize him. In this sense, the romance novel is mythical and archetypal in that it "celebrates the power of the female to heal and civilize the male."[35] Another contributor to Krentz's anthology, romance author Kathleen Gilles Seidel, had sharp words for those who identified as feminist but expressed little more than disdain for the literary habits of other women: "Feminists talk about sisterhood; I do not know how deeply they feel it. The undercurrent throughout feminist criticism of romances is that these scholars and critics know what is right for other women—and oh my, do they feel the 'us/them' distinction acutely.... They, those scholars, aren't like you and me, and they're mighty glad of it. Nonetheless, they know what you and I should be doing with our lives." She stresses that romance novels "are not self-help books. They are fantasies. They are entertainment. They are pleasure."[36] Social roles and women's rights may have changed, but the need for escapist fiction has not. *Gothic Journal* reader Louise Pacheco echoed these sentiments in a letter to the September/October 1993 issue: "The reason I read gothics is because they are uplifting. Yes, there's a dark, brooding hero, a mystery, and a hidden staircase, etc., but these stories are very uplifting to me. Usually—no, often—

the 'dark mystery' is just a misunderstanding.... [Gothics] keep me sane from the stress of twentieth century living."

What can be gleaned from the juxtaposition of these two radically different approaches is that critics like Russ (who did not come to study the gothic out of affection for the genre, but as a sort of anthropological foray into an unknown land) start with a profound misunderstanding of the average woman's purpose for reading gothics (and other types of romances). Far from picking up a book of popular fiction to experience political catharsis or explore modes of gender-based repression, gothic readers sought a mysterious, intriguing atmosphere, a few light puzzles to solve (perhaps involving the location of a lost treasure within the castle or saving a loved one's life, both common and timeless fantasies), and a few scares and thrills to keep the plot boiling. The castle or manor house setting also provides a combination of fairy tale elements, familiar to every reader from the simpler days of childhood storytelling, with the romance of the past, potent even for 18th-century gothicists. As Elsa Radcliffe noted in the introduction to her gothic bibliography,

> The key to an empathy for Gothic fiction is, to my mind, the idea that from the very beginning to the present day, these writers have not been "novelists" in the literary sense, but storytellers, in the most ancient and venerable of traditions.... They are not attempting to edify, enlighten, impress or persuade. Their sole *raison d'etre* is to entertain. Such a humble goal has not particularly impressed the literary establishment which seems to have done its best to relegate this literature, surely in the twentieth century, to oblivion by neglect. But the storytellers and their devoted reading public tend to ignore all that and happily go their way, writing and reading what entertains.[37]

Since gothic novels appeared en masse in the late 1960s, women have made great strides. Far from hampering them, popular culture has empowered them. Single, married, and everything in between, they now work as writers, professors, and publishers. It is unreasonable to think, given the numbers of romance sales, that none of these successful women ever read and enjoyed a romance or a mass market gothic. They obviously did not become passive, confused, or dependent on male authority. The gothic's pleasures are harmless and the specifics of any individual book may be fleeting, though readers have no difficulty recalling their favorite books and authors, even after many years. Romance readers may be perceived as less educated and unsophisticated by critics who disdain the form,[38] but their passion for the genre and deep familiarity with its tropes, traditions, and authors suggest a literary awareness that rivals that of many academics. In fact, the tendency of aficionados to amass and read, in serial fashion, vast numbers of similar

9. Critics on the Gothic

novels suggests that the effect of the gothic (and the romance in general) is cumulative, akin to the world-building used to establish a science fiction universe or a long-running series shared by multiple authors (for example, the *Star Trek* universe or the world of James Bond). This is why, as Pamela Regis suggests, critical studies based on limited samples of only two to five novels fail to provide genuine insight into the romance's intricacies.

In this world, every seaside cliff is crowded with manor houses in need of a governess or mistress, North America is dotted with medieval-style castles (some transported brick by brick from the old world and reassembled), and every village on both sides of the pond can recall the unsolved murder of a previous occupant of the local grand house. Despite what Russ and other critics believe, it is in fact a female-centered world; men may own the castles, command the villages, and take in the heroine as a poor relation or employee, but by the end of the novel the heroine is the one who has saved the estate from ruin, solved the murder, and reversed the hero's downward spiral into depression or depravity. Her nurturing, civilizing (some might say feminizing) influence is felt both within the castle walls and within the hearts of its inhabitants: troubled children heal emotionally, curses dissipate, and demons are vanquished. In most cases, too, heirs are born in a revived atmosphere of family affection and social justice. The sins of the past are vanquished not through battle or political coup, but solely through the heroine's capacity to love. Old-world patriarchy will give way not to matriarchy, which would simply bring with it a new set of problems, but a restructured dynamic and a modernized way of living with the opposite sex.

It is to this world of optimism, shaped and presided over by the heroine in her new role as mistress of the manor,[39] that women readers return again and again. For them, the romance novel was (and is) a living entity that has spoken to generations of women and will continue to do so. They do not approach their reading with rage or in a state of unhappiness, but as an enjoyable hobby, perhaps akin to crafting. Their modest efforts at quilting or embroidering may never end up in the Metropolitan Museum of Art, but the act of creation, much like reading a romance, proves a pleasant and uplifting way to spend an afternoon. Later, reactions can be shared with friends online, in a reading group, or informally. Readers, and especially women, want to enter the castle—not to be locked inside, but to stride in without flinching, purify the place, and claim a mate. The process is empowering and fulfilling—possibly the very opposite of spending an afternoon reading reductionist gender-based criticism.

10

Fading Shadows
Where Did the Gothic Go?

> It is this scene I think of when I think of that summer at Castle Mallow. The Castle is gone now; the bulldozers stamped it into the ground that fall.
> —*Farewell to the Castle* by Jane Corby, 1967

In 1974, Isabelle Holland described the plight of a male friend who, waiting to board a flight with nothing to read, stepped into the airport shop in search of a book to carry onboard. As he scanned the shelves, he grew bewildered to find almost nothing available except scores of paperbacks featuring women in flowing gowns running away from houses.[1] Holland's scenario was scarcely an exaggeration: Elsa Radcliffe's bibliography *Gothic Novels of the Twentieth Century* lists some 1,973 titles published by 1979, and is by no means complete. Nearly every major publishing company had its own gothic line, each releasing several gothics each month.

Yet, at the time Holland's article appeared in print, the popularity of the mass market gothic had peaked. Publishers were pumping out several books a month, with little attention to quality or genuine gothic elements. Many of the books from 1971 on seemed almost slapdash efforts (though Zebra tried to do something new with its "Illustrated Gothics" line in the late 1970s, recalling the ill-fated gothic magazines earlier in the decade). By the middle of that decade, the increasing apathy of large publishers toward the genre, motivated by an apparent decrease in readers, would hobble and eventually kill the genre.[2] By the mid–1980s, the classic mass market gothics were already the stuff of nostalgia, quaint souvenirs of an era when women demanded careers and equal treatment while wearing go-go boots and colorful miniskirts that barely hid their undergarments.

In 1991, Mary Stewart, still widely considered one of the queens of the gothic, released one of her final novels, *The Stormy Petrel*. Not even Stewart's

10. Fading Shadows

fluid prose can disguise her obvious weariness with the old tropes. *Petrel's* heroine wanders somewhat aimlessly around a treacherous landscape, investigates a ramshackle manor house, and is courted by two mysterious men, but no surprise twist and little true excitement awaits either the reader or the protagonist. The male characters turn out to be nothing more or less than the reader suspected from the very beginning and the novel's peaceful resolution seems too easily won. The light in the tower, burning steadily since the mid–1960s, was beginning to flicker; in a few short years it would blink out altogether. Harlequin Gothics, which had been late to the party, released only 18 books over the course of five years and ceased publication in 1988. Six years later, Kensington Press, the last popular fiction publisher dedicated to the traditional formula and covers, closed down their Zebra Gothic line. Silhouette Shadows, which had offered a few traditionally styled gothics along with paranormal romances and romantic suspense, followed suit in 1996.[3]

Gothic Journal, the desktop-publishing venture created to serve fans of the sputtering genre, unwittingly charted the demise of the mass market gothic by following the relevant publishing trends from 1992 to 1997. The *Journal's* readers, hungry for gothics, were not shy about writing to various publishers to make their feelings known. They would then report the results in the letters column, stimulating much discussion between gothic fans and authors alike. In late 1992, an editor at Leisure Books assured the *Journal* that, while that they loved gothics, the lack of orders from retailers could not justify publishing more (or perhaps any) of them.[4] A year earlier, the largest romance press in the world had apologized for their lack of new gothics. According to Harlequin Editorial Manager Karin Stoecker in 1991, "Gothics have been consistently published. However ... [due to] changing readers' tastes ... readers may want a gothic story now and then, but not necessarily six every month."[5] The publishers had tried to modernize gothic fare, but to no avail; readers were skeptical of their ideas for improvement. Signet had apparently tried adding sex scenes into some 1986 books, but the move sparked angry reader letters to *Gothic Journal*. As one from reader Georgia Walden pointed out, "Injecting sex into otherwise stupid books is not the answer."[6] On the topic of erotic content in traditional gothics, another contributor, Marion Schultz, agreed. "Nay, nay!" she exclaims, somewhat in the manner of her favorite heroines, championing the "essential innocence" of this type of book[7] and insisting that such content would be particularly inappropriate in gothics with Victorian settings.

Some contributors, such as Rachel Cosgrove Payes, a successful gothic author in the 1960s, disputed publishers' claims that readers were no longer looking for gothics. There were plenty of readers out there, she insisted, but publishers were ignoring them. Her logic seemed irrefutable: "If they don't advertise, they don't increase their reading base."[8] Payes and other authors also countered that acquisitions editors and publishers were partly to blame for reader boredom, since they were not taking a more flexible approach to the genre. She lamented in early 1993, "if you deviate more than a few millimeters from the old tried and true gothic plot, they don't want it. Basically, what they want is the same story over and over, just with different heads on the characters."[9] A devoted audience still existed, Payes believed, and quality gothic tales were well received when made available. However, the major paperback houses were no longer interested in serving this section of the reading public. They preferred to call their books something else, such as "romantic suspense," even if gothic elements were present. "[S]ome publishers are afraid to call a book a gothic because of the bad press when they declined in popularity in the early 1970s," editor Kristi Lyn Glass suggested in *Gothic Journal*.[10] "Poor writing and formula plots contributed greatly to their demise."

Gradually, *Gothic Journal* began to shift toward reviews of contemporary romantic suspense novels, though not all the readers were pleased with this direction. The lack of new material labeled "gothic" seems to have been behind the change. Apparently having run dry of subject matter, the *Gothic*'s final issue focused on Nancy Drew novels. It finally ceased publication in 1998.

The termination of the gothic lines at Ace, Zebra, and Harlequin (among others) meant that the mass market Gothic would no longer be written, printed or distributed in large numbers. Department store clearance bins held huge numbers of them, each for sale for a quarter or five for a dollar, in the late 1970s as publishers remaindered their leftover stock. Today many of the books available on eBay (at collectible prices) and at garage and library sales bear faded "clearance" stickers on the covers. Gothic became fodder for parody, pastiche, and wistful nostalgia. Examples include Philip Jose Farmer's *The Evil in Pemberley House* (2009—complete with a woman posing, though not running, in front of a house) and Rick Abbot's comic play, *The Bride of Brackenloch! A Ghastly Gothic Thriller?* (1987), advertised 20 years after *Mercy at the Manor Manor* as a "cheerily goofy spoof of all those gothic novels where the heroine is brought to the ancient manor by her handsome, brooding groom."[11]

It is impossible to speculate whether a renewed marketing push in the Reagan era might have restored the gothic to prominence. Publishers had no

10. Fading Shadows

interest in finding out, either, as they rushed to promote sexy full-length "bodice rippers" in the vein of *The Flame and the Flower*. Writers like Payes, finding that the historicals paid better and received a better marketing push in bookstores, moved on. Romance readers seeking a touch of mystery and danger with their love stories were forced to turn to "a nebulous category of novels that we are calling 'romantic suspense,'" noted Glass in *Gothic Journal*. "It is the modern term for 'gothic.'"[12] Meanwhile, in the mid-1970s, Stephen King began to reclaim gothic tropes from women writers and readers just as Scott had reshaped the historical in the early 19th century. King's stories are aggressively masculine; his vampire Barlow is no romantic hero, and must be destroyed after he kills Susan, the closest thing *Salem's Lot* has to a heroine. The hardcover version of *The Shining* had featured a gothic-style manor/hotel on the jacket, but the story focuses not on the bewildered wife, Wendy, but on Jack Torrance as he descends into homicidal madness. King's success inspired many imitators, mostly men or at least authors using masculine names; Clive Bloom notes that by the 1980s, every big-name horror writer except for Anne Rice (whose given name is, oddly, Howard) was male.[13] Gloomy houses were now the setting not for angst-ridden love affairs between a brooding master and a governess, but for graphic, blood-soaked mayhem.

The decline of gothics may represent not just the changing tastes of editors in New York, but the influence of a broader culture that could no longer take refuge in the tame fantasies of earlier decades. If the 1950s represented modern America's childhood and the turbulent '60s its teenage years, all that was left for the '70s and '80s were post-adolescent ennui and the cynicism of workaholic adulthood. Politics, fashion, and entertainment became more conservative, cable news channels hammered viewers incessantly with real-life stories of domestic violence, AIDS, and serial killers, while explicit sexuality in books and other media became less controversial and even unavoidable. As the 20th century entered its final decade, women were taking greater control of their own lives and careers. This brought new types of stress but also greater awareness of the world outside the home and the traditional marital bedroom. The genie summoned by the "women's liberation" movement and the sexual revolution had exploded from the bottle, shattering it so thoroughly that returning was impossible. In the romance novels of the 1990s, it was common to see never-married heroines who had sexual experience (mostly off stage) before meeting the hero and who seldom hesitated to bed the hero without a ring. The quaintness of gothics struggled to find a place in an increasingly fast-paced modern world. With the specter of the 21st cen-

The Gothic Romance Wave

tury hovering over her half-bared shoulder, the ingénue heroine slipped out of the castle in her bare feet and flowing nightdress for the last time and kept running.

In 1979, as the traditional gothic gradually began to disappear from bookstore shelves, Elsa Radcliffe suggested that the genre might not be going extinct, but simply evolving: "It is my view that from the seeds sown by Walpole, Radcliffe, Maturin, Lewis and so many others has grown an immense garden of literature which, by the twentieth century, has diverged into a rich variety of sub-species. In spite of some cross-breeding, there are to this day a large number of books being written which are identifiable as Gothic."[14]

Four decades later, Radcliffe's observation is as true as it was at the dawn of the 1980s. Gothic elements can currently be found in literary fiction, such as Diane Setterfield's *The Thirteenth Tale* (2006), Deborah Lawrenson's *The Lantern* (2011), and Wendy Webb's *The Vanishing* (2014), among many others; cozy mysteries like Julia Buckley's *A Dark and Stormy Murder* (2016) and its sequels, which feature an aging gothic author who resembles Phyllis Whitney, and Laura DiSilverio's *Murder at the Gothic Gala* (also 2016), in which a murder occurs at a celebration for Victoria Holt, Phyllis Whitney, Joan Aiken, Barbara Michaels, and Mary Stewart; and urban fantasy such as Laurel K. Hamilton's *Anita Blake, Vampire Hunter* series, which has sold millions of copies. Anita is no conventional gothic heroine—she is sexually adventurous in the extreme and eager to investigate paranormal mysteries involving vampires and werewolves, some of them reformed and some of them vicious killers. Other successful series are harder to categorize, but certainly have gothic roots. For example, in her Sookie Stackhouse novels, Charlaine Harris has combined the Southern gothic subgenre with light mystery and paranormal romance to create a fictional town where vampires and shapeshifters walk in public and romance humans. The books spawned a popular cable series, *True Blood*, that was as explicit and raw as *Dark Shadows* was naïve and guileless.

Of course, romance novels of all kinds continue to carry the mass market gothic's legacy forward. The subgenre *Gothic Journal* identified as closest to the original gothic, romantic suspense, has endured from the release of *Rebecca* in 1938 to the present day, and there is even a current line called, bluntly, Harlequin Romantic Suspense. Though the story in these books may still revolve around a wealthy man with a large house of some sort, and might even contain ambiguously paranormal elements, the form is flexible enough to encompass everything from light mystery to police procedural. Generally, there is at least some attempt at realism and a mix of the love story with a cozy mystery-style plot. Another subgenre, which achieved its greatest popularity in the first decade of the 21st century, is the paranormal romance, in which heroines become involved with vampires, werewolves, angels, demons, and other mythological creatures. Unlike the original gothics, these books can be and usually are sexually explicit (this, in fact, seems to be one of their chief draws). J.R. Ward's Black Dagger Brotherhood is just one example of many ongoing and highly successful series. A few authors have great fun tipping the quill to their gothic foremothers. Many Regency-set tales show the heroine (and sometimes the hero) reading or attempting to write gothic novels in the style of Ann Radcliffe. Author Brooklyn Ann's *Bite Me, Your Grace* (2013) goes even further, with a heroine who disguises herself as a man in order to publish gothic fiction; *The Vampyr*'s author, John Polidori himself, appears as a minor but pivotal character (and supplies a twist ending more cheerful than the one that befell him in real life).

Young adult publishers in search of the next Harry Potter probably regret the day they rejected Stephenie Meyer's *Twilight*. At least 14 of them passed up Meyer's manuscript before the series became incredibly popular, spawning blockbuster films and earning millions for its creator. Gothic fans would have no trouble recognizing the basic setup of this story, with its echoes of the tried-and-true gothic plot: a young, insecure girl arrives in a spooky, unfamiliar town and is courted by both a reformed vampire and a jealous werewolf while supernatural rivals plot her death. After *Twilight* sold over 50 million copies between 2008 and 2009 alone, paranormal romance exploded in the Young Adult section of every chain bookstore. A number of gothic-style YA novels have appeared in recent years, many featuring teen girls interacting with vampires, mermen, ghosts and other creatures while investigating suspicious goings-on in gloomy buildings. One author, Sarah Rees Brennan, deliberately set about to create a modern gothic, considering herself a fan of the genre[15] and has since released ten novels with gothic themes and settings. Other YA authors have adapted *Rebecca* and fictionalized the lives of the Brontës to form the basis for their novels. Others have updated the stories of Doctors Frankenstein, Jekyll, and Moreau—all of whom, it turns out, had teenage daughters eager for new gothic adventures. Last but not least, as is now well known, *Twilight* itself birthed an unlikely heir to the gothic in the adult bestseller *Fifty Shades of Grey*, with its Byronic hero who plays erotic games in his isolated world of unlimited wealth and power.

Emboldened by these successes, a few mainstream publishers have experimented with reviving the traditional gothic. Harlequin, the largest publisher of romance novels in the world, has occasionally published a traditional gothic as part of its Suspense, Intrigue, or Historical lines, though it has dispensed with the old-style cover cues and uses typical Harlequin clinch poses for the male and female models. In 2010, Harlequin released a stand-alone trade paperback edition of Deanna Raybourn's *The Dead Travel Fast*, which the author describes as "an homage to the classic Gothic with a heroine who fears domesticity and a hero who might or might not be undead."[16] The book, which makes use of both a Transylvanian castle and plot elements from Virginia Coffman's original *Moura*, garnered good reviews and proved popular with Raybourn's fans, but did not lead to any large-scale revival of the gothic genre.

Christian presses have apparently had better success releasing imitation gothic romances, though they do not generally use that term as part of the branding. The titles are reminiscent of old-style gothics: *Shadows of Lanbrooke*, *The Courier of Caswell Hall*, and *Chateau of Secrets* are a few recent entries. "Inspirational" gothics do, in fact, feature updated versions of the traditional 1960s covers, with a manor house in the background and an innocent-looking young woman in the foreground. A few differences, though, distinguish this modern incarnation from its predecessor. The house is shown in daytime and the familiar single light is gone, as is any suggestion of a frightening tower or imposing male figure in the background. The sea, if shown, shimmers bright blue and invites rather than threatens. The woman is not running in fear, and is never in her nightgown, but is demurely clad in respectable street clothes and is usually looking toward the house, showing curiosity but no fear. Back-cover blurbs that mention Cornish settings and suitors who cannot be fully trusted complete the picture. As with old-style gothics, there is no overt sexuality and the suspense is low-key and psychological rather than demonic. Since the focus is on the heroine's (and the reader's) Christian identity, in these stories the heroine's faith helps her cope with unpleasant secrets, mystery, and ultimately leads her into a happy, traditional marriage.

An even more recent development is the proliferation of gothics published in digital form. Whether old-school gothics will ever reappear on bookstore shelves is a matter of conjecture, but an audience—admittedly of an indeterminate size—continues to exist. EBooks, easy to buy and download on a variety of software platforms, are perhaps the perfect solution for genres that have fallen from favor in chain stores or serve small niche audiences.

10. Fading Shadows

Because eBooks are low overhead products and are distributed via digital download, they have no printing costs and need not appeal to large audiences. Instead, ePublishers can experiment with genre and form while targeting specialized groups and still turn a profit. Lovers of the traditional gothic can still find their reading material of choice, both in the form of digital re-issues of some of the classic gothics, such as those by Virginia Coffman, Dorothy Fletcher, and Anne Stuart, and new releases from small publishers who are more attentive to their interests than publishers depending on high-volume sales.

As in the days of Ann Radcliffe, eBooks have allowed women without agents or industry connections to offer their writing directly to the public. Countless small presses have sprung up, many run by women working from home, and romance has quickly claimed this market as its own too. Because of intense competition and lightning-fast turnaround times for manuscripts, eBook authors must and do produce at the rates the old pulp writers reached, sometimes turning out a 20,000-word novella every month, if not more often. Thanks to digital technology, they can finish a story and upload it for purchase on the same day. Independent imprints and self-publishers currently offer gothics ranging widely in content and quality, including both traditional "ingénue at the manor" tales and paranormal-themed romances featuring vampires, werewolves, and witchcraft. Some of these resemble old-style gothic romance down to the last detail; others have been updated to include explicit sex scenes.

Another interesting direction for gothic romance involves the gay and lesbian publishing marketplace. Same-sex love in gothics is not an entirely new concept: in 1980, just as the paperback gothic craze was winding down, Avon Books (home of many gothics as well as *The Flame and the Flower*), released Vincent Virga's *Gaywyck*. In this full-length historical blockbuster, innocent Robert Whyte comes to work at Gaywyck Manor at the turn of the 20th century and finds love with his mysterious master, Donough Gaylord. Cheerfully campy, but passionate and respectful in its homage to gothic tradition and grand romance, this groundbreaking and meticulously researched book employed gothic conventions to forge a new path for diverse popular fiction. The book's title and setting pay tribute to Anya Seton's classic *Dragonwyck*, while its storylines and situations pay tribute to *Jane Eyre*, *Rebecca*, *The Mysteries of Udolpho*, and others.

Virga's book received mass market treatment from Avon, complete with a dramatic cover painting showing Robert and Donough on the rocks in front of the manor house as a stormy sea rages around them. The dark-haired Donough wears a black frock coat and carries his top hat in one hand while he rests the other on Robert's shoulder. Robert, blond and youthful, wears light clothing and looks pensively away from Donough's entreaties. He could be any gothic heroine—and like his female counterparts he accepts the hero's love and, after the book's central mystery is resolved, decides to live with him openly. The book was an instant hit, selling 45,000 copies in the first printing and prompting a second.[17] The doorstopper-sized novel is now a collector's item, though modern readers with modest budgets can access it digitally, along with a few companion volumes by the same author.

Another male/male gothic, Max Pierce's *Master of Seacliff* (2006), boldly re-envisions Holt's original 1960 Gothic, the seminal *Mistress of Mellyn*, with the young tutor Andrew coming to a Gaywyck-style manor on the Hudson in 1899 to teach a young boy and hopefully repair the child's relationship with his father. As in *Mistress of Mellyn*, an unexpected enemy threatens the hero's life, having already done away with Duncan's first male lover. A dour and hateful butler complicates things for Andrew. After a series of gothic adventures and a houseful of secrets uncovered, the two men commit to one another. As the story progresses, Andrew teaches Duncan how to understand and talk to his son, while Duncan shows Andrew how to accept and take pride in his alternative sexuality. Other gothic classics have been given gender-swapping facelifts: a 2012 release, *Timothy* by Greg Herren, is a re-envisioning of *Rebecca* in the era of legal gay marriage, with the male model Timothy taking Rebecca's place in the plot and Mrs. Danvers transforming into a hostile butler; *James Eyre* by Jade Astor (Painted Hearts Publishing, 2016) is a reworked all-male version of Charlotte Brontë's original. This press offers a line of modern same-sex gothics called Dark Desires.

Virga's *Gaywyck* opened with Robert arriving to catalog Donough's rare book collection. This scenario likewise sets up *Castle of Dark Shadows*, self-published by Patty G. Henderson in 2012.[18] The title playfully echoes the Marilyn Ross books of the '60s, as well as the series that still enjoys a cult following today. This story features no gentleman vampire, however; the ingénue is female and so is the love interest, who is the elder daughter of the declining patriarch who owns the estate. In the 1960s and 1970s, gothics had occasionally hinted at or even depicted same-sex love, but almost always used it as shorthand for pathology (as indeed it was considered before the declassification of homosexuality as a mental illness in 1973). For example, a sadistic lesbian affair is the seed of the evil in *Towers of Fear* by Caroline Farr [Richard

10. Fading Shadows

Wilkes-Hunter] (Signet, 1972); the newer books, like Henderson's, are more optimistic. After discovering their love and surviving the usual gothic challenges, including a deadly falling bookshelf and a kidnapping, the two women leave the gloomy castle and its shadows to set up their own home in the city of Boston. There, they become involved with the suffragette cause and spend their afternoons in the symbolic, paranormally fertile garden they build. Henderson has written other novels in the same vein, with covers that echo the classic "woman running from the house" motif. In all of them, the heroine chooses as a love object a strong, independent woman who takes the place of the usual brooding master of the house.

These new gothics, which feature same-sex love affairs, challenge the notion that the genre depends on the subjugation of a weak female by a rage-filled alpha male. As it happens, when the ingénue is male, the story proceeds much like any regular mass market gothic. In *Master of Seacliff*, Duncan starts off as a rude brute who harangues Andrew with more tantrums than any of his 1960s prototypes would have dared. Yet he gradually softens toward Andrew and learns to express his emotions constructively as their relationship grows. The conflict, in turn, hones Andrew's personality and makes him a man. After Andrew has become Duncan's partner, he muses about their future in a reverie that could easily have come from any vintage mass market gothic romance: "What was important to us was that the dark shadow hanging over Seacliff was vanquished, and the promise of a new dawn was on the horizon."[19] In *Castle*, the two women exist in a delightful, politically progressive (if somewhat anachronistic) world in which they delight in what they can do and seldom think about restrictions that might be imposed on them.

Whether the existence of the same-sex gothics affirms or refutes some feminist critics' insistence that gothics (along with other mass market romance lines) were used to turn consumer readers into complacent Stepford wives remains an open question. However, books like Henderson's provide evidence that it is, in fact, possible to construct a satisfying gothic that does not privilege patriarchy or lionize a brutish, domineering man. In this story, the heroine's journey is one of affirmation, and at its end she is able to take her rightful place in society and a household in which she is fully equal. Even better, she is now in a position to use her newfound knowledge to improve the world for other women. Few readers will find this in any way surprising: many of the classic gothics reach the same denouement, albeit by different means. Ultimately, none of the malevolent family members, servants, or even suitors can keep the gothic heroine from self-actualizing. The gothic novel

The Gothic Romance Wave

is, in the end, not about creepy houses or brooding men or even marriage, though each of those elements has its place. Its overarching message is that all worldly (and even some otherworldly) problems can be solved by the power of feminine courage and love.

Could a gothic exist without doomed attractions, a churlish hero, twisted family relationships, surly servants, and the bitterness of social inequality? If so, it might read something like the following hypothetical synopsis:

> *A young woman without fortune or family is surprised when a long-lost relative emerges to inform her that she does indeed have living relatives who are eager to offer her permanent shelter. Gratefully she buys a train ticket and travels to the address she has been given to find that, to her delight, her family owns a magnificent castle with a staff of servants and the means to accommodate her in style. Because they are just, socially-minded people, they use their wealth to do good deeds and run charities; the nearby villagers and servants regard them with a kind of awe due to their generosity and fair-mindedness, a tradition that reaches back several centuries.*
>
> *Everyone is excited and happy to welcome the heroine into the fold. Her new cousins and extended family members immediately form strong bonds with her and express great regret over never knowing of her existence earlier, but a bureaucratic error caused the estrangement without their knowledge. They eagerly make it up to her by ensuring that she gets her fair share of the estate as well as access to a proper education and career. Her social class and gender prove to be no impediment to her advancement.*
>
> *In time, the heroine settles into her new life, working alongside her relatives to enhance the public good and further various social causes. The servants love her and the housekeeper, a matronly woman who has raised strong, independent daughters of her own, becomes a surrogate mother to her. Eventually, a fine young man who is a trusted acquaintance of the family begins a slow, respectful courtship and asks for her hand in marriage. She accepts and everyone is thrilled for the couple, who seem ideally matched. The wedding is lovely and the honeymoon even better. The two settle into the manor house with the rest of the family and continue doing charitable works that endear them to everyone they come in contact with. Of course the heroine continues with a satisfying personal career long after marriage and children, who are well-behaved additions to the family. Their life continues happily until they are well into old age, during which time they never quarrel or think ill of one another even for a moment. Their intelligent, responsible children carry on their legacy.*

No doubt everyone reading this summary, whether skilled in the nuances of literary criticism or not, can see the problems with such a story (unless it is written as a parody). As with Kurt Vonnegut's hobbled ballerinas in "Harrison Bergeron," perfect equality and emotional harmony has been achieved. Yet the plot seems bland at best. A story in which all characters work together with nobility and fairness may fulfill political fantasies, but it does not approach even minimum standards of literary entertainment (whether or

10. Fading Shadows

not it could reflect any possible permutation of human behavior is another question entirely). No challenges have tested the heroine's mettle, no doubts have been raised about her suitor's motives, and no obstacles disrupt the family's happiness. Worse still, the hero is dull and passive, and their happy marriage means nothing to us (and perhaps not even to the couple) because neither has had to struggle for it or perform any grand gesture to win the other's love. Without the claustrophobic gloom of the gothic setting, and a little genuine fear (of the hero, the house, or some other plot element), the scenes avoid melodrama. They also fail to pack any emotional (or even a metaphorical) punch. The vast majority of readers would reject such a story, assuming any author could stay awake long enough to complete it and any publisher would be foolish enough to accept it.

Clearly, unproblematic social relations and instant interpersonal harmony are incompatible with the requirements of gothic fiction and the needs of the reader. Any story, especially one involving mystery and suspense as its driving force, requires conflicts and misunderstands; any mystery requires suspects and red herrings. The conflicts, misunderstandings, and outright dangers the heroine faces as she tries to solve the novel's central puzzle generate reader sympathy and interest, however fleeting and superficial. Her romantic entanglements, likewise, must involve misunderstandings, hurt feelings, and compromise. True, such scenes sometimes (or even often) tend toward excessive sentimentality, but that does not dilute or negate either their purpose or effect. Critics' expectations notwithstanding, most readers do not pick up a paperback gothic in search of a cool political examination of gender roles and the dynamics of heterosexual (some might even say heterosexist) marriage. Their main goal is escape and entertainment, mostly in the form of vicarious empowerment through the heroine's triumph in love and life.

As most romance novelists (and publishers) have realized, women love to talk about their relationships. For whatever social, psychological, or biological reason, finding dates and scoring mates occupies a large part of women's time today, just as it did in the 1960s and '70s, the heyday of the mass market gothic romance. Many of the feminist critics who loathe the interest romance heroines show in the hero probably don't stop to consider that while they are earnestly lecturing about Woolf and Foucault, many more women outside the faculty lounge are busily rating mutual acquaintances as potential mates, planning weddings and baby showers, or complaining about a forgotten anniversary. Plenty of darker conversations go on too—is he cheating? How can she convince her sister to leave her abusive mate? The world

The Gothic Romance Wave

of the romance hero, supposedly so dangerous and misogynistic, seems a virtual paradise compared to what some real-world women go through to earn, keep, or sometime escape their real-world relationships.

In stark contrast, the world of the gothic novel offers a hero and heroine who emerge from their adventures having learned enough about themselves and each other to redefine marriage in a way that shakes off the chains and injustices of the past. Readers most likely sought out gothic after gothic not to experience the lead character's victimization (though some may have been able to identify with it), but to share in the triumph of a heroine who is determined and spunky enough to overcome obstacles, figure out the mystery, and win the love of the male lead, whose motives she has misjudged all along. His strength will only be used for benign purposes where she is concerned; the greater influence is hers. "[N]owhere is the heroine's power over her man more evident than in their sexual relationship," writes one of Krentz's essayists. Yes, "there is danger for her," in that the typical romance hero is both "fierce" and physically powerful. However, because the novel's obstacles have honed her self-awareness and other abilities (detection, sword-fighting, or whatever), "[i]nstead of hurting her, he cherishes her."[20] It is most likely this message, if any, that readers of the 1960s and 1970s gleaned from the mass market gothic romance. Though it may not meet the high standards of theoretical literary feminism, it seems an appropriately empowering one for light popular fiction.

It is probably true that many gothic characters and situations seem outdated and sexist when viewed through 21st-century eyes. In retrospect, however, the novels offer an interesting glimpse of the fledgling women's rights movement in the Nixon era. Whether or not they considered themselves "women's libbers," American women were moving toward greater social power and demanding equality within their marriages as well. The gothic heroine's quest to purify the castle and recalibrate the hero into a supportive mate reflect these two concerns, even if the metaphor was sufficiently subtle that many readers—and apparently most critics—remained entirely unaware of it. Yet the heroine of one gothic after another literally risks her life to restructure the patriarchal castle and its inbred social order to reflect a more egalitarian modern reality. She battles centuries-old curses, evil spirits, and most of all her own fear and despair with courage and determination. Only by holding fast to her values and beliefs, while at the same time opening her heart to love, does she finally gain respect and sexual satisfaction (which is always implied if seldom fully dramatized).

10. Fading Shadows

The gothic hero is likewise transformed by the plot's emotional and physical challenges. Though he often does rescue the heroine from the villain's clutches, she has already rescued him in a less tangible way. By the end of the novel, he has become a more compassionate, less selfish, more understanding man without sacrificing his dynamic personality or romantic charisma. He is caring and giving, both economically and in the bedroom, and he will usually declare his new outlook to the heroine with pride in his own transformation. Her magic has worked on him and restored the castle in a way his angry masculine approach could not. Together they will restore stability and peace to the castle and the community around it. Taking things further, the gothic implies, applying this feminine principle could most likely restore the world.

Many decades have passed since the gothic romance in its original form was the hottest commodity to hit the publishing world. Society and publishing have both moved on, and the innocence of the typical gothic seems out of place in the modern world. On the other hand, the market may have cooled just enough that it's time to turn up the burner again. Will young readers who have most likely never read Victoria Holt and Phyllis Whitney spark a new wave of popular gothics? Vintage paperbacks have strong nostalgic value as cultural artifacts, but there is no denying that a genuinely good story will grab readers at any time. The continuing popularity of *Jane Eyre*, *Rebecca*, and *Wuthering Heights* attest to audiences' ongoing taste for gothic situations, settings, and characters.

If mass market paperback houses do decide to revive the traditional gothic, no doubt they will be sharper, sexier, and probably more feminist than the first wave in the 1960s, even if they are set in the past (and of course setting old plots in the present reinvigorates them). They will feature openly supernatural characters instead of pranks played on the heroine. It remains to be seen whether they will feature women—and perhaps even a man or two—running from a brooding house in bare feet and flimsy nightwear.

Chapter Notes

Preface

1. Jennifer McKnight-Trontz, *The Look of Love: The Art of the Romance Novel* (New York: Princeton Architectural, 2001), 19–20.
2. Ken Gelder, *Popular Fiction: The Logics and Practices of a Literary Field* (New York: Routledge, 2005), 52. One female romance author, Yvonne Roberts, specifically argued against using feminism in her books, prompting Gelder to admit that perhaps a more traditional approach was closer to women's lives and spoke to them more directly—and the message wasn't necessarily to remain subservient.
3. Joanna Russ, *To Write Like a Woman: Essays in Feminism and Science Fiction* (Bloomington: Indiana University Press, 1995), 95. According to Russ, "These are the Modern Gothics. If you look inside the covers, you will find that the stories bear no resemblance to the literary definition of 'Gothic.' They are not related to the works of Monk Lewis or Mrs. Radcliffe, whose real descendants are known today as Horror Stories." Though Russ may be correct about Lewis, whose lurid horror tale *The Monk* is hardly a romance novel in any sense of the word, it is my belief that she is mistaken about Radcliffe, as I hope this study will demonstrate.
4. See, for example, Maya Rodale, *Dangerous Books for Girls: The Bad Reputation of Romance Novels Explained* (Maya Rodale, 2015), 12–13. Bestselling romance author Rodale points out that, to her chagrin, most everyone she meets responds to any mention of the romance industry with a single word: "Fabio!" She wonders, "Why is such a massively powerful and profitable female-driven industry exemplified by a dude?" Ultimately, she decides most people are just too uncomfortable talking about women's sexuality and power, topics the romance novel routinely tackles, so they shrug off the entire issue with embarrassed titters.
5. This common error suggests, at least to me, that people are conflating the gothic genre with its current incarnations, like *Twilight*, or are thinking of the "Satanic gothics" that became popular after the success of *Dark Shadows* and *Rosemary's Baby* in the late 1960s.
6. Pamela Regis, *A Natural History of the Romance Novel* (Philadelphia: University of Pennsylvania Press, 2003), 5–7.
7. Krentz's groundbreaking and enormously successful *Dangerous Men and Adventurous Women* (Philadelphia: University of Pennsylvania Press, 1992) gathered bestselling romance authors to write essays defending the genre and explaining their purpose in writing their stories. The book is a far cry from the first major romance study done by Janice Radway, *Reading the Romance* (1980), in which Radway clearly struggles to conceal her disdain for the novels she describes. A number of romance enthusiasts have followed Krentz and Regis in championing the genre and explaining its empowering message to women.

Chapter 1

1. Kay Mussell, *Women's Gothic and Romantic Fiction: A Reference Guide* (Westport, CT: Greenwood, 1981), 75.
2. Victoria Nelson, *Gothicka* (Cambridge: Harvard University Press, 2012), 2.
3. Clive Bloom, *Gothic Histories: The Taste for Terror, 1764 to the Present* (London: Continuum, 2010), 100–101.
4. "Varney the Vampyre," 9 May 2016, https://dlsummers.wordpress.com/tag/varney-the-vampire/. The blogger reports: "Throughout the novel, the titular hero is villainous, sympathetic, romantic, and even interviewed. In 1166 pages, he embodied just about every major vampire trope I can think of. If I had to tell you what *Var-*

Notes—Chapter 2

ney most reminded me of, it was *Dark Shadows*—not necessarily in the sense of quality, but in the sense that reading Varney was not a little like following a Gothic soap opera!"

5. A Google search "gothic cover art" brings up a number of well-illustrated Pinterest boards, Facebook pages, and blogs devoted to the topic.

6. One of the great ironies of gothic literature is that the book called "A Light in the Window" doesn't seem to have one! (noted on the web page http://flashbak.com/loads-of-women-running-from-houses-the-gothic-romance-paperback-150/). Another variation occurs on the cover of "House in Munich" by Walter Popp Avon. On this cover, the heroine walks toward the house (noted by poster "Ben Grim" on the same web page).

7. According to Piet Schreuders, *Paperbacks, U.S.A.: A Graphic History, 1939–1959* (San Diego: Blue Dolphin, 1981), Donald A. Wollheim is "the hand that lit the mysterious lamp." An editor of Ace Books, Wollheim claimed he could increase sales 5 percent if there was a single light in one upstairs window of the otherwise dark house (114). Conversely, one artist is said to have complained that he once forgot the light and sales of that novel dropped like a stone.

8. http://bookscans.com/Oddities/gothicromance.htm. It seems possible that the author in question was Joan Aiken, who was known to have a sense of humor about her adventures in gothic publishing, and the description of the book's contents seems to fit her novel *The Fortune Hunters*.

9. Bloom, *Gothic Histories*, 130–131.

10. Bloom, *Gothic Histories*, 77.

11. Geoffrey O'Brien, *Hardboiled America: the Lurid Years of Paperbacks* (New York: Van Nostrand Reinhold, 1981), 6.

12. *The Look of Love* points out that the first popular mass-market romance might have arrived as early as 1860, when audiences snapped up 65,000 copies of Ann S. Stephens' *Malaeska, an Indian Princess* (McKnight 10).

13. *The Sheik* is still considered shocking by modern critics, since Hull's heroine and the storyline embraced sexuality in a way that is distasteful today. Interestingly, some of the criticisms leveled at it echo those hurled at Woodiwiss's *The Flame and the Flower* half a century later, most because of the scenes of what is sometimes coyly referred to as "forcible deflowering." It seems odd to mention female liberation and rape as part of the same story, but,

as so often happens, the book was both controversial and popular. It, too, must read in the context of its own time and within its extreme setting and melodrama to be understood (Regis 115). Today, romances set in the Middle East featuring sheiks and virginal ladies are called "sand" romances and are still occasionally published by Harlequin, among others.

14. Mussell, *Women's Gothic and Romantic Fiction*, 16, 62.

15. McKnight-Trontz, *Look of Love*, 12.

16. Margaret Ann Jensen provides a lively history of Harlequin's rise to the pinnacle of romance publishing in her book *Love's $weet Return: The Harlequin Story* (New York: Popular Press, 1984).

17. An excellent and entertaining resource for "nursie" history and reviews can be found at http://vintagenurseromancenovels.blogspot.com/.

18. See https://hauntedhearts.wordpress.com/category/web-of-evil-by-lucille-emerick/ for an image of the cover and a discussion of the novel and cover artist.

19. McKnight-Trontz, *Look of Love*, 13–15.

20. Kathryn Falk, *How to Write a Romance and Get It Published* (New York: Signet, 1990), 304–305 (the agent in question was Jay Garon).

21. Russ, *To Write Like a Woman*, 94.

22. "Magazine Extras: Victoria Holt Feature from the Second Issue of Romantic Times," *RT Book Reviews*, 15 November 2012, http://www.rtbookreviews.com/rt-daily-blog/magazine-extras-victoria-holt-feature-second-issue-romantic-times.

23. This plot was resurrected in Deanna Raybourn's gothic throwback novel, *The Dead Travel Fast* (Ontario: Harlequin, 2010).

24. Dean Koontz, *Writing Popular Fiction* (New York: Writer's Digest, 1972), 5–6.

25. "Ace Cameo Gothic Series," 2010, https://hauntedhearts.wordpress.com/category/ace-cameo-gothics/.

26. "Gothic Lending Library," n.d., https://www.gothicjournal.com/gothic-lending-library/.

Chapter 2

1. Good introductions to Radcliffe's thought and influence may be found at http://academic.brooklyn.cuny.edu/english/melani/novel_18c/radcliffe/ and https://www.bl.uk/romantics-and-victorians/articles/an-introduction-to-ann-radcliffe.

Notes—Chapter 2

2. Krentz, *Dangerous Men*, 63.
3. Jane Austen, *Northanger Abbey* (Project Gutenberg), Chapter 14.
4. Nelson, *Gothicka*, 93.
5. Nelson, *Gothicka*, 99; Ellen Moers coined the term "female gothic" in 1976 in her book *Literary Women*.
6. Horace Walpole, *Castle of Otranto* (Project Gutenberg), Chapter 1.
7. Clara Reeve, *The Old English Baron* (Project Gutenberg), Part 12.
8. Ann Radcliffe, *The Mysteries of Udolpho* (Project Gutenberg), Chapter 4.
9. Regis, *Natural History*, 60.
10. Radcliffe, *The Mysteries of Udolpho*, Chapter 19.
11. Diana Wallace, *Female Gothic Histories: Gender, History and the Gothic* (Cardiff: University of Wales Press, 2013), 19.
12. Radcliffe received £500 for Udolpho while Lane paid about £30 per novel; the usual going rate was £5 to £20, See Martin Tropp, *Images of Fear: How Horror Stories Helped Shape Modern Culture* (Jefferson, NC: McFarland, 1990), 14–15.
13. Russ, *To Write Like a Woman*, 95.
14. Edward Jacobs, "Ann Radcliffe and Romantic Print Culture," in *Ann Radcliffe, Romanticism and the Gothic*, ed. Dale Townshend and Angela Wright (New York: Cambridge University Press, 2014), 55.
15. Franz Potter, *The History of Gothic Publishing, 1800–1835: Exhuming the Trade* (New York: Palgrave Macmillan, 2005), 23.
16. Tropp, *Images of Fear*, 15.
17. Bloom, *Gothic Histories*, 11.
18. Tropp, *Images of Fear*, 16.
19. Tropp, *Images of Fear*, 3.
20. Potter, *Images of Fear*, 23.
21. Tropp, *Images of Fear*, 16.
22. Potter, *History*, 2.
23. Bloom, *Gothic Histories*, 100–101.
24. Mussell, *Women's Gothic and Romantic Fiction*, 5.
25. Mussel, *Women's Gothic and Romantic Fiction*, 8.
26. Several Austen fan web pages contain info on Mrs. Radcliffe, and an imaginary meeting between the two novelists was dramatized in the film *Becoming Jane* (2007); Valancourt Press, an independent publisher based in Richmond, Virginia, and named for the male lead in Ann Radcliffe's *Mysteries of Udolpho*, is currently reissuing many classics of the genre, reprinting the so-called Horrid Novels in the book—books that were often thought to have been Austen's invention but which actually existed (http://www.valancourtbooks.com/jane-austens-northanger-abbey-horrid-novels.html).
27. Tropp, *Images of Fear*, 25.
28. Diana Wallace, in *Female Gothic Histories*, has also pointed out that the plot of *The Sicilian* seems to be what Catherine had in mind with respect to the plot of General Tilney against his wife. It is largely because of Northanger Abbey that Anne Radcliffe is remembered and read today; *Udolpho*, or abridged versions of it, are often bound with *Northanger* for study.
29. Wallace, *Female Gothic Histories*, 58.
30. Nelson, *Gothicka*, 18.
31. The reader review by "Jillon" notes, "Mausoleums, dungeons, bloodletting, sexy priests. Ms. Greer, kindly step out of my brain please. ;)" (https://www.amazon.com/Come-Tower-Love-Lisa-Greer/dp/1475234872).
32. Nelson, *Gothicka*, 3.
33. See, for example, Jan Cohn, *Romance and the Erotics of Property* (Durham: Duke University Press, 1988), 176–177:

> Romance attempts to have it both ways: it seeks in marriage to the supremely attractive and powerful hero the answer to woman's powerlessness, but in doing so it deconstructs itself through an unanswerable contradiction: to reestablish the power relations between men and woman through love and marriage is finally to accede to the conditions imposed by patriarchal society. Marriage remains woman's sole means of access to power, and romantic love—the supreme value in romance fiction—relentlessly defends women against economic self-interest in marriage. Thus, romance ends where it began, its resolution endlessly reenacting the contradiction it exists to dispel.

Cf. Mussell, *Fantasy and Reconciliation* (Westport, CT: Greenwood, 1984), 164: "[R]omances cannot provide permanent reconciliation with [gender] roles and dilemmas, however, for the situations are too extreme and the solutions too shallow. Relief is only temporary, because the reality of women's experience in society is so massive that only repeated reading can assuage the felt discontinuities."
34. Eric Bentley, *The Life of the Drama* (New York: Applause, 2000), 199.
35. Bloom, *Gothic Histories*, 126.
36. Dan J. McNutt, *The Eighteenth Century*

Gothic Novel: An Annotated Bibliography of Criticism and Selected Texts (New York: Garland, 1975), 79.

37. Falk, *How To*, 303.

38. Phyllis Whitney, "Writing the Gothic Novel," *The Writer*, February 1967, 45.

39. Bentley, *Life*, 199.

Chapter 3

1. The Hammer horror films and the lovingly staged Victorian time-travel sequences from the *Dark Shadows* series are good examples from the 1960s; 2015's *Crimson Peak* in the movies and the TV series *Penny Dreadful* (2014–2016) are two more recent examples. Modern novels using Victorian and gothic elements are too numerous to mention, but the entire Zebra Gothic Romance series of the 1990s used this setting, as do many throwback-style modern gothics.

2. Medieval settings, of course, were and still are highly popular in non-gothic historical romance. Additionally, during the heyday of the gothic paperback, some routine costume dramas were packaged or repackaged as mass market gothic romances, complete with the traditional "woman fleeing the castle" covers. For example, Jean Bellamy's *Prisoner of Ingecliffe* (Dell, 1971) is touted as a typical gothic, but is instead a somewhat dreary story of Elizabethan treachery and courtly intrigue. As Elsa Radcliffe puts it in her annotated bibliography of the gothic, "I found this a dull tale—essentially historical romance…. Historical Gothic, maybe, but with emphasis on the historical" (15).

3. Carol A. Senf, *The Vampire in Nineteenth Century English Literature* (Madison: University of Wisconsin Press, 1988), 78.

4. Senf, *The Vampire*, 28.

5. Regis, *Natural History*, 64.

6. Nelson, *Gothicka*, 101.

7. See, for example Julie Pfeiffer, "John Milton's Influence on the Inspired Poetry of Charlotte Brontë," *Brontë Studies* 28, no. 1 (2003) and Peter McInerney, "Satanic Conceits in Frankenstein and Wuthering Heights," *Milton and the Romantics* 4, no. 1 (1980), 10. He quotes Winifred Gerin, the Brontë biographer: "The Brontës' interest in *Paradise Lost*, and particularly Emily's, was intense. Milton's importance was equalled only by Byron's."

8. Kate Ferguson Ellis calls 18th- and early 19th-century gothicists from Walpole to Emily Brontë "Milton's Progeny" in Chapter 3 of *The Contested Castle* (Urbana: University of Illinois Press, 1989).

9. Harold Bloom qtd. in Regis, *Natural History*, 86.

10. James Twitchell, "Heathcliff as Vampire," in *Nineteenth-Century Gothic: At Home with the Vampire (Critical Concepts in Literary and Cultural Studies)*, ed. Fred Botting and Dale Townshend (London: Routledge, 2004), 87. Twitchell stresses that Heathcliff's vampirism is a metaphor, but no small number of modern readers and writers make the connection to vampire literature more explicit, as the publication of novels like Sarah Gray's *Wuthering Bites* (Kensington, 2010) and Amanda Paris's *Heathcliff, Vampire of Wuthering Heights* (CreateSpace, 2010) attests. A vampire-themed *Jane Eyre*, Sherri Browning Erwin's *Jane Slayer*, came out from Gallery Books in the same year.

11. Even today, it is rare to find a blond hero in a traditional romance novel.

12. It is worth noting that Charlotte's other novels, which also lack memorable heroes, have failed to achieve the same success and widespread appeal as *Jane Eyre*.

13. A useful overview of the penny dreadful trade can be found at https://www.bl.uk/romantics-and-victorians/articles/penny-dreadfuls#.

14. Christopher Frayling, *Vampyres: Lord Byron to Count Dracula* (London: Faber and Faber, 1991), 40.

15. Frayling, *Vampyres*, 38.

16. Mussell, *Women's Gothic and Romantic Fiction*, 4.

17. Mussell, *Women's Gothic and Romantic Fiction*, 7, 10. The United States' first homegrown gothic author (who also used American settings for his gothics) was Charles Brockden Brown (1771–1810), who published several successful novels in 1798 and 1799. Mussell notes that his novels differed from those of the female gothic authors by subordinating the romantic relationships in favor of psychological suspense (5).

18. Mussell, *Women's Gothic and Romantic Fiction*, 8.

19. Mussell, *Women's Gothic and Romantic Fiction*, 4.

20. Janice A. Radway, *Reading the Romance: Women, Patriarchy, and Popular Culture* (Chapel Hill: University of North Carolina Press, 1984), 27.

21. O'Brien, *Hardboiled*, 33–35. The connection between paperback romance and typical periodical consumption would prove central to the success of publishers like Harlequin, Dell, and Avon, all publishers of popular mass market gothic romance lines. Readers, they hoped, would start to think of paperbacks the way they thought of magazines, buying a new issue or book each month or perhaps even more often. To this day, Harlequin romances with eye-catching covers are rotated on store shelves once a month, with each separate line of romances instantly recognizable by cover style, title font, and general content.

22. Her grandfather, George du Maurier, was an author and *Punch* cartoonist who created the well-known character of Svengali in the novel *Trilby*, an 1895 bestseller. Interestingly, George was accused of plagiarism, just as his granddaughter Daphne would be with respect to *Rebecca*.

23. See, among other sources, Matthew Dennison, "How Daphne du Maurier Wrote Rebecca," *The Telegraph*, 19 April 2008, http://www.telegraph.co.uk/culture/books/3672739/How-Daphne-du-Maurier-wrote-Rebecca.html.

24. Russ, *To Write*, 94.

25. Controversy later arose when du Maurier was accused of plagiarizing certain elements of *Rebecca*, including the sinister housekeeper, from a 1934 Brazilian novel, *A Sucessora* by Carolina Nabuco, which Du Maurier's publisher had supposedly made available to her while she was struggling to finish her own manuscript (http://mybookgoggles.blogspot.com/2012/06/authors-behaving-badly-daphne-du.html). When the movie came out, another author, Edwina Levin MacDonald, sued over supposed similarities between Rebecca and her novel, 1927's *Blind Windows* (http://www.fractiousfiction.com/rebecca.html). Neither allegation has ever been proven, and du Maurier denied any influence on her novel beyond the basic plot elements and gothic tropes that were common to many other published novels already in print.

26. Guy Barefoot, *Gaslight Melodrama: From Victorian London to 1940s Hollywood* (London: Bloomsbury Academic, 2001), 69–70.

27. From McDermid's useful overview of "Women Crime Writers: Eight Suspense Novels of the 1940s and 1950s" (https://www.nytimes.com/2015/11/01/books/review/women-crime-writers-eight-suspense-novels-of-the-1940s-and-1950s.html).

28. Many identifications of paperback gothic authors can be made with Adrian Room, *Dictionary of Pseudonyms: 13,000 Assumed Names and Their Origins* (Jefferson, NC: McFarland, 2010), 383.

29. "Magazine Extras."

30. A reproduction may be viewed at https://thedwsblog.com/2014/10/26/mistress-mellyn-victoria-holt/.

31. *The Man in Grey*, retitled *A Dark and Splendid Passion*, is one such example. See a reproduction mass market gothic romance style cover at https://www.goodreads.com/book/show/875912.A_Dark_and_Splendid_Passion.

32. Phyllis Whitney, *Guide to Fiction Writing* (Boston: The Writer, 1982), 6.

33. Whitney, *Guide to Fiction Writing*, 8. She goes on to note of 1960s mass market gothic romance publishing: "Now there was a 'bandwagon'—and I was aboard."

34. A useful overview on the clear delineation between female and male literary gothic can be found at https://www.saylor.org/site/wp-content/uploads/2011/04/The-Female-Gothic.pdf.

Chapter 4

1. O'Brien, *Hardboiled*, 130.

2. In fairness, O'Brien points out that Hemingway modeled his sparse style on that of Gertrude Stein, who, he notes wryly, "would make an interesting creation goddess for hard-boiled detective fiction" (66).

3. L. V. Kepert, "'Little Old Lady' Whose Books Sell Millions," *The Sydney Morning Herald*, February 24, 1974, 73.

4. Falk, *How To*, 303.

5. Noted in http://guides.library.unr.edu/nvwriters-hall-of-fame/coffman-1990. The title was also applied to Whitney, among others.

6. In the 18th century, Ann Radcliffe described what constituted, in her view, the difference: "Terror and Horror are so far opposite that the first expands the soul, and awakens the faculties to a high degree of life; the other contracts, freezes and nearly annihilates them.... And where lies the difference between horror and terror, but in the uncertainty and obscurity that accompany the first, respecting the dreading evil?" (http://academic.brooklyn.cuny.edu/english/melani/gothic/terror_horror.html).

7. I am personally in possession of two copies of this strange hybrid book but have no information on how many copies were mis-

Notes—Chapter 5

printed this way, or what (if anything) was done to correct the problem.

8. Rachel Cosgrove Payes, *Gothic Journal*, January/February 1993, 12. This suggests that editors, librarians, and perhaps Payes herself, had a low opinion of gothics even in their heyday, or at least considered them little more than exercises in formula.

9. Elsa J. Radcliffe, *Gothic Novels of the Twentieth Century: An Annotated Bibliography* (Metuchen, NJ: Scarecrow, 1979), 36. *Kirkus Review* was kinder in 1946, when the story was released as a simple cozy: "A gripping, unnerving mystery of a gloomy English mansion with hidden rooms and unused tunnels, whose inmates are not at all above suspicion of three unsolved murders.... Effective mystery atmosphere, with intricate multiple plot" (https://www.kirkusreviews.com/book-reviews/alice-campbell-4/with-bated-breath/).

10. An amusing anecdote appears at https://joanaiken.wordpress.com/tag/joan-aiken-gothic-romance/:

> Authors like Joan Aiken, who might be perfectly aware of the conventions of the genre, and who were more likely to be writing parodies of the style, in the manner of Jane Austen in her own *Northanger Abbey*, could nevertheless find that paperback copies of their novels featured startling images on their covers that bore no relation to the content. Even if your heroine was a jeans-wearing, car-driving, educated working girl, she could still find herself depicted at a complete loss, running away from a haunted house in her nightdress, if the publisher thought this would sell more copies.... Joan Aiken was delighted to discover a copy of one of her own early novels on a New York book stand, with its dramatic Gothic cover showing a girl hot-footing it away from an imprisoning past, the book now hygienically shrink-wrapped and labelled:
> *Used, sanitised, yours for One Dollar!*
> Reader, she bought it....

11. Jane Blackmore, *That Night* (New York: Lancer, 1963), 23.

12. Other "nursie" gothics, with the uniformed nurse fleeing the castle or manor, include *House of Hate* by Dorothy Fletcher (1967), Lois Eby's *House on Nightmare Island* (1966), Joanne Holden's *Nurse at the Castle* (1965), and Peggy O'More's *Seacliff Nurse* (1966), among many others.

13. Radcliffe, *Gothic Novels*, 243.

14. Hester Jane Mundis, *Mercy at the Manor Manor* (New York: Parallax, 1967), 12.

15. Mundis, *Mercy*, 13.

16. For a complete list of *Dark Shadows* titles with synopses and commentary, see http://www.darkshadowsonline.com/pap_lib_books.html.

17. Alice Brennan, *Castle Mirage* (New York: Unibooks, 1971), 34.

18. Qtd. at http://quotesgram.com/jonathan-frid-quotes/.

19. Marilyn Ross, *The Peril of Barnabas Collins* (New York: Paperback Library, 1969), 57–58.

20. This figure is cited in several places, including http://www.darkshadowsonline.com/victoria/dan_ross.html

21. Jane McCarthy, *Carlotta's Castle* (New York: Dell, 1968), 107. Post–*Dark Shadows* vampire protagonists, many of them depicted as attractive and desirable romantic heroes, became the forebears of Anne Rice's Louis and Lestat as well as Stephenie Meyer's Edward Cullen (whose last name echoes that of Barnabas Collins). Contemporary horror author P. N. Elrod even wrote her Jonathan Barrett vampire series with Frid in mind as her hero: "Jonathan was named after actor Jonathan Frid," she tells us on her web page, enthusiastically adding, "Barnabas Collins, YAY! love-you-love-you, woooo-hooo-hooo, yowzah!" (http://www.vampwriter.com/barretts_parlor.htm).

Chapter 5

1. Harry Benshoff, *Dark Shadows* (Detroit: Wayne State University Press, 2011), 83.

2. Nineteen seventies statistics can be found at https://www.thoughtco.com/1970s-feminism-timeline-3528911 and http://www.thepeoplehistory.com/1970.html.

3. Radway, *Reading*, 33.

4. See http://truelovecomicstales.blogspot.com for gothic comic reproductions and commentary on the form. The gothic format was by then so entrenched in popular culture that even Batman got in on the action in 1970 with "The Demon of Gothos Mansion" (reviewed at https://hauntedhearts.wordpress.com/tag/batman/).

5. These blurbs appear on, among many others, a 1968 edition of *The Minerva Stone* by Anne Maybury and Lancer Gothic's *The Ashes of Falconwyk* by Angela Gray in 1971.

6. Isabelle Holland, "'Jane Eyre' Type 'Goth-

Notes—Chapter 6

ics' Flood Bookshelves," *Sarasota Herald Tribune*, August 4, 1974, 11E.

7. A 1969 article notes that "the new trend [in gothics] is toward the supernatural. You can blame *Rosemary's Baby* for that." See Lewis Nichols, "The Gothic Story," *New York Times Book Review*, July 27, 1969, 25.

8. Examples can be viewed at https://haunted hearts.wordpress.com/category/astrological-birthstone-gothics/.

9. *Tule Witch* appears to be unique, as every other gothic cover I found features a Caucasian heroine.

10. Radcliffe, *Gothic Novels*, 61.

11. Dorian Winslow, *The Sorcerers* (New York: Avon, 1973), 104.

12. See http://mysteryfile.com/blog/?p=380.

13. Louisa Bronte [Janet Louise Roberts], *Her Demon Lover*, 18.

14. Louisa Bronte [Janet Louise Roberts] *Her Demon Lover*, 53.

15. Louisa Bronte [Janet Louise Roberts] *Her Demon Lover*, 35.

16. Elna Stone, *Secret of the Willows* (New York: Unibooks, 1970), 68–69.

17. Radcliffe, *Gothic Novels*, 57, 193.

18. Koontz, *Writing*, 116.

19. From http://www.georgerrmartin.com/about-george/speeches/editors-the-writers-natural-enemy/.

20. Dilys Winn, *Mistress Ink* (New York: Workman, 1979), 83.

21. These figures are from Woodwiss's author page at Amazon.com.

22. Pam Proctor, "Phyllis Whitney: She Writes Best Sellers the Old-Fashioned Way." *Parade Magazine*, November 2, 1975, 19.

23. Sarah Wendell and Candy Tan, *Beyond Heaving Bosoms: The Smart Bitches' Guide to Romance Novels* (New York: Fireside, 2009). Wendell and Tan humorously characterize *The Flame and the Flower* as "the Platonic ideal of the bodice ripper.... Woodiwiss works simile and metaphor to limp exhaustion" (11).

24. Jules Archer reports that a survey in 1968 revealed that 64 percent of unmarried college-aged women were willing to engage in premarital sex and 87 percent felt no guilt about specific sexual activities. Of the sexually active women, however, 78 percent insisted on love as a prerequisite (as it is in every popular romance novel). See Jules Archer, *The Incredible '60s: The Stormy Years That Changed America* (New York: Harcourt Brace Jovanovich, 1986), 121.

25. Koontz, *Writing*, 128 (italics his).

26. Radcliffe, *Gothic Novels*, 100.

27. Mussell, *Women's Gothic and Romantic Fiction* (16) notes the explosion of Harlequins at the same time.

28. Elaine Booth Selig, *Mariner's End* (New York: Pocket, 1977), 24–25.

29. Radway, *Reading*, 33.

Chapter 6

1. Nowadays, readers demand the hero's perspective as well. Several chapters will explain how he sees the heroine and why he acts the way he does. In a gothic, the heroine must figure all this out for herself, and her deductions generally lead up to a confession scene. In a multiple point of view book, the reader would perhaps know the answer ahead of the heroine, ruining the suspense (as if a mystery gave away the murderer early on by letting him or her self-identify and describe the crime).

2. Wallace, *Female Gothic Histories*, 17.

3. Ellis, *Contested Castle*, xiii.

4. Mussell, *Women's Gothic and Romantic Fiction*, 6.

5. Regis, *Natural History*, 63.

6. Austen, *Northanger Abbey*, Chapter 29.

7. Du Maurier, *Rebecca*, Chapter 27.

8. Satanic gothics with a more explicit description of the heroine's orgasmic awakening are rare exception, though by modern standards these scenes do not seem especially startling.

9. This has changed in modern gothics, as seen in a 2017 throwback romance, *Deadly Fall* by Elle James, published by Harlequin in its Romantic Suspense line. This novel features a heroine who is a former soldier and professional fighter turned bodyguard: "In a Gothic mansion on a windy coast, former soldier Dixie Reeves and her client, billionaire Andrew Stratford, are in grave danger. The single dad has hired her to help him protect his daughter from a mysterious threat."

10. A typical nursie gothic, *Nurse Missing* by Elizabeth Kellier (1961), is reviewed at http://vintagenurseromancenovels.blogspot.com/2016/04/nurse-missing.html:

When Anne Leatherington, a young R.N., accepted a private case at Craigash, an isolated ancient estate in the Scottish Highlands, she found herself confronted by one mystery after another. Suddenly, a torrent of questions overwhelmed her as she became a victim of her own curiosity. Why was he patient, the seemingly harmless, senile Mrs. McGray, terrified of her own stepson, Charles, the brooding owner of Craigash? And why was his past such a grim secret? But the darkest mystery of all was what had become of Anne's predecessor, the previous nurse who had disappeared in curious circumstances. As Anne glimpsed the terrifying answers she would realize that the truth could destroy her and the man she had come to love.

11. Back cover of Pyramid Gothic edition, 1965.

12. Roberts, *Ravenswood* (New York: Pocket, 1978), 17–18.

13. Amusingly, Dean Koontz cautioned aspiring gothic novelists from using "a real Women's Lib heroine" since most likely such a heroine "would probably not be in the old house, the target of a murderer, consumed by her own terror; instead, she would take matters into her own hands as any man would do, and settle them quickly. She'd end your novel on page thirty! You won't face such problems if you keep that heroine with stereotypical female fears—a fear of the dark, of being alone and ending up an old maid, of rape, of losing the man she loves—and hopes—for a good marriage, love, perhaps children, religious and social contentment" (124).

14. Mona Farnsworth, *The Castle That Whispered* (New York: Award, 1976), 23.

15. Emma Mai Ewing, "Gothic Mania," *New York Times Archives*, http://www.nytimes.com/1975/05/11/archives/gothic-mania.html. This is, incidentally, the same Michael Hinkemeyer whose book *Summer Solstice* disgusted Elsa Radcliffe with its supposedly coarse sexual descriptions.

16. Janice Radway, "The Utopian Impulse in Popular Literature: Gothic Romances and 'Feminist' Protest," in *Locating American Studies: The Evolution of a Discipline*, ed. Lucy Maddox (Baltimore: Johns Hopkins University Press, 1999), 253, 255.

17. Mussell, *Fantasy and Reconciliation*, 74.

18. Mussell, *Fantasy and Reconciliation*, xi.

19. Cohn, *Romance*, 176–167.

20. Mussell, *Fantasy and Reconciliation*, xii.

21. Mussell, *Fantasy and Reconciliation*, xi.

22. Published in *Gothic Journal*, January/February 1992, 3.

23. Radcliffe, *Gothic Novels*, 48.

24. Review of *The Crimson Roses of Fountain Court*. *Gothic Journal*, September/October 1991, 11.

25. See, for example, the definition provided at http://smartbitchestrashybooks.com/2005/03/too_stupid_to_live_double_standards/.

26. Mussell, *Fantasy and Reconciliation*, 97.

27. The domestic test is altered for plain women, Mussell says (98). Intellect and kindness are weighed more heavily than physical attractiveness.

28. Regis, for example, frequently points out the structural connection between comedy and romance novels in her scholarship on the form.

Chapter 7

1. This figure was reported by Andy Lewis in the news item "*Fifty Shades of Grey* Sales Hit 100 Million" (http://www.hollywoodreporter.com/news/fifty-shades-grey-sales-hit-683852).

2. According to Bob Minzesheimer and Anthony DeBarros, "Stephenie Meyer sold more books in 2008 than any other author (22 million, according to her publisher) and did what no one else—not even J.K. Rowling—has done in the 15 years of *USA Today*'s Best-Selling Books" ("Sellers Basked in Stephenie Meyer's *Twilight* in 2008," *USA Today*, January 16, 2009, http://usatoday30.usatoday.com/life/books/news/2009-01-14-top-sellers-main_N.htm).

3. Calculated at http://www.statisticbrain.com/total-twilight-franchise-sales-revenue/.

4. Reported by, among many other sources, http://www.businessinsider.com/fifty-shades-of-grey-started-out-as-twilight-fan-fiction-2015-2.

5. One cannot help but wonder if the Cullen family saga, with its ongoing parade of vampires and werewolves, might have been inspired by the similarly-named Collins family of *Dark Shadows*.

6. The influence of Milton's Satan may be at work here—readers and critics alike have long noticed (and sometimes lamented) that Satan is the most appealing character in the work. Some heroes trace their lineage via Byron's other literary spawn, Lord Ruthven the Vampyr.

7. Kristin Ramsdell, *Romance Fiction: A Guide to the Genre* (Englewood, CO: Libraries Unlimited, 1999), 82.

8. Krentz, *Dangerous Men*, 56.

9. Phyllis Whitney admitted in *The Writer*

Notes—Chapter 7

in February 1967 that she experimented with "giving all these qualities to the villain, and making my hero blond and cheerful, as well as strong, with the result that the villain became the more interesting character" ("Writing the Gothic Novel," 12).

10. In fact, Radcliffe's own *A Sicilian Romance* revolves around the tribulations of Julia Mazzini, but the narrator is a male who relates the story from one remove, much as Lockwood would later narrate *Wuthering Heights*.

11. Radcliffe, *The Mysteries of Udolpho*, Chapter 4.

12. Radcliffe, *The Mysteries of Udolpho*, Chapter 12.

13. As more than one critic has noted, in a modern mass market gothic romance, the sweet and solicitous suitor almost always turns out to be the scheming villain at the end of the story, while the more frightening figure turns out to be misjudged hero whose intentions are pure.

14. Anne Maybury, *Shadow of a Stranger* (New York: Ace, 1960), 76.

15. Maybury, *Shadow of a Stranger*, 46.

16. Maybury, *Shadow of a Stranger*, 65.

17. McCarthy, *Carlotta's Castle*, 43. *Carlotta's Castle* involves a career woman, Brooke, who discovers that she is the long lost heir to a castle. Located in California, the castle was moved brick by brick from Europe by a man who wanted to please his European bride, Carlotta. Alas, the marriage went bad and Carlotta died in the castle under circumstances recalling the demise of Countess Montoni in *Udolpho*. Brooke realizes she cannot possibly maintain the castle and plans to donate it to some nuns who raised her in an orphanage. Her suitor, Piers, seems to have other ideas. As an architect, he would prefer to restore the castle to enhance his professional reputation. He marries her abruptly, leading her to wonder if he is seeking legal control of the castle.

18. Koontz, *Writing*, 128.

19. It might also be noted that Mr. Collins seemed odious to Elizabeth (and the reader), but perfectly adequate as far as Mrs. Bennett, and no doubt many of her peers, was concerned. Charlotte Lucas, an aging spinster, found him tolerable and in some ways a good catch; like the house carpenter's wife, she is about to give him an heir at the close of *Pride and Prejudice*. No demon lover waits for Charlotte in the wings, rendering her a somewhat pitiful figure as she sends her husband into the garden to achieve some relief from his nattering.

20. McCarthy, *Carlotta's Castle*, 203–204.

21. McCarthy, *Carlotta's Castle*, 204.

22. McCarthy, *Carlotta's Castle*, 206–207.

23. Roberts, *Ravenswood*, 174–175.

24. Jean DeWitt Fitz. *The Devon Maze* (New York: Pyramid, 1971), 223.

25. Rita Felski, *Literature After Feminism* (Chicago: University of Chicago Press, 2003), 152.

26. Krentz, *Dangerous Men*, 163.

27. Toni Reed, *Demon-Lovers and Their Victims in British Fiction* (Lexington: University Press of Kentucky, 1988), 7.

28. Like "House Carpenter," this song was popularized by Joan Baez in 1960 (same year as the publication of *Mistress of Mellyn*).

29. The Ross version of Barnabas Collins suggests Ruthven as he might have been if Ruthven had retained his humanity and controlled his thirst for blood. At the end of *The Vampyr*, Ruthven claimed a bride and delights in the idea of destroying both her innocence and her life; Barnabas, unwilling to bind a young and vital woman to a revenant, leaves the heroine and wanders on, a lonely Byronic figure.

30. Krentz, *Dangerous Men*, 65.

31. Sometimes, as in Scott's *Count of Van Rheeden Castle*, the author playfully reverses readers' expectations. For most of the novel, the title (in both senses of the word) seems to refer to one man, who is presented as the hero, while the foil character appears to be a surly, unpleasant sort best avoided. Then, when the heroine uncovers an unsavory truth about the family bloodlines, the former hero shows his true and unsavory colors and the real count emerges to take his place both in the castle and in the heroine's life.

32. Heathcliff's unique combination of erotic allure and undeniable brutality has long presented a dilemma for the readers and authors of derivative popular fiction. The mass market gothic romance solves the problem by splitting him into two men. One really is nasty but looks like a friend. Meanwhile, his ostensibly cruel foil, the Heathcliff figure, is declawed; his supposed transgressions against decency are all the result of a misunderstanding.

33. Victoria Holt, *The Time of the Hunter's Moon* (New York: Fawcett Crest, 1983), 117–118.

34. Holt, *The Time of the Hunter's Moon*, 133–135.

35. Holt, *The Time of the Hunter's Moon*, 138.
36. Holt, *The Time of the Hunter's Moon*, 233–235.
37. Holt, *The Time of the Hunter's Moon*, 364–366.
38. Whitney, "Writing the Gothic Novel," 43.

Chapter 8

1. In her estimation, "a certain kind of low-level but potent theological rumination is constantly taking place" (Nelson, *Gothicka*, 18).
2. One particularly entertaining use of nuns comes in *Carlotta's Castle*, in which the coarse, villainous nuns are hiding a startling secret that is perhaps obvious to the reader long before it is to the heroine.
3. Nelson is able to demonstrate a thread that runs through Gothic cathedrals, medieval manuscripts, and modern popular culture. In *Jane Eyre*, for example, she finds "the classic happy ending of a medieval romance oddly grafted onto the shell of a horror story" (101).
4. For a tongue-in-cheek overview, see http://www.newyorker.com/books/page-turner/bad-romance (which uses Woodiwiss's 1972 *The Flame and the Flower* as a humorous example): "New research suggests that romance novels are deeply dangerous: addictive, mood- and mind-altering, adultery-inducing distractions that make it impossible for women to put down their books and start worshiping their real husbands."
5. This allows the reader to vicariously experience the adventure but without lasting effect—something Gans attributes to popular culture. Its effects are not intended to be transformative, at least not in the short run. Possibly this accounts for the tendency of gothic readers—and romance readers in general—to purchase similar types of novels again and again and again.
6. Krentz, *Dangerous Men*, 57.
7. Bentley, *Life*, 217–218. In their dream lives, people who eschew melodrama often contort themselves like a ham actor, Bentley says. The exercise and perhaps the exorcism of strong emotions in modern orderly society is necessary for psychic health. Women are more in touch with such emotions than men: "Good little boys who keep still and quiet under a rain of blows may pay for their stoicism twenty years later on a therapist's couch" (199). One cannot help but speculate on the implications of male readers' preference for of "tough guy" books.
8. Bentley *Life*, 24; cf. "And a main reason for going to a play, as for reading a novel, will always be the need for emotions that are coherent and continuous as well as strong" (Bentley, *Life*, 39).
9. Bloom, *Gothic Histories*, 133–134.
10. See, for example, Paula R. Backscheider, *Spectacular Politics: Theatrical Power and Mass Culture in Early Modern England* (Baltimore: Johns Hopkins University Press, 1993) and Diane Long Hoeveler, *Gothic Feminism: The Professionalization of Gender from Charlotte Smith to the Brontës* (University Park: Pennsylvania State University Press, 2007). Hoeveler's conclusion is that, "in short, melodrama is a version of the female gothic while the female gothic provides the undergirding for a species of victim feminism, a hyperbolic ideology bent on depicting women as the innocent prey of a corrupt and evil patriarchal system" (9).

An opposing view might be that, although the gothic heroine is occasionally victimized in the course of her adventures, the romance genre's insistence on a happy ending ensures that she will eventually triumph (usually with the hero's help). Romance readers assuredly do not see themselves as victims and do not read gothics or any sort of romance to bask in victim status. Those have written about their enjoyment of the genre have stressed this point over and over. For example, Susan Elizabeth Phillips writes about her life in the late 1970s as a young wife and mother. She and a friend actively read romances, wrote letters of protest to the purveyors of books with rape scenes, and still loved the books, seeing no conflict with their feminism (Krentz, *Dangerous Men*, 53).

11. Peter Brooks, *The Melodramatic Imagination: Balzac, Henry James, Melodrama, and the Mode of Excess* (New Haven: Yale University Press, 1976), 25.
12. As many critics have pointed out, Jane Eyre's famous line "Reader, I married him" is Jane's defiant conclusion to her rollercoaster story. It is not "Reader, he married me"—as one would expect in a Victorian society where women were supposed to be passive, or even "Reader, we married." Instead Jane asserts herself; she is the driving force of her narrative (see, for example, Tracy Chevalier, http://www.huffingtonpost.com/entry/charlotte-bronte-reader-i-married-him_us_5717f9cfe4b0c9244a7acaaf).

13. In more than one gothic, an annoying secondary character takes a fateful step from an upper floor into nothingness.

14. Felski, *Literature After Feminism*, 154.

15. As time went on and books in the "pure" gothic genre became harder to find, the magazine broadened its definition, much to the chagrin of some fans, who did not like reading about books they felt were too far removed from their personal tastes. The emphasis on crime-related suspense turned many off, to judge from the letters column. The journal folded without publishing either an announcement or explanation for its demise. The final issue featured a Nancy Drew retrospective. Possibly material had run dry or subscribers had dropped away, displeased with the publication's new direction. Today, *Gothic Journal* exists only a webpage selling back issues and suggesting other sites for gothic lovers, advertising vintage book stores, and promoting the Gothic Lending Library, an archive of vintage gothic novels readers can rent books from. Back issues of this excellent publication can also be purchased there.

Interestingly, the inclusion of an article on Nancy Drew in the final issue suggests a connection between the teenaged girl mystery series, which debuted in 1930, and the mass market gothic romance of the 1960s. Are gothic heroines just variations on Nancy all grown up and ready to marry? Were the light mysteries Nancy is asked to solve, sometimes involving missing friends and secret passages in creaky old houses, a blueprint for similar gothic plots?

16. Regis, *Natural History*, 60.

17. Krentz, *Dangerous Men*, 55. "[T]he fantasy these novels offered me was one of command and control over the harum scarum events of my life—a fantasy of female empowerment." Other women she talked to confirmed this response as common.

18. Krentz, *Dangerous Men*, 56–57.

19. Krentz, *Dangerous Men*, 57.

20. On the other hand, this plot suits readers perfectly well when the inexperienced young man falls in love with the powerful man who owns the estate where he is employed. Vincent Virga's *Gaywyck* was the first of many male/male gothic romances to follow this trope.

21. Some Gothics do feature a more commonplace hero and a charming, aristocratic villain (for example, Joan Aikin's *The Fortune Hunters* and Claudette Nicole [Jon Messmann]'s *Mistress of Orion Hall*, in which the heroine climbs cliffs, wields a gun, and incapacitates various male characters while wearing only a bikini that miraculously stays in place). These were the forerunners of today's romantic suspense novel, which combines a more or less standard mystery plot with heightened melodramatic situations and sometimes a castle or other gothic setting.

22. Herbert Gans, *Popular Culture and High Culture: An Analysis and Evaluation of Taste* (New York: Basic, 1999), 71.

23. Wendell and Tan note, as have many others, that mystery novels might also be called formulaic. After all, in most cases there is a murder, some suspects are considered, and eventually the correct perpetrator is unmasked and brought to justice. "Of course, Mystery novels are socially and culturally acceptable reading material," they say, perhaps because "they are often about violence, crime, murder and bloodshed rather than "sex, emotions, happiness, and love" (*Beyond Heaving Bosoms*, 123).

24. The (Protestant) Grimm brothers' stripping away of most of the "fairy" elements from the original French (Catholic) versions brings to mind Victoria Nelson's observations about the gaping psychic hole left by post–Age of Reason society's rejection of the numinous, especially in Protestant countries (see, for example, https://fairycolumbine.wordpress.com/about/fairy-tales/). England and Germany, not coincidentally, are where gothics flourished. In the modern era, many mass market gothic romances from the 1960s and 1970s have been translated into German and still turn up frequently on eBay.

25. It should be noted that retelling and reinterpreting a popular fairy tale like "Beauty and the Beast" or "Cinderella" is a standard trope in romance novels of all stripes.

26. Jack Zipes, *The Irresistible Fairy Tale: The Cultural and Social History of a Genre* (Princeton: Princeton University Press, 2012), 2.

27. Radcliffe, *Gothic Novels*, x.

28. Waverly Fitzgerald, "The Heroine's Quest in the Gothic Novel," *Gothic Journal*, September/October 1993, 16.

29. Fitzgerald, "The Heroine's Quest," 14.

30. "[I]f art did not treat violence, it could not go to the heart of things. Without violence, there would be nothing in the world but goodness, and literature is not mainly about goodness: it is mainly about badness" (Bentley, *Life*, 221).

Chapter 9

1. Qtd. in http://smartbitchestrashybooks.com/2015/10/plagiarism-the-pattern-and-the-response/.
2. http://smartbitchestrashybooks.com/2015/10/plagiarism-the-pattern-and-the-response/.
3. Mussell, *Women's Romantic*, 8. Interestingly, and perhaps ironically, Demi Moore's recent film version of *The Scarlet Letter* decided to inject some sexy "bodice ripper" action to interest modern audiences.
4. Sociology professors Jen Lois and Joanna Gregson also note that "we've interviewed *New York Times* bestselling romance authors who still get told, 'That is so great you are successful at this; maybe someday you'll write a *real* book'" (http://popularromanceproject.org/stigma-surprise/).
5. Sarah S.G. Frantz and Eric Murphy Selinger, eds., *New Approaches to Popular Romance Fiction: Critical Essays* (Jefferson, NC: McFarland, 2012), 60. Mary Bly herself provides an interesting case study. An interview with her reveals that "Mary Bly is a Shakespearean scholar at Fordham University, with degrees from Harvard, Oxford, and Yale. Unbeknownst to nearly everyone except her family—which famously includes her father, the poet Robert Bly, and her mother, the short-story writer Carol Bly—for the past five years she's been living a parallel life as the best-selling historical-romance author Eloisa James, whose eight novels include titles such as *Fool for Love, Your Wicked Ways*, and the just-published *Much Ado About You*" (http://nymag.com/nymetro/arts/books/10870/).
6. http://womenrunningfromhouses.blogspot.com/.
7. Koontz, *Writing*, 116.
8. Proctor, "Phyllis Whitney," 20.
9. Gans, *Popular Culture*, xii.
10. Regis, *Natural History*, 207; she goes on to "assert that [these values] are the impossible dream of millions of women in many parts of the world today" and to defend that dream as an entirely proper basis for literary entertainment.
11. Gans, *Popular Culture*, 35.
12. Gans, *Popular Culture*, 76.
13. Krentz notes Radway's bias, such as mocking one of her interviewees for wearing a lavender pantsuit (surely unremarkable in the late 1970s).
14. Russ, *To Write*, 95.
15. Russ, *To Write*, 96.
16. Russ, *To Write*, 96; capital letters and italics in original.
17. Russ, *To Write*, 111; italics hers.
18. Russ, *To Write*, 108–109.
19. Russ, *To Write*, 111.
20. Russ, *To Write*, 115–118. Her main target is Susan Howatch, who went on to be considered a master of suspense novels and is ironically far better known than Russ, who also wrote fiction.
21. Seidel specifically notes that

    Mystery readers don't expect much description of hair styles and sleeve length.

    Romance readers do. They are interested in the physical detail of the fantasy world. They want to know what the characters look like; they want clothes and rooms described.

    Critics often ridicule as trivial this attention to detail in romances, particularly in regard to setting, but, as in any work of fiction, a carefully presented setting helps the reader suspend disbelief. Moreover, in a romance the setting itself may be part of the fantasy [Krentz, *Dangerous Men*, 165].

22. Susan Howatch, "Realism in Modern Gothics," *The Writer*, 87 no. 5 (May 1974), 11.
23. Tania Modelski, *Loving with a Vengeance* (Hamden, CT: Archon, 1982), 60.
24. Modelski, *Loving*, 61.
25. Notably, parents are seldom depicted in the gothic, though the hero may have a ward or motherless child living with him. Mussell's *Fantasy and Reconciliation* posits the main portion of the heroine's domestic test as making this orphan avoid the heroine's pain in this respect.
26. Russ again presages (and probably inspired) Modleski when she characterizes the plots as dependent on "a kind of justified paranoia: people are planning awful things about you" (Russ, *To Write*, 108).
27. Modelski, *Loving*, 61–62.
28. Regis, *Natural History*, 12–13.
29. Glen Thomas, "Happy Readers or Sad Ones? Romance Fiction and the Problems of the Media Effects Model," in *New Approaches to Popular Romance Fiction: Critical Essays*, ed. Sarah S.G. Frantz and Eric Murphy Selinger (Jefferson, NC: McFarland, 2012,) 207.
30. Thomas sees the variety of romance types on the market as evidence of this—such as historical, suspense, inspirational, Regency, contemporary and gothic ("Happy Readers," 211–213).

31. Gans, *Popular Culture*, 43, 46.
32. Yankelovich, qtd. in Mussell, *Women's Gothic*, 107; Cf. Thomas 210:
> Bonnie Williams argues that romance readers have better sex lives than non-readers because romance novels allow their readers to "get in the mood." She cites a staggering statistic from *Psychology Today* that asserts that women who read romances "make love with their partners 74% more often than women who don't, which does suggest that men everywhere could save money on flowers and chocolates in favor of the latest release from Harlequin…. Here, no-fun critics of romance fiction have allowed their anti-libidinal prejudices to blind them to the fact that when it comes to what Caitlin Flanagan calls the whoopee hour, the behaviorist effects of romance fiction make women's lives a lot more interesting.

33. As just one example, *The Feminine Mystique* by Betty Friedan came out in 1963, sparking mainstream discussion of feminism, only three years after the first mass market gothic romances were published under that label.
34. Krentz, *Dangerous Men*, 64–65.
35. Krentz, *Dangerous Men*, 27.
36. Krentz, *Dangerous Men*, 172.
37. Radcliffe, *Gothic Novels*, x.
38. As Gans notes, people who perceive themselves as high culture would not dream of enjoying the popular culture embraced by the lower class, except to study or criticize it (Gans, *Popular Culture*, 144).
39. For example, the title of Holt's *Mistress of Mellyn* refers to both the heroine and the crime victim she must avenge.

Chapter 10

1. Holland, "'Jane Eyre' Type 'Gothics,'" 11E. By the late 1970s, Isabelle Holland (1920–2002) was herself an acclaimed gothic author. *Gothic Journal* profiled her in its April/May 1995 issue.
2. While publishers who wrote to the *Journal* claimed sales were down, authors and readers complained they could not find the titles in stores, inevitably resulting in low sales and creating a vicious supply/demand circle that ultimately doomed the gothics.
3. Information about various gothic lines, authors, and titles can be found at http://www.romancewiki.com/.
4. Jo-Ann Power, "Reading Between the Lines," *Gothic Journal*, November/December 1992, 14.
5. Karin Stoeker, Letter, *Gothic Journal*, May/June 1991, 3.
6. Georgia Walden, Letter, *Gothic Journal*, September/October 1991, 5.
7. Marion Schultz, "Writing Sexy for the Gothics," *Gothic Journal*, July/August 1992, 7.
8. Rachel Cosgrove Payes, Letter, *Gothic Journal*, July/August 1992, 9.
9. Rachel Cosgrove Payes, "Gothics: The Stepchildren of the Romance Field," *Gothic Journal*, January/February 1993, 13.
10. Kristi Lyn Glass, editorial note, *Gothic Journal*, July/August 1992, 6.
11. A summary can be found at http://www.samuelfrench.com/p/1157/the-bride-of-brackenloch-a-ghastly-gothic-thriller.
12. Kristi Lyn Glass, editorial note, *Gothic Journal*, July/August 1992, 6.
13. Bloom, *Gothic Histories*, 181.
14. Radcliffe, *Gothic Novels*, x.
15. See http://www.signature-reads.com/2012/10/a-qa-with-sarah-rees-brennan-author-of-the-gothic-inspired-unspoken/.
16. See the author's home page at http://deannaraybourn.com/blog/in-which-it-wouldnt-be-october-without-the-dead-travel-fast/.
17. Falk, *How To*, 307.
18. The earliest openly lesbian gothic may have been *The Marquise and the Novice*, published in 1981 by Naiad Press. To date, Patty G. Henderson has released a total of four retro-style historical gothics featuring all-female love stories.
19. Max Pierce, *Master of Seacliff* (New York: Haworth, 2007), 177. Of course, Andrew and Duncan have a few more hair-raising adventures before they find real peace together.
20. Krentz, *Dangerous Men*, 129.

Bibliography

"Ace Cameo Gothic Series." https://haunted hearts.wordpress.com/category/ace-cameo-gothics/. 2010.

Archer, Jules. *The Incredible '60s: The Stormy Years That Changed America*. New York: Harcourt Brace Jovanovich, 1986.

Austen, Jane. *Northanger Abbey*. 1818. Project Gutenberg, 1994. http://www.gutenberg.org/ebooks/121.

Barefoot, Guy. *Gaslight Melodrama: From Victorian London to 1940s Hollywood*. London: Bloomsbury Academic, 2001.

Bellamy, Jean *Prisoner of Ingecliffe*. New York: Dell, 1971.

Benshoff, Harry. *Dark Shadows*. Detroit: Wayne State University Press, 2011.

Bentley, Eric. *The Life of the Drama*. New York: Applause, 2000.

Bloom, Clive. *Gothic Histories: The Taste for Terror, 1764 to the Present*. London: Continuum, 2010.

Brennan, Alice. *Castle Mirage*. New York: Unibooks, 1971.

Bronte, Louisa [Janet Louise Roberts]. *Her Demon Lover*. New York: Avon, 1973.

Brooks, Peter. *The Melodramatic Imagination: Balzac, Henry James, Melodrama, and the Mode of Excess*. New Haven: Yale University Press, 1976.

Claudia, Susan [William Johnston]. *Madness at the Castle*. New York: Signet, 1966.

Cohn, Jan. *Romance and the Erotics of Property*. Durham: Duke University Press, 1988.

Dennison, Matthew. "How Daphne du Maurier Wrote *Rebecca*." *The Telegraph*, April 19, 2008. http://www.telegraph.co.uk/culture/books/3672739/How-Daphne-du-Maurier-wrote-Rebecca.html.

du Maurier, Daphne. *Rebecca*. New York: Modern Library, 1938.

Ellis, Kate. *The Contested Castle: Gothic Novels and the Subversion of Domestic Ideology*. Urbana: University of Illinois Press, 1989.

Elrod, P.N. "Welcome to Barrett's Parlor." http://www.vampwriter.com/barretts_parlor.htm. 2011.

Falk, Kathryn. *How to Write a Romance and Get It Published*. New York: Signet, 1990.

Farnsworth, Mona. *The Castle That Whispered*. New York: Award, 1976.

Felski, Rita. *Literature After Feminism*. Chicago: University of Chicago Press, 2003.

Fitz, Jean DeWitt. *The Devon Maze*. New York: Pyramid, 1971.

Fitzgerald, Waverly. "The Heroine's Quest in the Gothic Novel." *Gothic Journal*, September/October 1993.

Frayling, Christopher. *Vampyres: Lord Byron to Count Dracula*. London: Faber & Faber, 1991.

Frenier, Miriam Darce. *Good-Bye Heathcliff: Changing Heroes, Heroines, Roles, and Values in Women's Category Romances*. New York: Greenwood, 1988.

Gans, Herbert. *Popular Culture and High Culture: An Analysis and Evaluation of Taste*. 2nd ed. New York: Basic, 1999.

Gelder, Ken. *Popular Fiction: The Logics and Practices of a Literary Field*. New York: Routledge, 2005.

"Gothic Lending Library." https://www.gothicjournal.com/gothic-lending-library/. n.d.

"The Gothic Romance." http://bookscans.com/Oddities/gothicromance.htm. n.d.

Hamrick, Craig. "A Conversation with Dan Ross." Dark Shadows Online. 2004. http://

Bibliography

www.darkshadowsonline.com/victoria/dan_ross.html.

"Harlequin Gothic Romance." https://www.romancewiki.com/Harlequin_Gothic_Romance. 2008.

Henderson, Patty G. *Castle of Dark Shadows*. CreateSpace, 2012.

Holland, Isabelle. "'Jane Eyre' Type 'Gothics' Flood Bookshelves." *Sarasota Herald Tribune*, August 4, 1974, 11E.

Holt, Victoria. *Mistress of Mellyn*. New York: Fawcett Crest, 1960.

———. *The Time of the Hunter's Moon*. New York: Fawcett Crest, 1983.

Howatch, Susan. "Realism in Modern Gothics." *The Writer*, May 1974.

Jacobs, Edward. "Ann Radcliffe and Romantic Print Culture." *Ann Radcliffe, Romanticism and the Gothic*, edited by Dale Townshend and Angela Wright, 49–66. New York: Cambridge University Press, 2014.

Jennings, Gary. "Heathcliff Doesn't Smoke L & Ms." *New York Times Book Review*, July 27, 1969.

Jensen, Margaret Ann. *Love's $weet Return: The Harlequin Story*. New York: Popular Press, 1984.

Jones, Ann Rosalind. "Mills and Boon Meets Feminism." *The Progress of Romance: The Politics of Popular Fiction*, edited by Jean Radford. New York: Routledge, 1986.

Kepert, L. V. "'Little Old Lady' Whose Books Sell Millions." *The Sydney Morning Herald*, February 24, 1974.

Koontz, Dean. *Writing Popular Fiction*. New York: Writer's Digest, 1972.

Krentz, Jayne Ann, ed. *Dangerous Men and Adventurous Women: Romance Writers on the Appeal of Romance*. Philadelphia: University of Pennsylvania Press, 1992.

Lamb, Joyce. "Romance, Gender, and the Measure of a 'Real Book.'" *USA Today*, August 12, 2013. http://happyeverafter.usatoday.com/2013/08/12/joanna-gregson-jen-lois-romance-sociology/.

"Loads of Women Running from Houses: The Gothic Romance Paperback." Flashbak. http://flashbak.com/loads-of-women-running-from-houses-the-gothic-romance-paperback-150/, 13 June 2014.

Lois, Jen, and Joanna Gregson. "Stigma and Surprise." 2014. Accessed 6 June 2016. http://popularromanceproject.org/stigma-surprise/.

"Magazine Extras: Victoria Holt Feature from the Second Issue of *Romantic Times*." *RT Book Reviews*, November 15, 2012. http://www.rtbookreviews.com/rt-daily-blog/magazine-extras-victoria-holt-feature-second-issue-romantic-times.

Maybury, Anne. *Shadow of a Stranger*. New York: Ace, 1960.

McCarthy, Jane. *Carlotta's Castle*. New York: Dell, 1968.

McInerney, Peter. "Satanic Conceits in Frankenstein and *Wuthering Heights*." *Milton and the Romantics* 4, no. 1 (1980): 1–15.

McKnight-Trontz, Jennifer. *The Look of Love: The Art of the Romance Novel*. New York: Princeton Architectural, 2001.

McNutt, Dan J. *The Eighteenth Century Gothic Novel: An Annotated Bibliography of Criticism and Selected Texts (Garland Reference Library of the Humanities vol. 4)*. New York: Garland, 1975.

Modleski, Tania. *Loving With a Vengeance*. Hamden, CT: Archon, 1982.

Moers, Ellen *Literary Women: The Great Writers*. New York: Anchor, 1977.

Mundis, Hester Jane. *Mercy at the Manor Manor*. New York: Simon & Schuster, 1967.

Mussell, Kay. *Fantasy and Reconciliation: Contemporary Formulas of Women's Romance Fiction (Contributions in Women's Studies)*. Westport, CT: Greenwood, 1984.

———. *Women's Gothic and Romantic Fiction: A Reference Guide (American Popular Culture)*. Westport, CT: Greenwood, 1981.

Nelson, Victoria. *Gothicka*. Cambridge: Harvard University Press, 2012.

Nichols, Lewis. "The Gothic Story." *New York Times Book Review*, July 27, 1969.

O'Brien, Geoffrey. *Hardboiled America: the Lurid Years of Paperbacks*. New York: Van Nostrand Reinhold, 1981.

Payes, Rachel Cosgrove. "Gothics: The Stepchildren of the Romance Field." *Gothic Journal*, January/February 1993.

———. Letter. *Gothic Journal*, July/August 1992.

Pfeiffer, Julie. "John Milton's Influence on the

Inspired Poetry of Charlotte Brontë." *Brontë Studies* 28, no. 1 (2003): 37–45.

Pierce, Max. *The Master of Seacliff.* New York: Haworth, 2007.

Potter, Franz. *The History of Gothic Publishing, 1800–1835: Exhuming the Trade.* New York: Palgrave Macmillan, 2005.

Power, Jo-Ann. "Reading Between the Lines." *Gothic Journal*, November/December 1992.

Proctor, Pam. "Phyllis Whitney: She Writes Best Sellers the Old-Fashioned Way." *Parade Magazine*, November 2, 1975, 19–20.

Radcliffe, Ann. *The Mysteries of Udolpho.* 1794. Project Gutenberg, 2002. http://www.gutenberg.org/ebooks/3268.

Radcliffe, Elsa J. *Gothic Novels of the Twentieth Century: An Annotated Bibliography.* Metuchen, NJ: Scarecrow, 1979.

Radway, Janice A. *Reading the Romance: Women, Patriarchy, and Popular Culture.* Chapel Hill: University of North Carolina Press, 1984.

———. "The Utopian Impulse in Popular Literature: Gothic Romances and 'Feminist' Protest." *Locating American Studies: The Evolution of a Discipline*, edited by Lucy Maddox. Baltimore: Johns Hopkins, 1999. 235–260.

Ramsdell, Kristin. *Romance Fiction: A Guide to the Genre.* Englewood, CO: Libraries Unlimited, 1999.

Raybourn, Deanne. "In Which It Wouldn't Be October Without *The Dead Travel Fast*." http://deannaraybourn.com/blog/in-which-it-wouldnt-be-october-without-the-dead-travel-fast/. 2014.

Reed, Toni. *Demon-Lovers and Their Victims in British Fiction.* Lexington: University Press of Kentucky, 1988.

Reeve, Clara. *The Old English Baron.* 1778. Project Gutenberg, 2009. http://www.gutenberg.org/ebooks/5182.

Regis, Pamela. *A Natural History of the Romance Novel.* Philadelphia: University of Pennsylvania Press, 2003.

Roberts, Janet Louise. "An Expert Takes the Mystery Out of Writing and Selling the Gothic." *Writer's Digest*, January 1973.

———. *Ravenswood.* 2nd ed. New York: Pocket, 1978.

Rodale, Maya. *Dangerous Books for Girls: The Bad Reputation of Romance Novels Explained.* Maya Rodale, 2015.

Room, Adrian. *Dictionary of Pseudonyms: 13,000 Assumed Names and Their Origins.* 5th ed. Jefferson, NC: McFarland, 2010.

Ross, Clarissa [William Edward Daniel]. *Barnabas Collins and the Mysterious Ghost.* New York: Paperback Library, 1970.

———. *The Peril of Barnabas Collins.* New York: Paperback Library, 1969.

———. *Secret of the Pale Lover.* New York: Lancer, 1969.

Russ, Joanna. *To Write Like a Woman: Essays in Feminism and Science Fiction.* Bloomington: Indiana University Press, 1995.

Samuel French, Inc. "The Bride of Brackenloch! A Ghastly Gothic Thriller?" http://www.samuelfrench.com/p/1157/the-bride-of-brackenloch-a-ghastly-gothic-thriller. n.d.

Schreuders, Piet. *Paperbacks, U.S.A.: A Graphic History, 1939–1959.* San Diego: Blue Dolphin, 1981.

Schultz, Marion. "Writing Sexy for the Gothics." *Gothic Journal*, July/August 1992.

Scott, Annjeanette [Scott Wright]. *Count of Van Rheeden Castle.* New York: Popular Library, 1976.

Selig, Elaine Booth. *Mariner's End.* New York: Pocket, 1977.

Senf, Carol A. *The Vampire in Nineteenth Century English Literature.* Madison: University of Wisconsin Press, 1988.

"Silhouette Shadows." http://www.romancewiki.com/Silhouette_Shadows. 2008.

Spectergirl. "Women Running from Houses: A Gothic Novel Reading List." http://womenrunningfromhouses.blogspot.com/. 2013.

Stoecker, Karin. Letter. *Gothic Journal*, May/June 1991.

Stone, Elna. *Secret of the Willows.* New York: Unibooks, 1970.

Sullivan, Kate. "A Q&A with Sarah Rees Brennan, Author of the Gothic-Inspired Unspoken." http://www.signature-reads.com/2012/10/a-qa-with-sarah-rees-brennan-author-of-the-gothic-inspired-unspoken/. 2012.

Thomas, Glen. "Happy Readers or Sad Ones? Romance Fiction and the Problems of the

Bibliography

Media Effects Model." *New Approaches to Popular Romance Fiction: Critical Essays*, edited by Sarah S.G. Frantz and Eric Murphy Selinger, 206–217. Jefferson, NC: McFarland, 2012.

Thurston, Carol. *The Romance Revolution: Erotic Novels for Women and the Quest for a New Sexual Identity*. Urbana: University of Illinois Press, 1987.

Tropp, Martin. *Images of Fear: How Horror Stories Helped Shape Modern Culture (1818–1918)*. Jefferson, NC: McFarland, 1990.

Twitchell, James. "Heathcliff as Vampire." *Nineteenth-Century Gothic: At Home with the Vampire (Critical Concepts in Literary and Cultural Studies)*, edited by Fred Botting and Dale Townshend, 80–88. London: Routledge, 2004.

"Varney the Vampyre." https://dlsummers.wordpress.com/tag/varney-the-vampire/. 2016.

"Vintage Nurse Romance Novels." http://vintagenurseromancenovels.blogspot.com/. 2010.

Walden, Georgia. Letter. *Gothic Journal*, September/October 1991.

Wallace, Diana. *Female Gothic Histories: Gender, History and the Gothic*. Cardiff: University of Wales Press, 2013.

Walpole, Horace. *Castle of Otranto*. 1764. Project Gutenberg, 1996. http://www.gutenberg.org/ebooks/696.

"The Web of Evil." https://hauntedhearts.wordpress.com/. 2013.

Wendell, Sarah. "Plagiarism: The Pattern and the Response." 2015. http://smartbitchestrashybooks.com/2015/10/plagiarism-the-pattern-and-the-response/.

Wendell, Sarah, and Candy Tan. *Beyond Heaving Bosoms: The Smart Bitches' Guide to Romance Novels*. New York: Fireside, 2009.

Whitney, Phyllis. *Guide to Fiction Writing*. Boston: The Writer, 1982.

_____. "Writing the Gothic Novel." *The Writer*, February 1967.

Winn, Dilys. *Mistress Ink*. New York: Workman, 1979.

Winslow, Dorian. *The Sorcerers*. New York: Avon, 1973.

Zipes, Jack. *The Irresistible Fairy Tale: The Cultural and Social History of a Genre*. Princeton: Princeton University Press, 2012.

Index

Abbot, Rick 152, 177n
alpha hero 43, 106, 107, 141, 159
aristocracy, portrayal of in gothics 2, 16, 26, 27, 40, 43, 46, 49, 57, 68, 75, 85, 109, 131
Arnold, Matthew 39, 128
Austen, Jane 26, 59, 90, 91, 124; *Northanger Abbey* 3, 27, 30, 33, 34, 37, 41, 43, 53, 121
Avallone, Michael 61, 63, 70, 73, 77, 82
Avon Books 74, 77, 78, 84, 87, 157

Baez, Joan 116, 173n
ballads 7, 106, 116, 117
Bantam Books 73, 88, 98
The Beatles 20, 73
Bentley, Eric 36-37, 122, 165
Bloom, Clive 10, 16, 32, 33, 36, 123, 153
bodice rippers 15, 86, 136, 139
Bradley, Marion Zimmer 83
Brennan, Alice 77, 96, 120
The Bride of Brackenloch see Abbot, Rick
Brock, Rose see Hansen, Joseph
Brontë, Anne 110, 166; *Agnes Grey*, 44; *Tenant of Wildfell Hall* 44, 110
Brontë, Charlotte 39, 43-45, 117, 158; *Jane Eyre* 3, 4, 10, 19, 24, 40, 42-44, 48-51, 61, 66, 79, 92-94, 101-102, 109, 110, 124, 129, 143, 163
Brontë, Emily 39-40, 43, 48, 117; *Wuthering Heights* 3, 10, 40, 43-45, 52, 56, 90, 110, 163
Bronte, Louisa 79, 87; *see also* Roberts, Janet Louise
Brontë sisters 5, 15, 27, 39, 43, 46, 50, 52, 56, 90, 109, 116, 117, 119, 140, 155
Brown, Charles Brockden 33
Byron, Lord (George Gordon) 42-44, 54, 106, 109, 110, 155

Carlotta's Castle 71, 96, 103, 112, 114; *see also* McCarthy, Jane
The Castle of Otranto see Walpole, Horace
Coffman, Virginia 16, 20, 37, 63, 74, 78, 121, 126, 127, 157; *Moura* series 19, 56, 70, 85, 113, 124, 156
Coleridge, Samuel Taylor 15, 35
Collins, Barnabas 54, 67-71, 73, 77, 167; *see also Dark Shadows*

Collins, Quentin 67, 69, 70; *see also Dark Shadows*
cover art 2, 5-7, 10-11, 17, 21-23, 49, 52, 56-59, 63- 67, 71, 73, 75-77, 89, 96, 123-124, 127, 151, 156, 159

Danvers, Mrs. 93, 158; *see also* Du Maurier, Daphne
Dark Shadows 7, 20, 21, 56, 62, 65-71, 73-74, 77, 123
demonic hero 43, 117, 118, 156
De Winter, Mrs. 49, 92-94, 102, 103; *see also* Du Maurier, Daphne
dimwitted heroines 86, 127
Dracula see Stoker, Bram
Dragonwyck see Seton, Anya
du Maurier, Daphne 3, 27, 51, 52, 63, 75, 77, 93, 140; *Rebecca* 3, 10, 12, 17, 19, 48-52, 58, 61, 66, 87, 93, 102, 103, 110, 114, 123, 154, 155, 157, 158, 163

Edwardian era 15, 50, 75, 78

fairy tales 27, 125, 128, 131-133, 148
Fawcett-Crest Books 60, 73, 98, 166
feminism 3, 4, 7, 31, 36, 146, 162
feminists 73, 90, 120, 136, 147; critics 49, 85, 86, 110, 139, 140, 159, 161
feudalism 4, 28, 39, 75, 103, 108, 113, 125, 128, 130
Fielding, Henry 25, 26
Fifty Shades of Grey see James, E.L.
Fitzgerald, Waverley 132, 133, 165
The Flame and the Flower see Woodiwiss, Kathleen
Fontaine, Joan 49, 66
Frankenstein see Shelley, Mary
Frenier, Miriam Darce 112, 113, 139, 165
Freudianism 12, 27, 64

Gans, Herbert 103, 104, 125, 126, 130, 138, 140, 145
gargoyles 39, 77
gay characters in gothics 157, 158
Gaywyck see Virga, Vincent

183

Index

Gothic Journal 6, 11, 21, 93, 126, 132, 146–147, 151–154
governesses 14, 15, 19, 21, 41- 45, 51, 66, 77–78, 86–87, 92, 94, 101, 124, 130, 149, 153
graphic content 21, 84, 86, 153
Gregson, Joanna 35, 135, 136

Hammet, Dashiell 48, 55
hardboiled mysteries 16, 48, 55, 83, 104, 166
hardcover editions 17, 48, 137, 153
Harlequin Romances 17, 18, 21, 36, 53, 57, 74, 83, 86, 126, 139, 142–143, 151–156
Haworth 37, 43, 56, 79, 167; *see also* Brontë sisters
Hawthorne, Nathaniel 33, 47, 50, 136, 138
Hibbert, Eleanor *see* Holt, Victoria
Holland, Isabelle 98, 150
Holt, Victoria 12, 16, 19, 27, 51, 55, 94, 101, 117, 139, 158
horoscopes 77, 97
"House Carpenter" (ballad) 116–117, 173*n*
Howatch, Susan 21, 142, 166

imprisonment 30, 39, 44
independent heroines 18, 29, 31, 60, 91, 92, 99, 104, 112, 128, 146–147, 157, 159–160
industrialism 40, 90
innuendo in gothics 15, 45, 133
inspiration for gothics 3, 26, 45, 48, 105
Ivanhoe see Scott, Sir Walter

James, E.L. 105–106; *Fifty Shades of Grey* 3, 4, 71, 85, 105, 106, 155
Jane Eyre see Brontë, Charlotte
Jekyll, Dr. Henry 70, 155
"John Riley" (ballad) 116, 117, 119, 173*n*

knights 39, 101, 136
Koontz, Dean 5, 20, 53, 83–85, 113, 137, 138
Krentz, Jayne Ann 6, 147, 162

labyrinths 5, 26, 35, 81, 125, 129
Lewis, Matthew 46, 47, 154; *The Monk* 3, 25, 35, 36, 53, 121
Lois, Jen 35, 135, 136
London in gothics 15, 23, 39, 41, 68, 69, 168
Lovelace, Mr. 25, 30, 109, 116, 117; *see also* Richardson, Samuel

madness in gothics 49, 61, 80, 81, 90, 143, 153
Master of Seacliff *see* Pierce, Max
Maybury, Anne 61, 63, 110
McCaffrey, Anne 83
McCarthy, Mary 9
McKnight-Trontz, Jennifer 2, 3, 18
medieval settings 9, 25–28, 33, 34, 39, 40, 47, 58, 75, 76, 121, 127, 149

Meyer, Stephenie 31, 105, 122, 155; *Twilight* series 8, 31, 69, 71, 106, 119, 155
Michaels, Barbara 73, 126, 154
Minerva Press 23, 32
misogyny 5, 136, 162
Modleski, Tania 99, 110, 139, 142–145, 147
The Monk see Lewis, Matthew
The Monkees 20, 67
monsters 20, 67, 75, 122, 128
Moura series *see* Coffman, Virginia
Mundis, Hester Jane 63, 89
Mussell, Kay 47, 90, 99, 101, 102, 139, 145
The Mysteries of Udolpho see Radcliffe, Ann

Nelson, Victoria 9, 35, 36, 39, 42, 97, 109, 121, 128
Northanger Abbey see Austen, Jane
Norton, Andre 73, 83
nursies (nurse romances) 18, 57, 62, 77, 82, 94, 96, 112

O'Brien, Geoffrey 16, 54
The Old English Baron see Reeve, Clara

Pamela see Richardson, Samuel
paranormal romances 3, 21, 119, 121, 151, 154, 155, 157
parodies of gothics 2, 3, 23, 25, 53, 56, 63, 65, 102, 123, 152, 160
penny dreadfuls 10, 11, 33, 35, 45, 46
Phillips, Susan Elizabeth 122, 128, 129
Pierce, Max 158–159
plagiarism 135, 136
Polidori, John: *The Vampyr* 10, 15, 42, 45, 46, 123, 155
Potter, Franz 31, 32

Queen-Size Gothics 19, 73, 76

Radcliffe, Ann Ward 5, 7, 9, 14, 26–28, 34, 37, 39, 46, 47, 57, 64, 90, 109, 117, 120, 121, 123–125, 138, 147, 150, 154, 155, 157; *The Mysteries of Udolpho* 3, 27, 30, 31, 33, 41, 42, 91, 108, 157, 167; *A Sicilian Romance* 26
Radcliffe, Elsa 59, 64, 77, 82, 100, 132, 148, 150, 154
Radway, Janice 73, 87, 98, 99, 139, 144, 146
Raybourn, Deanna 156
Rebecca see Du Maurier, Daphne
Reeve, Clara 7, 26–28, 39, 47, 108; *The Old English Baron* 26, 28, 29
Regency romances 17, 21, 48, 59, 79, 92, 123, 126, 133, 139, 155
Regis, Pamela 6, 30, 35, 41, 91, 128, 138, 144, 149
Rhys, Jean 143
Rice, Ann
Richardson, Samuel 24–26, 41, 48; *Pamela* 30, 41, 42, 48, 90, 91, 109

Index

Roberts, Janet Louise 75, 79, 114; *see also* Bronte, Louisa
Ross, Marilyn [W.E.D.] 3, 7, 54, 61, 66, 73, 74, 77, 158
Russ, Joanna 5, 19, 31, 49, 85, 94, 110, 124, 140–143, 147–149
Ruthven, Lord 40, 42, 43, 45, 106, 109; *see also* Polidori, John
Rymer, James Malcolm 45, 46; *Varney the Vampire* 10, 11, 45–47, 56, 168

Scott, Sir Walter 32–34, 120, 153; *Ivanhoe* 39
Seton, Anya: *Dragonwyck* 17, 50, 157
Shelley, Mary: *Frankenstein* 10, 41, 155, 166
Shelley, Percy Bysshe 32
A Sicilian Romance see Radcliffe, Ann
sorcery 70, 77, 78
stagecraft and the gothic 15, 36, 37, 46, 114, 119, 123, 124
Star Trek 8, 149
stereotypes 87, 98, 102, 135, 139
Stewart, Mary 3, 6, 51, 52, 61, 63, 74, 150, 154
Stoker, Bram 46; *Dracula* 3, 10, 39–41, 46, 139
supernatural in gothics 9, 14, 21, 27, 33, 35, 39, 45–47, 66, 71, 76, 77, 104, 106, 118, 119, 121, 130, 131, 155, 163
superstition 35, 121

taboos in gothics 85, 101
Tan, Candy 131
Tenant of Wildfell Hall see Brontë, Anne
theater and gothics 15, 26, 37, 48–49, 68, 112, 122, 123, 140
Toombs, Jane 74, 77; *Tule Witch* 77
Transylvania 40, 156; *see also Dracula*
Tropp, Martin 32, 33
Tule Witch see Toombs, Jane

Twilight series *see* Meyer, Stephenie
Twitchell, James 43, 168

vampires 6, 10, 15, 20, 35, 36, 39–43, 46, 73, 76, 77, 85, 109, 119, 121, 122, 128, 130, 133, 144, 153–155, 157, 158, 167, 168; erotic portrayal of 3, 45; Heathcliff as 43; as metaphor 40, 42; in romances 31, 42, 56, 67–71, 105–107; study of 8
Varney the Vampire see Rymer, James Malcolm
Virga, Vincent 157, 158

Wagner, Sharon 70, 76, 127
Wallace, Diana 30, 34, 90
Walpole, Horace 7, 34, 39, 40, 46, 122–125, 154; *The Castle of Otranto* 3, 9, 25, 26, 28, 29, 42, 47, 53, 108, 124
Wendell, Sarah 131, 136
werewolves 6, 11, 41, 67–71, 119, 121, 139, 154, 155, 157
Whitney, Phyllis 3, 19–21, 37, 51, 56, 90, 119, 126, 137, 154, 163
witchcraft in gothics 59, 67, 70, 77–79, 107, 132, 157
Wollstonecraft, Mary 30, 31, 90
Woodiwiss, Kathleen 84, 85, 120; *The Flame and the Flower* 84, 87
Wuthering Heights see Brontë, Emily

Yorkshire 37, 41, 56

Zawadsky, Patience 72, 78
Zebra Gothics 10, 15, 21, 126, 150–152
Zipes, Jack 131, 168
Zodiac Gothics 77

www.ingramcontent.com/pod-product-compliance
Lightning Source LLC
Chambersburg PA
CBHW021356300426
44114CB00012B/1249